DEATH AND DESTRUCTION
ON THE
THAMES
IN LONDON

Anthony Galvin

SAPERE
BOOKS

DEATH AND
DESTRUCTION
ON THE
THAMES
IN LONDON

Published by Sapere Books.

11 Bank Chambers, Hornsey, London, N8 7NN,
United Kingdom

saperebooks.com

ISBN: 978-1-912786-69-5

INTRODUCTION

The Thames dominates London, splitting the city in two. Winding in serpentine coils across the capital, it is both the giver of life to the city, and the bringer of destruction. Trade depends on the river. It brings the boats with their cargoes, it allows people to travel. But it also brings pollution and sewage from upstream, it causes floods, and its inky blackness is a siren call to suicides.

The history of London is a history of the Thames — but the Thames is far older and more elemental than the city it defines. It rises in the Cotswolds and, at 346 kilometres (215 miles), is the longest river in England (and the second longest in the UK). The name Thames is ancient and comes from the Middle English Temese, which in turn derives from the Celtic name for the river, Tamesas. It means darkness. There is evidence the name is at least two thousand years old.

Flowing from the Cotswolds through Oxford and Windsor, among other towns, the river reaches Greater London, passing Hampton Court, Surbiton, Kingston, Teddington, Twickenham, Richmond, Syon House and Kew, before flowing through central London. It forms one of the principal axes of the city, from the Palace of Westminster to the Tower of London, and is the southern boundary of the medieval city (now the financial district, and still known as the City). On the opposite bank is Southwark.

The river winds on past Greenwich and the Isle of Dogs, before flowing through the Thames Barrier and by Dagenham, Dartford, Tilbury and Gravesend, before entering the estuary and flowing into the North Sea. The Thames is tidal up to

Teddington Lock, on the west of the city. The entire river in central London is tidal and subject to a 7 metre (23 feet) water level fluctuation daily.

London grew around the Thames. There were small settlements over two thousand years ago, but things began to develop when the Romans arrived in AD 43, under the Emperor Claudius. Within four years, they had a trading post at Londinium. They chose a site where the Thames was narrow enough to bridge, but deep enough to handle sea-going marine vessels. Archaeological digs have found the remains of a massive Roman pier dating from that period, close to the modern London Bridge.

This early settlement, no larger than Hyde Park, was burnt to the ground by Queen Boudicca, but after her defeat, the Romans consolidated their hold on the city and the country. After the Romans left, the Anglo Saxons let the first London Bridge fall into disrepair, but they kept up the settlement. It came under frequent attack from the Vikings, until Ethelred the Unready drove them from the city in 1014. However, the Anglo Saxons were not destined to hold on for long; in 1066 the Normans, descendants of the Vikings based in northern France, invaded.

At the Battle of Hastings, King Harold was defeated and killed, and William the Conqueror had himself crowned. The Normans, unlike the Romans and the Vikings, stayed the course. William quickly realised the importance of London, and at the battle of Ludgate (near present day St Paul's Cathedral), he defeated the city. He built a fortification at what is now the Tower of London, and in 1078 built the White Tower.

Under the Normans, London became a centre of commerce and was established as the capital. There was a royal palace at the Tower, and another was built at Westminster. Over the next few centuries, London became a diverse melting pot of different nations. The Normans mixed with the Saxons and the remaining Vikings. Added to this were the slaves brought over from Africa from the end of the fifteenth century, the Jewish and Muslim traders who settled in the city, and Dutch traders.

Colourful monarchs came and went, including Henry VIII, who married six times and beheaded two of his wives. His daughter, Elizabeth I, entertained more gentleman friends than is normal for a Virgin Queen.

London had its ups and downs; the plague wiped out a huge portion of the population in 1665-6, and the Great Fire months later, destroyed a third of the city. Ironically, this heralded a golden era. Sir Christopher Wren's genius blossomed and some of the most magnificent buildings the world has ever seen were erected to replace the smouldering ruins. The dome of St Paul's is one of the most distinctive landmarks in the city, and Wren built another fifty churches to go with it.

By the 1800s, the slave trade had been abolished and London's black communities had grown considerably. People flowed in from South Asia and China. The Jewish population continued to grow as people fled persecution in Eastern Europe. One of the refugees may well have been the infamous Jack the Ripper — at least four identified suspects were from Eastern Europe. London had become the centre of a worldwide British Empire. The empire grew to such proportions that the sun never set on it.

London survived World War I relatively unscathed in a physical sense, but the conflict changed society for ever. Women had been pressed into work, and now demanded equal rights with men. And a generation of the best and the brightest men had been wiped out. Although Britain was on the winning side of the conflict, the days of the empire were numbered.

The Second World War was devastating for London. First came the Blitz, then four years later, in a last desperate throw of the dice, Hitler launched the world's first guided missiles at the city. The fifties saw London rebuilt. Today it is a vibrant, modern metropolis. No longer the heart of a great empire, it is still a great city, one of the most important in the world. In the summer of 2012, it hosted the Olympic Games, focusing the world's attention once more on it.

But with all the changes, one thing has remained constant. When people visit, they are drawn to the river. The Thames is the heart of London. On the following pages, I hope to throw light on the darker side of the dark river — death and destruction on the Thames in London.

CHAPTER ONE: LONDON'S BURNING!

FIRE! Few cries evoke more terror. There is something primal about how fire engulfs us. It is our servant, but it can quickly become a murderous master. Cities have always been vulnerable to fires. In the past, when wooden construction was popular and buildings were heaped densely on top of each other, fires spread with the rapidity of flowing water, destroying all in their path.

The Thames has boiled and bubbled under many an inferno over the past thousand years. Each major fire marks a turning point in the city's history, allowing rebuilding and renewal. The modern landscape of London owes much to the work done to rebuild after the Great Fire of 1666. But that fire was by no means the first. It was just one more in a long succession of great fires.

Early Fires

The city has suffered a number of devastating infernos, from Roman times to the Blitz. In earlier times, wooden buildings and the lack of a fire service meant that fires could rage uncontained. The congestion of the city also hindered efforts to control conflagrations.

However, each time London has risen, phoenix-like, from the ashes. Some of the greatest architects have contributed to rebuilding the city after each inferno.

But to those who lived through them, every fire was a great fire. There were major blazes in AD 60, 125, 764, 798, 852, 893, 961, 982, 1077, 1087, 1093, 1130, 1132, 1136, 1203, 1212, 1220, 1227, 1299, 1635, 1666 and 1940. There were minor blazes — some killing dozens of people and destroying hundreds of houses — in as many other years.

The first of those great fires was back in the days of the Roman occupation.

Londinium Sacked and Torched

The first recorded fire in the capital occurred in AD 60, when Queen Boudicca sacked the Roman settlement of Londinium. The settlement was on the northern shore of the river, close to what is now London Bridge, and was around the size of Hyde Park. Her Iceni warriors overran the settlement, slaughtered the traders, then torched all the buildings. To this day, the layer of red ash from that fire survives, and is used by archaeologists to date strata when they undertake digs near London Bridge. The layer of ash stretches down to the river on the northern bank.

The Romans swiftly defeated Boudicca at the Battle of Watling Street, near present day King's Cross. The victorious Romans rebuilt their trading town. London had risen from the ashes for the first time.

The Hadriatic Fire

London survived less than a century before fire struck again. Some few short years after the visit of the Roman Emperor Hadrian in AD 122, a huge fire swept through the town, destroying a huge portion of it.

It is not known what caused it, but it spread rapidly, consuming over 100 acres before dying out. It spread in a sheet of flame between what is now Newgate Street and the Tower of London. All the wooden buildings were destroyed, and only a handful of sturdier stone structures survived. One of the buildings that remained was the Roman fort at Cripplegate.

Archaeologists believe the area was so badly damaged that it remained uninhabited for more than a century. By the time London rose from the ashes a second time, the Roman Empire was in terminal decline.

Anglo-Saxon Fires

London continued to be occupied after the fall of the Roman Empire, but the Anglo-Saxons were no better at keeping it safe from the flames. In 675, a fire broke out between the river and Ludgate Hill, destroying many homes and razing the cathedral to the ground. The cathedral, on the site of what would become St Paul's, was just seventy-years-old. It was rebuilt within a decade, but the roof contained too many wooden supports, and when fire struck in 962, it was destroyed again.

Other great fires of that period occurred in 798 and in 982. The final great fire of the Anglo-Saxon period occurred in 989. It broke out at Aldgate and spread wildly, destroying street after street. It only stopped when it reached the junction of the Thames and the Fleet, at Ludgate. Houses, churches and civic buildings were all destroyed.

Normans Fail to Stop the Flames

Aware of its history, the Norman conquerors tried to ensure that London would never burn again. They introduced a curfew, banning the use of fires and candles after 8 p.m. It was to no avail. In 1077, a fire caused extensive damage and loss of life, while in 1087, another fire broke out, spreading quickly from the Fleet to the Thames. St Paul's Cathedral was destroyed once more, as was the Palatine Tower built by William the Conqueror on the banks of the Fleet. This blaze was so devastating that it was referred to as The Great Fire of London for decades — until the next great fire.

The Great Fire of 1135

The fire of 1135 was so severe, it eclipsed all the previous ones. It broke out on the feast of Pentecost, the seventh Sunday after Easter (May 26). The fire started on Cannon Street, at the home of the Sheriff of London, Gilbert Becket. He was a mercer (fabric importer) and the father of Thomas Becket.

The fire quickly swept down to the river, and the wooden London Bridge began to burn. This happened so swiftly that many people thought the fire broke out on the bridge itself.

It then swept west, engulfing all the streets and lanes leading towards Ludgate Hill and St Paul's Cathedral. At its height, the blaze stretched in a half mile wall of flame from the church of St Clement Danes in Westminster, to St Paul's — which was one of the few buildings to survive. London Bridge did burn down, and had to be replaced yet again.

An interesting footnote is that records indicate that Gilbert Becket lost much of his fortune as a result of the Great Fire. Most of his wealth had been tied up in property which was destroyed. It is ironic that the man who inadvertently caused the Great Fire should have been impoverished by it.

The Worst Bridge Disaster Ever

The Guinness Book of Records is a bit squeamish when it comes to the gory records, but they do recognise one record no one is vying to beat. The Great Fire of 1212 killed up to 3,000 people on London Bridge alone.

The fire broke out on 10 July on the south bank of the river, at Southwark. Very quickly it spread, destroying the cathedral, St Mary Overie. The day was dry with strong southerly winds that blew the flames towards the river, igniting the thatched roofs of houses along the way. Soon the whole southern bank was ablaze, and the fire had reached London Bridge.

Back then, London Bridge was not what it is now. Built just three years earlier, in 1209, it was a thriving thoroughfare, with houses crowding both sides. It was prime real estate, and King John had rented it all to raise much needed funds for its upkeep.

It could take an hour to cross because there was only a thin ribbon of road weaving between the two rows of houses and shops. The buildings tottered over the superstructure of the bridge to four or five storeys. Some merchants built bridges from windows of upper storeys to cross from one side to the other.

An overturned cart could be enough to bring traffic to a standstill.

As those on the north side of the river saw the fire spreading, some crossed the bridge to help. Others just crowded the bridge for a better view, their voyeuristic instincts roused by the burning city. It was quite a sight. Such massive fires cause a natural phenomenon called a fire bow, an arc of flame that reaches across the horizon, often stretching for hundreds of yards. The flames can jump to flammable points such as roofs, allowing a big fire to spread at an alarming rate.

As the crowd gathered on the bridge, they were blocked by the advancing flames and could not exit into Southwark. But before they managed to turn and retreat, the flame arced across the river, igniting the northern side of London Bridge.

No one knows how many people were on the bridge at the time. The Guinness Book of Records for years carried the claim that there were 3,000 trapped, though historians believe that this number is exaggerated. Many tried to escape the flames by jumping into the river, but the swiftly flowing waters drowned them.

The *Book of Ancient Laws* (1274) is the oldest book among the records of London Corporation, and it records: "In this year (1212) was the Great Fire of Southwark, and it burned the church of St Mary Overie, as also the Bridge, with the chapel there, and the great part of the city."

Another account said: "An exceeding great multitude of people passing the Bridge, either to extinguish or quench it, or else to gaze at and behold it, suddenly the north part, by blowing of the south wind, was also set on fire, and the people which were even now passing the Bridge, perceiving the same, would have returned, but were stopped by the fire."

London Bridge itself, which was stone, survived the fire. But all the buildings on the bridge were lost. However, it was many years before the bridge was fully usable again.

London Bridge is Burning Down
In 1635, a fire broke out on the north side of London Bridge. It was nowhere near as serious as the earlier fires in the city, being contained before it could become a citywide conflagration. But it did destroy forty-two buildings on the northern third of the bridge, along with eighty buildings on nearby Thames Street. Dozens of people were killed, and the embers remained hot and smouldering for a week after the blaze was put out.

Some of the destroyed buildings were not replaced, particularly on the bridge. This left gaps which formed an accidental fire block.

When the Great Fire broke out thirty years later, this accidental firebreak was what saved the bridge and prevented the fire spreading to Southwark.

The Great Fire

The Great Fire of 1666, recorded in detail by diarist Samuel Pepys and others, did more to define London than any other event in the city's history. The skyscape we are now familiar with — the dome of St Paul's Cathedral and the other classic buildings designed by Sir Christopher Wren — were built on the smouldering remains of the medieval city.

The blaze laid waste to a huge part of central London. The banks of the Thames on the north were a wall of flame for days. The city inside the old Roman City Wall was destroyed. The fire stretched from the Tower to almost as far as Westminster.

Only blind chance prevented it flowing across London Bridge and laying waste to Southwark as well. A smaller fire in 1635 had destroyed forty houses on the northern portion of the bridge, and the gap formed a natural fire block. Had it not been in place, the damage would have been vastly magnified.

As it was, the fire consumed 13,200 houses, eighty-seven parish churches, St Paul's Cathedral and most of the buildings that administered the kingdom. Between 70,000 and 80,000 people were rendered homeless.

But one of the most remarkable things about the Great Fire is that so few were killed during it. The fire of 1212 claimed several thousand lives. The Great Fire killed half a dozen. More people were killed in the aftermath by maddened crowds looking for someone to blame, than died in the blaze itself.

London Before the Fire

London was by far the largest city in Britain, with a population of half a million — more than the next fifty towns combined. Inside the medieval defensive City Wall, it was overcrowded. Slums such as Shoreditch, Holborn and Southwark took the overflow.

London had stretched west to absorb the independent town of Westminster. The City, then as now, was the commercial heart of the capital and the empire. It was surrounded by a ring of inner suburbs where most people lived, and the docks along the Thames formed the busiest port in England.

The aristocracy lived further out, congregating in Westminster, near the Whitehall residence of King Charles II.

The centre of London was full of narrow streets and high buildings, many with thatched roofs. The large public buildings were made of stone, but most of the meaner structures were constructed of wood.

There was a severe drought in the summer of 1666 — long, hot weeks of sweltering heat with no rain. London was a tinder box, waiting for the spark.

The majestic river also contributed to the problem. It offered water for firefighting, and a route to escape the conflagration, but it also offered plenty of fuel to feed the dancing flames. In the poorer districts along the riverfront, there were stores and cellars crammed with combustibles. All along the wharves, the rickety wooden tenements had thatch and tar paper (heavy paper soaked in tar for strength and waterproofing) as core materials.

Tar, pitch, hemp, rosin and flax were among the goods warehoused by the water's edge. Lumber yards abounded. And there was an even more deadly hazard: black powder. Many of the citizens still had supplies of gunpowder left over from the Civil War. The Tower of London was an arsenal, with almost six hundred tonnes of the explosive stored there. The ships chandlers along the wharves also held their own supply, stored in flammable wooden barrels.

If London went up, it could go up with a bang.

Beginnings

The fire started in a bakery on Pudding Lane. Pudding Lane, off Eastcheap in the City, was a small road leading towards the Thames. It was the route the butchers of Eastcheap used for bringing carts of offal and entrails to the waste barges on the river. The Pudding in the name refers to those entrails.

Like most citizens, the baker Thomas Farriner (or Farrynor) was a cautious man who knew the dangers of naked flames. As he told a parliamentary inquiry after the event, on the evening of Saturday, 1 September 1666, he had: "gone through every room and found no fire but in one chimney, where the room was paved with bricks, which fire he diligently raked up in embers."

It is thought he raked some of those embers out into a waste bucket outside the bakery, and the sparks from this was what caused the blaze. It had been a long, hot summer, and August had been a particularly dry month, so the wooden beams and thatch of the houses were prime tinder.

A little after midnight (Sunday, 2 September), the fire was detected and the alarm raised. The family was trapped upstairs, but managed to scramble through an upstairs window to the house next door. But their maid lost her nerve and would not climb out onto the window ledge. She was soon overcome with smoke and became the first victim of the fire.

Neighbours up and down the street quickly got dressed and came out to battle the blaze before it could reach their houses. Within an hour, it was obvious the blaze was going to consume the bakery entirely. The Parish Constables (part-time unpaid police) arrived and recommended the adjoining houses should be demolished immediately to form a firebreak.

The neighbours naturally objected and the matter was left to the Lord Mayor, Sir Thomas Bloodworth, to decide. He arrived, looked at the flames, and indecisiveness took over. He could see that the adjoining houses were already lost, and the flame, fanned by a strong easterly wind, was creeping towards the paper warehouses and other flammable stores on the water front. Experienced voices were calling for houses to be pulled down, but he knew better.

"Pish," he said. "A woman could piss it out." Then he went home and left the firefighters to cope as best they could, without permission to create firebreaks. It was a fatal error.

Sunday

Samuel Pepys, a naval administrator who kept a detailed diary of national events during the period, was at his home on Seething Lane, near Tower Hill, when his panicked maid woke him at 3 a.m. He looked out and saw the fire stretching from Pudding Lane towards Billingsgate, a distance of roughly 150 metres. The flames were halfway to his house, but he decided the danger was minimal and went back to bed.

But when he woke up the following morning, he was told that 300 houses had been destroyed and the flames were threatening London Bridge. He immediately walked to the Tower, a very short distance from him, and climbed it to see the extent of the problem. The fire had spread from Pudding Lane towards Fish Street, and was licking around the bridge. It had passed through Thames Street on to Old Swan Lane, St Lawrence Lane and Dowgate. Pepys took a boat upriver to Whitehall to report to the king.

As he recorded: "I down to the water-side, and there got a boat and through bridge, and there saw a lamentable fire. Poor Michell's house, as far as the Old Swan, already burned that way, and the fire running further, that in a very little time it got as far as the Steelyard, while I was there. Everybody endeavouring to remove their goods, and flinging into the river or bringing them into lighters that layoff; poor people staying in their houses as long as till the very fire touched them, and then running into boats, or clambering from one pair of stairs by the water-side to another. Having staid, and in an hour's time seen the fire rage every way, and nobody, to my sight, endeavouring to quench it, but to remove their goods, and leave all to the fire, and having seen it get as far as the Steeleyard, and the wind mighty high and driving it into the City; and everything, after so long a drought, proving combustible..."

The diary was written in shorthand, and its grammar might be questionable, but not the scenes of panic Pepys recorded. He went on to Whitehall and informed the king and the Duke of York of the situation. The king asked him to go to the Lord Mayor and tell him to begin pulling down houses as firebreaks.

A young schoolboy, William Taswell, left the service in Westminster Abbey to view the excitement. He told the Parliamentary Inquiry that he saw refugees arriving at the Westminster Stairs, covered in blankets after fleeing their homes naked. The services of the Thames ferrymen were suddenly very expensive, and only those who could afford the extortionate fees could escape across the river.

The wind had grown to a gale, spreading the fire rapidly westwards, away from the Tower and towards Westminster. Pepys took a coach from Whitehall back to the city, but only reached St Paul's Cathedral before he was forced to get out and walk. The human traffic fleeing against him — with all their goods and possessions — made progress difficult.

He found the mayor, who had already begun pulling down houses. "Lord! What can I do? I am spent: people will not obey me. I have been pulling down houses; but the fire overtakes us faster than we can do it," he complained.

However, his efforts were too little too late, and he retired, frustrated. That afternoon, King Charles II sailed down from Whitehall on the royal barge and saw how little had been done. He furiously overrode the authority of the mayor and ordered wholesale demolition of everything in the path of the fire. But the order came too late; the blaze was already out of control.

The firestorm created a strong updraft, increasing the power of the easterly wind and fanning the flames further. Pepys records going to the river that Sunday night and seeing that the extent of the fire was increasing. They rowed as close as possible to the blaze: "So near the fire as we could for smoke; and all over the Thames, with one's face in the wind, you were almost burned with a shower of fire drops."

Afterwards, sitting in an alehouse on the bank of the Thames in Southwark, he described: "a most horrid, malicious bloody flame, not like the fire flame of an ordinary fire.

"We could see fire on London Bridge and across the river, as only one entire arch of fire from this to the other side of the bridge, and in a bow up the hill for an arch of above a mile long. It made me weep to see it."

This was the terrifying fire bow, the phenomenon that allows fires to jump from building to building, even across firebreaks. Pepys described it as "A bow with God's arrow in it, with a shining point."

Monday

By dawn on Monday, 3 September, the fire was still spreading north and west, driven by the easterly gale. But turbulence created by the updraft helped the fire creep east as well. South, the river formed an effective block. The fire failed to get across London Bridge because of the gaps left by the 1635 fire. The few houses left on the north side of the bridge, and the few restored after the earlier fire, did burn.

Some embers floated across the river, and a fire broke out in Southwark. But the inhabitants were ready and it was quickly doused.

A minor panic was caused on Monday when the houses of bankers on Lombard Street began to burn. Some of them contained the gold reserve, crucial to the wealth of the city and nation. The gold was removed to safety before it could melt away.

Despair gripped the city, with citizens moping around listlessly, at a loss as to how to fight the fire and save their possessions. Wealthy, fashionable districts such as The Royal Exchange (an upmarket shopping and commercial centre) and the shopping streets of Cheapside, were now under threat. The Exchange was lost that afternoon.

Another noted diarist, writer and courtier, John Evelyn, recorded the events. Evelyn lived in Deptford, on the estuary about four miles from the city, so was not a witness to the early stages of the fire. But on Monday, he wrote: "The conflagration was so universal, and the people so astonished, that from the beginning, I knew not by what despondency or fate, they hardly stirred to quench it, so that there was nothing heard or seen but crying and lamentation, running about like distracted creatures without at all attempting to save even their goods, such a strange consternation was upon them."

With many other upper class people, he took a coach to Southwark to watch the chaos. He wrote: "The whole city in dreadful flames near the water-side; all the houses from the bridge, all Thames Street, and upwards towards Cheapside, down to the Three Cranes, were now consumed."

By evening, the river was covered with barges and boats trying to flee. The city gates were a bottleneck and roads out were strewn with people and carriages.

"Oh the miserable and calamitous spectacle," wrote Evelyn.

Fires began breaking out all over the city, throwing people into a panic. The fires were caused by windborne embers, but people naturally suspected arson. Britain was at war with Holland, and France was still the old enemy. Foreigners in the city found themselves being followed and set upon. There were a number of lynchings.

Schoolboy William Taswell told the Inquiry about a mob looting the shop of a French painter and demolishing it. He was horrified to see a blacksmith walk up to a Frenchman in the street and hit him over the head with an iron bar.

As the panic grew, the cost of hiring a cart went from a couple of shillings on Saturday night, to £40 (the equivalent of nearly £5,000 today) on Monday evening. Every cart, carriage and boat owner within miles was making their way towards London, eager to cash in. Things got so bad that the magistrates ordered the gates of the city to be shut, in the hopes that people would stop panicking and start fighting the fire. This extreme measure proved fruitless, and the gates were opened again on Tuesday.

But on Monday, some order began to creep into the firefighting efforts. Lord Mayor Bloodworth had fled the city, and the king put his brother James, Duke of York, in charge, overriding the city corporation. James set up command posts and began press-ganging any men he found loitering into teams of well-paid and well-fed firemen. They formed chains to throw water on the flames and began pulling down buildings in the line of the fire.

They were also busy saving foreigners from lynch mobs, and gradually some order returned to the streets. The king himself turned up and helped demolish buildings in the at-risk areas. But on Monday evening, the small spark of optimism was extinguished when Baynard's Castle, Blackfriars, began to burn. It was hoped the massive stone walls would resist the fire, but the historic royal palace was completely consumed, burning through the night.

Pepys recorded that, at around 4 p.m., he realised his own home was under threat. He sent his precious diary and a number of other valued possessions to a friend in the naval office at Bethnal Green, and ordered a cart for the following day to remove everything else.

Then he settled down to a cold dinner, not having a fire to cook upon. The ordinary people of London, too late, were taking precautions against further outbreaks.

Lynchings

In the panic, people misinterpreted what they saw. Houses were catching fire dozens or hundreds of yards away from the wall of flame, and people reported seeing strangers throwing incendiary devices and grenades. The blame fell on the French, old enemies from the Hundred Years' War, and on the Dutch.

Britain was in the middle of the second Anglo-Dutch war (1665-67). But many Dutch traders and merchants had settled in London, where they ran their businesses for years, integrating into the local community. Now, those years of integration meant nothing.

One French man was beaten senseless because he was carrying a bag of grenades: the grenades turned out to be tennis balls. A Dutch merchant was ostracised by his neighbours because he could afford a cart to save his possessions. He was almost lynched when he returned. It was only when he began to tear down his own home to form a firebreak that they trusted him again.

A French woman was attacked by a mob and had her breasts slashed off.

The Coldstream Guards, who should have been fighting the flames, were roaming the streets rounding up foreigners — and saving foreigners from the marauding masses.

Tuesday

September 4 was the day of greatest destruction. The fire reached a peak. The big push was to stop the westward sweep of the blaze, using the River Fleet as a fire block. If they could hold that line, they could save the Palace of Whitehall.

The Duke of York made a stand with his firemen from the Fleet Bridge down to the Thames. But early on Tuesday morning, the gale blew the flames across the Fleet. Now the firemen were trapped between two walls of flame and had to beat a hasty retreat.

"Oh, the confusion there was then at that court!" quipped Evelyn.

The firebreak to the north of the fire held until late afternoon, when flames leapt across and ignited the affluent shopping street of Cheapside.

St Paul's Cathedral at least seemed safe. Made of solid stone with a wide open space surrounding it, everyone packed the church with their most precious possessions. The crypt was crammed tight with the stock of the printers and booksellers in nearby Paternoster Row. But wooden scaffolding outside caught fire, and the church was lost.

All day, the firefighting efforts were concentrated on the western side of the fire, which was advancing rapidly under the strong gales. But the fire was also creeping east, towards Pepys's home and the Tower of London, with its supply of gunpowder. If that ignited, untold damage would be done. After waiting in vain for the firefighters to come to their aid, the garrison in the Tower took action.

They began using their stocks of gunpowder to blow up several houses close to the Tower to create a firebreak, and this did halt the creeping advance.

Pepys was taking no chances, though. He spent the day loading everything he could onto a cart for evacuation. He wrote: "I to Tower Street, and there met the fire burning three or four doors beyond Mr Howell's, whose goods, poor man, were flung all along Tower Street, the fire coming on both sides with infinite fury.

"Sir William Batten not knowing how to remove his wine did dig a pit in the garden and laid it there. And I took the opportunity of laying all the papers of my office that I could not otherwise dispose of. And in the evening Sir William Penn and I did dig another, and put our wine in it, and I my Parmesan cheese and some other things."

Christopher Wren — Destroyer and Creator

St Paul's should have survived, except for some restoration work that was being carried out by a young architect, Christopher Wren. Just thirty-three, he was two weeks into a restoration job on the cathedral and had constructed enormous wooden scaffolds to gain access to the roof. On Tuesday night, flying embers set this scaffolding on fire.

Young William Taswell saw it all from the bank of the river at the Westminster Stairs, the steps down to the river used to access the water taxis and other boats. He described how the flames crept round the cathedral, and the burning scaffolding ignited the timber roof beams. Within half an hour, the lead roof was melting, then the books and paper in the crypt suddenly ignited with a roar and a ball of fire.

"The stones of Paul's flew like grenados, the melting lead running down the streets in a stream and the very pavements glowing with fiery redness, so as no horse, nor man, was able to tread on them," John Evelyn recorded.

The cathedral was destroyed in hours.

However, when it came to rebuilding, the job went to the young architect whose scaffolding had led to the destruction of the building in the first place. The new St Paul's is one of the iconic buildings of London, and a fitting tribute to the genius of Sir Christopher Wren.

Standing on Ludgate Hill, the highest point in central London, it dominates the city. The church, at 111 metres (365 feet) high, was the tallest building in London until 1962. The dome is one of the largest in the world. The seat of the Bishop of London is one of the biggest tourist draws in the city.

It is also an imposing monument to the survival spirit of the people of London.

All Hallows-by-the-Tower

All Hallows-by-the-Tower (previously known as St Mary the Virgin) is the oldest church in London. It was built by the Saxons in 675, just 300 feet from the Thames on what is now Byward Road. Unusually for those days, it was built of stone, incorporating tiles and bricks from the abandoned Roman settlement of Londinium.

The seventh century Saxon arch of recycled Roman tiles is the oldest extant piece of church architecture in London. The church was expanded and rebuilt extensively a number of times between the eleventh and fifteenth century, and had many Royal associations due to its proximity to the Tower of London.

The heart of Richard the Lionheart, who died while returning from the crusades, is buried in the churchyard, and the heads of those executed in the Tower were often temporarily interred there. These included William Laud, Archbishop of Canterbury; Thomas More; and John Fisher.

The church suffered extensive damage in 1650. The yard was being used to store gunpowder and it exploded, destroying fifty nearby houses. There were a large number of fatalities. Rebuilt in 1658, the church escaped the Great Fire.

But it did not survive the Blitz. It was gutted by German bombers and required extensive reconstruction, not opening again until 1957.

Open to visitors today, All Hallows-by-the-Tower is an interesting snapshot of 1,500 years of history, a short hop from the more popular attraction of The Tower of London.

Wednesday

At 2 a.m., Pepys was woken by his wife in a panic. The fire had almost reached the church of All Hallows-by-the-Tower.

Sir William Penn had left over his digging of impromptu wine cellars, and was busy trying to save the church. The father of William Penn, founder of Pennsylvania, was an admiral and he had his men out in force, tearing down buildings wholesale to create a firebreak.

Pepys had more practical things on his mind. The fire was licking around the foot of Seething Lane, so he sent his wife to Woolwich. He also sent his gold — about £2,350 worth, which was a considerable fortune in those days — with her.

On Wednesday morning, the wind dropped. With the gale abating, the firebreaks created by the garrison at the Tower began to take effect, as did the firebreaks to the west, near Whitehall.

Because London Bridge had held, the fire had not spread into Southwark, so the southern banks of the river were all still functional. But from the north river bank into the city, all was wasteland. The fire still burnt strongly in areas, but it was not spreading any more.

Fire needs fuel, and as the last of the buildings were consumed to ashes, the flames across the city died down. There was nothing left to burn. Every thatched roof, every wooden beam, every scrap of furniture and storehouse full of wares, was reduced to embers. The embers continued to glow, and a pall of smoke hung over the charred wreckage of what had been a proud city.

But the fire was over. Whitehall and Westminster had been saved, as had the Tower of London. The Bridge was still standing. The king's brother, James Duke of York, was a hero to the people. The mayor hung his head in shame and told everyone who would listen that the extent of the damage was not his fault. Within a month, his time in office came to an end and with it, his public life.

The idle rich came to gawk; the poor remained to lament the loss of their meagre possessions.

Pepys walked the smouldering Dante-esque landscape, enduring the burning heat under his feet. He climbed the steeple of Barking Church and witnessed "the saddest sight of desolation that I ever saw."

The wall of flame was gone, and the searing heat had died down to the normal warmth of late summer. Several small fires were burning themselves out in the wreckage, but the Great Fire was over.

The Diarists

Samuel Pepys (1633-1703) was a naval administrator, and later a Member of Parliament. His work brought him into close contact with all the movers and shakers of the day. During a ten-year period when he was a young man (1660-69), he kept a detailed diary. It throws light on life during those turbulent times. He saw at first hand the second Anglo-Dutch war, the plague, and the Great Fire.

He also recorded the personal minutiae of his life, including his insatiable sexual appetites. These parts of the diary were censored in the first published versions as they were quite racy. He described being with the maid when his wife "coming up suddenly, did find me embracing the girl con my hand sub su coats; and indeed I was with my main in her cunny. I was at a wonderful loss upon it, and the girl also."

His mix of English, shorthand, and pidgin Latin is quaint, but the meaning is unmistakable!

Pepys stopped keeping his diary when his eyesight began to decline. He was elected MP for Castle Rising in Norfolk in 1673, then for Harwich in 1679, serving in the government until 1688. His diaries (minus the racy bits!) were published in 1825.

John Evelyn (1620-1706) was the other great diarist of the age. Unlike Pepys, who made his mark through hard work and graft, Evelyn was born a gentleman, and was a noted scholar and bibliophile. He wrote several books, but was particularly known for his works on horticulture.

Evelyn lived in Deptford, on the north bank of the Thames Estuary about four miles from the city. He kept his diary for more than sixty years and, like Pepys, he commented on all the great events of the day. He also chronicled the events of his own life.

The big difference (apart from the fact that he was more literate) was that his account of life in the seventeenth century was far less racy than Pepys's. It was first published in 1827.

Aftermath

Moorfields, near Moorgate, was one of the last pieces of open land in London, and in the aftermath of the fire, it became a refugee camp for the tens of thousands of homeless. King Charles encouraged those bereft by the fire to move out of London to the surrounding countryside and towns, but many built shanties in the park.

Both Pepys and Evelyn visited the refugee camp and left us harrowing descriptions.

Pepys wrote: "Poor wretches carrying their goods there, and everybody keeping his goods together by himself." He noted that the price of bread had doubled in a few days.

Evelyn was horrified at the numbers of desperate people living in the park, many in tents while others had makeshift shacks. "Many were without a rag or any necessary utensils, bed or board — reduced to extremist misery and poverty."

But the pride of the dispossessed impressed him: "Though ready to perish for hunger and destitution, yet not asking one penny for relief."

Evelyn was on hand to witness mass hysteria on the evening the fire finally died out. A rumour spread that a force of 50,000 French and Dutch immigrants were marching on Moorfields to finish what the fire had begun: to kill the men, rape the women and steal their few possessions. The terrified mob took to the streets, falling on foreigners of every description.

"Only with infinite pains and great difficulty" were the mob restrained, he recorded.

Rebuilding London

After the fire, London was a wasteland. Both Pepys and Evelyn mention that it was difficult to even recognise streets and districts, unless you identified a spire or a stone tower that had somehow survived, and used that as a landmark. People were disorientated. Only the river was a constant, the ribbon that had saved the south side from destruction.

But within a day, some people were back looking for the site of their former homes, erecting rough fences to reclaim their little portion of the city. King Charles was in favour of a quick rebuild, but he ordered that no work should begin for a few days, until some "order and direction" had been introduced.

Ambitious architects and engineers began submitting designs for the new city which would rise from the ashes. Christopher Wren wanted intersecting avenues like the grand cities of Europe. John Evelyn was more ambitious; he submitted a plan that turned London into a giant grid, dominated by twelve majestic piazzas. Neither plan was accepted.

What was needed was a quick solution. Four-fifths of the centre of London was gone. Fifteen of the city's twenty-six wards were in ruins. 460 streets, comprising over 13,000 houses, were reduced to ashes. Eighty-seven parish churches and four of the city's seven ancient gates were no more. Gone too was the Old Bailey, St Paul's, the Royal Exchange, the Custom House, the Bridewell Palace and several of the prisons. The heat was so intense, the bars melted and the locks gave way. It is not known whether the prisoners then walked away to freedom — or died unrecorded in the flames.

In today's money, the Great Fire caused well over a billion pounds of damage to a country just recovering from the plague, the civil war, and the second Anglo-Dutch war. The rebuild would stretch the economy to the limits.

Work began immediately on tearing down damaged buildings and clearing the wreckage. It was also important to get the quays and wharfs of the river trading again. Within a year, trade had returned to normal.

Christopher Wren was on the committee to oversee the work. The plan was simple: rebuild along the old lines, but make the streets wider. And houses had to be built of stone or brick. Householders had to pay for their own costs, while a tax on coal raised funds to pay for the public buildings. Within two years, 1,200 houses were rebuilt, and a year later, another 1,600.

Within a decade, most of the work had been carried out, but there were still gaps; several of the churches had not yet been replaced, and some of the new docks proposed for the banks of the river had not gone ahead.

Wren got to work on St Paul's. The structure he put in its place was magnificent; for three centuries it was the tallest structure in the city. The dome dominates the skyline. Wren was also responsible for the rebuilding of fifty-one other churches throughout the city, not just restoring London to its former magnificence but adding greatly to its glory.

Fire Fighting Techniques
Fires were frequent, but the city did not have a dedicated firefighting service like today. Instead, the local militia (volunteer army) could be called out in an emergency. A thousand militia men patrolled London by night, and one of the things they had to watch for was fires. They were known as Bellmen.

Usually, neighbours stepped in to help, and in the case of small fires, that proved sufficient. There were two techniques used: buildings were demolished to stop the fire, and water was thrown on the flames. Every parish church, by law, had to have equipment such as long ladders, axes, buckets and fire hooks (poles for pulling down roofs and walls), and these were available to the community as needed.

In drastic cases, gunpowder was used for bringing down buildings and creating firebreaks. It was the extensive use of gunpowder, especially by the garrison at the Tower, that finally stopped the spread of the Great Fire.

Water is the main weapon against fire. London was one of the few cities with a supply of pumped water four hundred years ago. However, the supply let them down during the Great Fire.

There was a high water tower at Cornhill, filled from the river at high tide, as well as a reservoir of Hertfordshire spring water at Islington. Both contained millions of gallons of water, which was supplied to the city through a network of wooden pipes. The pipes did not go to houses, but supplied a number of pumps on the streets, and public wells. It was often possible to hack through a pipe near a burning building and connect it to a hose, or use it to fill leather buckets and form a chain to fight the fire. And then there was the river itself.

Pudding Lane was so close to the Thames that, at quiet times during the night, you could hear the water lapping on the banks. Had the Parish Constables done their job properly (or the mayor issued the right orders), a double chain of men with buckets should have been working through the first night, dousing flames. That did not happen, according to witnesses such as Pepys. Instead of trying to fight the fire, people rushed about trying to save their own possessions: "to remove their goods, and leave all to the fire."

Once they let the fire reach the warehouses on the riverfront, the battle was lost. Now firefighters were cut off from their best source of water, the river. Worse was to follow.

Under London Bridge were two great waterwheels. One drove a mill wheel, while the other, on the northern side of the bridge, drove a water pump, supplying the pipes to the Cornhill water tower. But on day one, the flames reached London Bridge and the waterwheel began to burn. That rendered the river and the piped water supply useless to the firefighters, leaving them with only one option — wholesale destruction of buildings in the path of the conflagration to create firebreaks.

London also had primitive fire engines. But some of these were not even on wheels, but on wooden sleds. It took hours to drag them into position, and by then the water pipes they needed had already failed. Some efforts were made to drag the fire engines down to the river to get water, but several toppled into the Thames and were lost. Others were caught between the advancing flames and the river, and never got to be used at all.

London Bridge

The Great Fire of 1212 began in Southwark, then spread north across the bridge, engulfing the city. Several thousand people were killed. The big fear was that the 1666 fire would travel the other way, crossing the bridge and engulfing the slums of Southwark.

The bridge was still covered in medieval houses, which could form a fiery arrow to the heart of the southern suburb. On Sunday morning, hours into the fire, Samuel Pepys was convinced the bridge was lost. He was looking from the Tower of London and could see the whole hellish panorama.

It had been a deathtrap during the earlier fire of 1635, and now the flames were approaching again. In his diary, Pepys recorded his concern for friends living on the bridge.

But the open space on the north side of the bridge, where buildings demolished in the fire over thirty years previously had not been replaced, proved too big a jump for the fire bow. The strong easterly winds kept the fire moving west. Had the wind shifted to the north, it might have driven the flames across the gap. Some burning embers did cross the river, igniting several small fires in Southwark. But the unintended firebreak in the bridge itself was enough to prevent the fire spreading to the southern banks of the Thames.

Death Toll

The official death toll from the Great Fire was amazingly in single figures — a great tribute to the sagacity of the poor of the city who managed to abandon their tenements and move out through the overcrowded gates of the city ahead of the advancing flames. Some authorities give the exact figure as six, others as eight.

Although four-fifths of the centre of a great city, with a population of half a million, was destroyed, the loss of life was tiny. The first to die was the maid who refused to leap to safety from the home of Thomas Farriner, the house at the epicentre of the blaze. She lost her nerve and would not leap to safety.

Another man was identified as a watchmaker from Shoe Lane, because of the position of his corpse, and the fact that his keys survived the heat.

Officially, a handful more died over the next five days. More people were killed by lynch mobs seeking reprisals against foreigners than by the flames themselves. The number of foreigners lynched is not known, though the troops on the street from the second day kept this to a minimum too.

However, the actual death toll is certainly far higher than the official one. Many of the poor lived unrecorded lives.

Homeless and those without surviving relatives were not looked for in the aftermath, and many certainly perished. However, the intensity of the blaze was such that the corpses were reduced to unrecognisable ashes.

It is safe to say that the Great Fire probably claimed several hundred lives. But this is still far less than the lesser Great Fire of 1212. London had a lucky escape.

Dramatic End for Dramatist

One of the people displaced by the Great Fire was London dramatist James Shirley (1596-1666). Between 1625 and 1642, he carved out a successful niche as a playwright, turning out thirty tragedies and comedies over nearly two decades. He was the chief writer for the company Queen Henrietta's Men. That company was the main rival to The King's Men, the company Shakespeare had once been attached to.

But as the Puritans came to dominate public life, theatre went into a decline and Shirley had to make as good a living as he could, writing educational tracks and teaching. By 1666, he and his second wife were living in genteel poverty in the city. Then came the Great Fire, and he lost everything. Now aged seventy, he was a broken man.

He ended up in the refugee camp near Moorfields, and he and his wife both perished, officially of "fright and exposure".

Many, many others also died in the aftermath of the fire, from the effects of exposure to smoke, lack of sanitation in the camps and starvation. The price of food in the markets around the camps of the displaced was vastly inflated, as people tried to exploit the disaster for their own gain.

Monuments to the Great Fire

The most dramatic of the many monuments to the Great Fire is the 60 metre high stone Doric column near the northern end of London Bridge, at the junction of Monument Street and Fish Street Hill.

Towering above the houses, it stands just 61 metres from where the fire broke out in Pudding Lane. It was designed by Christopher Wren and Robert Hooke, under the instructions of the king.

The monument, still the tallest stone column in the world, was built on the site of St Margaret's, the first church to be lost to the flames. The top of the monument is a flaming gilded urn, though Wren favoured a golden phoenix rising from the ashes. The centre of the column is hollow, and the top can be reached by a winding stair of 311 steps. There is a viewing platform just under the gilded urn. This was caged in for safety in the mid-nineteenth century after a spate of suicides. Six people jumped between 1788 and 1842, forcing authorities to act.

For many years, the monument bore the inscription: "Here by permission of heaven, hell broke loose upon this Protestant city. The most dreadful burning of this city, began and carried out by the treachery and malice of the Popish faction… Popish frenzy which wrought such horrors is not yet quenched."

In 1830, after the passing of the Catholic Emancipation Act, this offensive inscription was chiselled out.

The Monument is open to the public daily from 9.30 a.m. to 5.30 p.m., and the cost of admission, at the time of writing, is £4.50. From the top, a great panoramic view over the river and the city is ample reward for the long climb. But for those who are unable for the steps, there is a webcam on the top of the Tower broadcasting the panorama constantly over the internet.

Another monument to the fire is the less impressive Golden Boy of Pye Corner, in Smithfield. This monument is a recessed arch in a limestone wall containing the small, golden figure of a young boy. It marks the spot where the fire stopped.

According to the inscription, the fire began in Pudding Lane and stopped at Pye Corner, indicating that the destruction of the city was evidence of God's wrath for the sin of gluttony.

The Burning of Parliament

The early nineteenth century was a dangerous time to be a parliamentarian in Britain. First, the Prime Minister, Spencer Perceval, was gunned down by a disgruntled constituent in 1812. Then the parliament itself burned to the ground in 1834. It was the biggest fire the city had seen since the Great Fire of 1666, and drew more crowds than a Cup Final.

The fire blazed for hours, and gutted most of the Palace of Westminster, including the converted St Stephen's Chapel where the House of Commons met.

It all began with an attempt to modernise the administration. For centuries, clerks, barely literate, used tally sticks to record finances and taxes. The tally sticks were notched wooden sticks which served as a record of monies owed or due. This began to be phased out in the early eighteenth century. It took 102 years to complete the phasing out, but by 1826 they were entirely removed from use.

An order was given in autumn of 1834 that the remaining tally sticks be burnt. The job went to Richard Whibley, Clerk of Works at the Palace. He decided against the sensible option of a bonfire as it might annoy the neighbours. So he ordered the tally sticks to be carried downstairs and put in the under floor stove that heated the House of Lords.

On the morning of 16 October, two workmen, Joshua Cross and Patrick Furlong, carried all the tally sticks downstairs and fired up the furnace. The job took all day, and the men toiled long hours, throwing the dry sticks into the stove, ignoring the fact that the copper-lined brick flues were becoming dangerously overheated.

First indications of a problem came in the afternoon as a housekeeper, Mrs Wright, was showing some visitors the chamber of the House of Lords. The chamber was full of smoke — a change from the usual hot air that filled the space. The floor seemed unnaturally warm. But Mrs Wright did not pursue the matter and went on with the tour.

Cross and Furlong piled the last of the tally sticks into the furnace in late afternoon, then went home, their job done. Mrs Wright closed the House of Lords at 5 p.m. Within an hour, it was found to be ablaze. The chimney flues had disintegrated, the wood close to them had ignited, and the fire had spread to the ancient wood panelling of the chamber.

The chamber was full of wooden chairs upholstered in flammable fabrics and ancient drapes ripe for the spark. Within minutes, it was an inferno.

The blaze began about an hour before dusk, and the evening sky over Westminster became red with the dancing flames. As word spread, huge crowds gathered to watch the drama unfold, including Prime Minister Lord Melbourne, and many of his cabinet.

The London Fire Engine Establishment, owned by the insurance companies, sent engines to the scene under director James Braidwood (later to be killed fighting the Tooley Street fire). They assessed the scene and realised that the palace was lost. They concentrated on saving Westminster Hall. Soon the fire spread to the House of Commons, whose chamber was situated in the former St Stephen's Chapel. Westminster Hall was now under serious threat.

Work continued through the evening and night, with civilian volunteers toiling shoulder to shoulder with the professional firefighters. Their main task was to dampen the great hall's fourteenth century roof with water, to prevent it from catching fire. This they succeeded in doing, and they brought the blaze under control after a number of hours. But by that stage, the majority of the old palace was no more.

Among the witnesses to the destruction was the painter William Turner, aged sixty-one at the time. He took a boat and went out onto the river to see the fire in its full glory. It was an image he kept coming back to; painting and repainting the scene in many spectacular canvasses over the next few years.

It could all have been avoided, as novelist Charles Dickens pointed out: "It would naturally occur to any intelligent person that nothing could be easier than to allow the tally sticks to be carried away for firewood by the miserable people who lived in that neighbourhood. However they never had been useful and official routine required that they should never be, and so the order went out that they were to be privately and confidentially burned. It came to pass that they were burned in a stove in the House of Lords. The stove, overgorged with these preposterous sticks, set fire to the panelling; the panelling set fire to the House of Commons; the two houses were reduced to ashes; architects were called in to build others; and we are now in the second million of the cost thereof."

Hasty reconstruction work began. The husk of the House of Lords was roofed (its four walls were still intact), and the Commons met there, among the damp and the stench of fire. The Lords met in the Painted Chamber, a hall of the palace that had not been completely gutted. It, too, needed a new roof for its temporary occupants, but the mother of Parliaments continued to meet in Westminster while construction went on all around the speakers.

It took years before the new building was ready for occupation. The first step was to pick a design. There was a competition, with ninety-seven architects submitting plans. Sir Charles Barry won out. His plan featured gothic revival detailing, supplied by Augustus Pugin.

The House of Lords was completed in 1847, with the Commons ready five years later. The building is one of London's most famous, sitting majestically along the banks of the Thames in the heart of the city. The eastern side, the Thames façade, is 267 metres (873 feet) long, and the complex has more than a thousand rooms. Perhaps its most famous feature is the large clock tower, housing Big Ben.

Although Westminster Palace is a working parliament with two houses sitting, it is still open to visitors. Guided tours of both Houses happen every Saturday throughout the year, and during the summer months when Parliament is in recess. It is also possible to arrange a tour of Big Ben, or to attend one of the parliamentary debates, though there can be a long waiting list for this, especially for the House of Commons.

Check out www.parliament.uk for more information.

The Yard Destroyed and the Pound Lost
One of the casualties of the Burning of Parliament was a very important yard in the Palace of Westminster. The yard was the small brass stick housed with the Clerk of the House of Commons, divided into three feet, one of the feet subdivided into 12 inches, and one of the inches further divided into tenths. The brass rod was the standard yard against which all others were to be measured and had been housed at

Westminster since an Act of Parliament in 1758.

The ends of the brass rod were marked with gold studs, and the yard was defined, by law, as: "The same straight line or distance between the centres of the said two points in the said gold studs in the said brass rod, the brass being at the temperature of sixty-two degrees by Fahrenheit's thermometer."

Unfortunately, that day, the temperature by Fahrenheit's thermometer exceeded sixty-two degrees by several hundred. The brass rod melted and distorted badly. It survived, but the gold studs were gone, and it was unusable as a measure.

The standard weight of a pound (16 ounces) was also destroyed in the blaze, as were the libraries, several centuries of records, some great works of art, and a great tapestry in the House of Lords commemorating the defeat of the Spanish Armada.

Tooley Street Fire

The last great peacetime fire in London was on Tooley Street in Southwark in 1861, and blazed for a fortnight. It caused massive damage, considerable loss of life and forced the city to rethink how it organised its firefighting services.

Now, with modern technology and proper health and safety precautions in place, such a blaze would be impossible. Short of war or a factory explosion, there will never be a calamity in the city such as that which beset Tooley Street in the summer of 1861. It was the last great fire of London.

Tooley Street runs through Southwark from the southern end of London Bridge past Tower Bridge and on to St Saviour's Dock. Today, it is part of the A200. In 1861 it was a busy thoroughfare running by equally busy docks.

The fire broke out on the afternoon of 22 June 1861, in a warehouse storing hemp and jute at Cotton's Wharf. A workman spotted smoke at four-thirty, and raised the alarm. Immediately a team began trying to battle the fire with buckets of water, but it was no easy task. It was low tide, and a spring tide, so the water was too far away for the chain of buckets to be effective. Within twenty minutes, they had admitted defeat and called in the fire brigade.

The first fire engine arrived within minutes. Others followed quickly. The head of the London Fire Engine Establishment, James Braidwood, galloped to the scene on his own horse-drawn fire engine. By six o'clock there were fourteen fire engines, between the horse-drawn land ones and the floating ones, at the scene. But the floating engines had to deal with the extreme low tide, and the fire was spreading. It had engulfed the upper storey of the warehouse and was creeping towards the neighbouring buildings. The spread was helped by the fact that the iron doors connecting the warehouses were left open during the day, only closing at night when the workmen had left.

The blaze was intense, and a little after 6 p.m., the Cotton Wharf warehouse suddenly collapsed onto nearby buildings which stored tar, tallow and resin, fuelling the conflagration. The head of the fire service, sixty-one-year-old James Braidwood, was caught by a falling wall and killed instantly.

By 8 p.m., the fire had spread to encompass the entire row of warehouses facing the river and all the buildings facing Tooley Street. The sky was lurid red, with smoke billowing thousands of feet into the air. The heat was so intense that it made approaching the warehouses almost impossible for the firefighters. By ten o'clock the blaze had reached a peak of intensity. Heat intensity was causing explosions in the packed warehouses, throwing blazing tallow into the air, and spreading the fire. Now the tide was coming in again. Burning oil floated along the river, which also contributed to the spread.

London Bridge and Tower Bridge were crowded with people eager to see the free illuminations. Throngs jostled for position, and over the course of the next few days, several people fell off the bridges and were drowned.

The fire was a great talking point in the city. Arthur Munby wrote in his diary a few days after 22 June: "Between Epsom and Cheam we saw from the train a great fire in the direction of London. A pyramid of red flame on the horizon, sending up a column of smoke that rose high in the air and then spread, like that over Vesuvius.

"As we drove along the arched way into town, the whole of Bermondsey was in a blaze of light. The fire was close to the station; dull brick-red fumes and showers of sparks rose high between it and the river. The station yard, which was as light as day, was crammed with people: railings, lamp posts, every high spot, was alive with climbers. The façade of St Thomas's Hospital, and the tower of St Saviour's were both fringed atop with lookers on."

Munby managed to secure a place on the roof of a bus to get a better view as they crossed the bridge. He saw: "struggling, screaming and fighting for a view, was a dense illimitable crowd, which even surged in heaps over the parapet of the bridge. For nearly a quarter of a mile the south bank of the Thames was on fire: a long line of what had been warehouses, their roofs and fronts all gone; and the tall ghastly sidewalls, white with heat, standing, or rather tottering, side by side in the midst of a mountainous desert of red and black ruin, which smouldered and steamed and sent up sheets of savage intolerable flame a 100 feet high.

"Burning barges lined the shore; burning oil and tallow poured in cascades from the wharfs, and flowed out blazing on the river."

It took half an hour for Munby's bus to cross the bridge; such was the throng of people trying to get a view of the blaze.

He later recorded: "No such fire has been known in London since the Fire of 1666: which, by the way, began at a spot exactly opposite this. Two millions, at least, of property destroyed: near eleven acres of ruin: many lives lost, among them the chief of the Fire Brigade. The fire was at his height two or three hours after I saw it: but it is still (Wednesday afternoon) burning furiously …"

Reynolds's Newspaper recorded: "And still the people came in fresh thousands to view the sight. Dawn of Sunday found London Bridge still thronged with cabs, omnibuses, carts, wagons and vehicles of every description. Peripatetic vendors of ginger-beer, fruit and other cheap refreshments abounded, and were sold out half a dozen times over. Public-houses, in defiance of Acts of Parliament, kept open all night long, and did a roaring trade, and so, for that matter, did the pickpockets, who blended business with pleasure, and had a ready hand for anything remunerative in their particular line. But the fire, fortunately, had done its worst, though the flames continued to surge and roar with unabated fury for some time, the intensity of the fire at length visibly slackened. The efforts of the firemen were redoubled, and by four o'clock on Sunday morning all danger of its further extension seemed at an end."

The fire was contained by Sunday, but it was not quenched that day — or the next. There were so many flammable materials in the warehouses that the firefighters had to content themselves with stopping the spread of the blaze, then wait until it burned itself out. That took more than two weeks. All through the end of June and into July, the blaze continued to smoulder, occasionally flaring up. Nearly three weeks passed before things cooled down enough for the clear up to begin.

Fire Insurance

Fire brigades in the nineteenth century were not like those today. The London Fire Engine Establishment was run by the insurance companies, not the local authorities. And for them, fire had to be profitable.

The Tooley Street fire blazed so long, it nearly broke them. So they raised their premiums and threatened to disband their fire service unless the government agreed to take over the work, or subsidise them properly. It took a few years to resolve the dispute, but in the end the Metropolitan Fire Brigade Act was passed, and London had its first real fire service.

Sugar Causes River of Flame

When a terrible fire broke out at Hawley's Wharf near Hermitage Wharf, Wapping, in December 1793, the entire wharf was destroyed, along with several neighbouring properties, three vessels on the river and a number of small craft on the docks. The heat was so intense that 1,400 casks of sugar were melted into one mass, which flowed through the streets and into the river as one bright stream of liquid fire.

Ratcliff Reduced to Ashes

In July 1794, a huge fire blazed at Ratcliff, destroying the area and several vessels in the river alongside. The fire was caused by the boiling over of a pitch kettle at a boatbuilder's yard, and it quickly spread to a neighbouring barge. The barge contained saltpetre, one of the key ingredients of gunpowder. Once the barge ignited, the conflagration was unstoppable.

The Ratcliff fire, near Wapping, was the largest fire disaster in London between the Great Fire of 1666 and the Blitz. Over 400 houses were destroyed, along with twenty warehouses. A thousand people were left homeless. A tented village was erected near St Dunstan's Church to accommodate them while the district was rebuilt.

The Last Great Fire of London

Between 6 p.m. on 29 December 1940 and 6 a.m. the following morning, the German Air Force, the Luftwaffe, dropped 100,000 incendiary bombs on the centre of London, obliterating much of the city. The damage stretched from Islington to St Paul's Cathedral.

1,500 individual fires broke out, spreading rapidly. Many joined up to form three major conflagrations which merged into a firestorm that devastated the city. 160 people were killed, and nineteen churches were destroyed, along with thirty-one Guildhalls, and all of Paternoster Row near St Paul's.

The incident, the worst single attack on the capital during the war, came to be known as the second Great Fire of London. It is described in detail in the chapter on the Thames during wartime.

CHAPTER TWO: SHIPPING DISASTERS ON THE THAMES

THE Thames is not a big river, though it is the second longest in Britain. However, the Port of London makes it one of the busiest shipping routes in the world. Stand on the banks and you will see everything pass by, from large cargo vessels and tankers, to huge industrial dredgers, hardy tugs, ferries, small tourist cruisers, Police and Fire Service RIBs and launches, rowboats, skulls and amphibious buses left over from the war. Two hundred years ago, it was even busier, with water taxis and small craft plying their trades. Collisions and sinkings were inevitable.

Thousands of small collisions occur every year, with boats bouncing off one another and off the piers of the bridges with alarming regularity. But some of the incidents on the river have been major tragedies that have caught the public imagination.

Royal Escort Accidentally Blown Up

Of the 1,100 ships that have gone down in the Thames, few were more prestigious than the HMS *London*, a 90-gun Royal Navy ship of the line that sank in 1665. Ships of the line were powerful gunboats that were the backbone of naval warfare. The HMS *London* had an added distinction. It was one of the ships that had escorted Charles II from Holland back to England during the Restoration in May 1660.

It was a very large ship by the standards of the day, with two gun decks and a crew of over three hundred, commanded by Captain John Lawson. Lawson had also been in charge during the restoration mission, and one of his passengers was James, Duke of York, and younger son of King Charles II.

HMS *London* was built at Chatham, launched in June 1656, and served with distinction for nearly a decade. On 7 March 1665, she was being fitted out at Chatham in preparation for a voyage. She then sailed from the Medway into the Thames and towards the city. But a sailor went down to the hold with a candle. The hold contained 14 tonnes of gunpowder, and the naked flame triggered an accidental explosion, blowing the ship asunder. Twenty-four men and one woman were thrown clear, and were rescued. But more than 300 lives were lost.

Samuel Pepys, the diarist, was a naval administrator at the time. He wrote: "This morning is brought to me to the office the sad news of the London, in which Sir J. Lawson's men were all bringing her from Chatham to the Hope, and thence he was to go to sea in her — but a little this side of the buoy of the Nower, she suddenly blew up.

"About 24 and a woman that were in the round house and coach saved; the rest, being 300, drowned — the ship breaking all into pieces — with 80 pieces of brass ordnance. She lies sunk, with her round house above water. Sir J. Lawson hath a great loss in this, of so many good chosen men, and many relations among them."

Lawson himself was not on board. But his luck was short-lived. Three months later, on 13 June, he was killed at the Battle of Lowestoft during the second Anglo-Dutch War.

Although the *London* sank in shallow water and parts of her superstructure were visible above water after the explosion, shifting tides caused her to be lost to history. Then, in 2008, the wreck was rediscovered. Because of its historic significance the port authorities changed the route of the shipping channel to prevent damage to the site, and to allow a full archaeological survey. It became the largest ever post-war salvage operation on the Thames, and uncovered remains of seven ships.

But within months of the rediscovery of the HMS *London*, thieves had dived at the site and recovered a brass canon. The wreck was then made a protected site. It didn't stop the looting. In April 2011, two men were arrested after a canon and other items were illegally raised, presumably for sale, on the black market.

Princess Alice — Britain's Biggest Peacetime Loss of Life

The Victorians were great day-trippers. The working classes and the growing middle classes liked to ape the gentry by going on little excursions. The growing rail network opened up the seaside resorts along the south coast and the Thames, the muddy sludgy highway through the centre of the city, proved an equally popular escape route.

But with few safety regulations, the dirtiest river in the empire and overcrowded boats, it was a disaster waiting to happen. On a sunny summer evening in 1878, the *Princess Alice* went down with the loss of 650 lives — the greatest loss of life in any Thames shipping disaster, and still the biggest peacetime loss of life in Britain.

The *Princess Alice*, a large paddle steamer, was bought by the Waterman's Steam Packet Company in 1867 and named after Queen Victoria's third daughter, the Grand Duchess of Hesse-Darmstadt. They put her to work on the profitable pleasure trips up and down the river. For the next decade, her distinctive three paddles were a familiar sight to Londoners. By 1875, she was owned and operated by the London Steamship Company and was regularly hired out for jaunts to the Boat Race and pleasure cruises.

September 3, 1878, was a balmy summer day, with clear skies and a warm breeze. A large crowd gathered at Swan Pier, near London Bridge, and boarded the *Princess Alice* for the two-hour trip down river to Sheerness and Gravesend. Rosherville Gardens was the big draw, a seventeen acre park that had ornamental gardens, wild animals, live music and fireworks every evening.

At 6 p.m. the *Princess Alice* pulled into the Rosherville Gardens pier and everyone piled back on board, paying their two shillings for the return to London — billed as the Moonlight Trip despite the early hour. No exact numbers are known, but it is thought that 750 people boarded. The capacity of the ship was 936 — though, she carried only two small lifeboats. The return trip would take almost two hours.

At 7.45 p.m., *Princess Alice* had steamed past Tripcock Point and was passing Gallions Reach, just before Woolwich Town. But at that moment, a large coal tanker, the 890-ton *Bywell Castle*, entered Gallions Reach from upstream. Riding high in the water because she was empty, she was moving at half-speed down the centre of the river. Captain Thomas Harrison knew that the river was wide enough — half a mile at that point — for both ships to pass safely. A rule had been introduced a few years previously, that ships should pass on the port side, but that was at sea. This was an inland waterway. So he kept the *Bywell Castle* on course, following a traditional path. He just veered slightly south, to avoid the passenger boat.

But on board the *Princess Alice*, Captain William Grinsted saw the large cargo vessel and swerved south too, straight into the path of the huge collier. Captain Harrison ordered a full-speed reverse of his engines, but it was too late. Moments later, the *Bywell Castle* ploughed into the *Princess Alice* just behind her starboard paddle wheel, splitting the smaller ship cleanly in two. Within four minutes, the *Princess Alice* was at the bottom of the river. Hundreds trapped inside went down with her. More were thrown into the river.

The *Bywell Castle* was floating high so there was no chance for survivors to scramble on board, but Captain Harrison did his best. Everything that could float was thrown overboard for survivors to cling to. He launched his lifeboats and was instrumental in saving some lives.

"We took immediate measures for saving life by hauling up over our bows several passengers, throwing overboard ropes' ends, life-buoys, a hold-ladder, and several planks, and getting out three boats. The *Princess Alice* turned over and sank under our bows. We succeeded in rescuing a great many passengers," Captain Harrison recorded in his log.

But the disaster was compounded by another problem. Just an hour before the collision, the Becton North Outfall Sewer, as well as sewers at Barking and Crossness, had discharged 75 million gallons of raw sewage into the river near the collision site — and with the waste, both industrial and human, already in the river, many of those who survived, later succumbed to the effects of the pollution.

One man did have an amazing escape; as the bow of the *Princess Alice* rose just before she plunged into the river, he calmly stepped from the bow onto the deck of the *Bywell Castle*. He didn't even get his feet wet. But there were few such good stories.

Only a hundred were saved. It was a disaster unparalleled in the history of the Thames. A newspaper man, W. T. Vincent, was one of those quickly on the scene. His account of that evening is harrowing: "Soon policemen and watermen were seen by the feeble light bearing ghastly objects into the offices of the Steampacket Company, for a boat had just arrived with the first consignment of the dead, mostly little children whose light bodies and ample drapery had kept them afloat even while they were smothered in the festering Thames. I followed into the steamboat office, marvelling at the fate which had brought the earliest harvest of victims to the headquarters of the doomed ship, and, entering the boardroom, the first of the martyrs was pointed out to me as one of the company's own servants, a man employed on the *Princess Alice*. The lifeless frames of men and women lay about, and out on the balcony, from which the directors had so often looked upon their fleet through the fragrant smoke of the evening cigar, there was a sight to wring out tears of blood from the eyes of any beholder. A row of little innocents, plump and pretty, well-dressed children, all dead and cold, some with life's ruddy tinge still on their cheeks and lips, the lips from which the merry prattle had gone forever."

The rescue operation soon switched to a recovery operation. Local watermen were paid five shillings for each body they found, and they were pulling victims out of the river for weeks afterwards. Some bodies were never recovered, but when the two halves of the *Princess Alice* were raised, they were full of bloated corpses, particularly around the exits to the salons. Hundreds had been trapped inside, drowned as they tried to battle their way onto the decks. 115 were buried unidentified, and at least 590 inquests were held. The death toll was probably between 600 and 650.

The first public enquiry, convened three days after the accident, found that the *Princess Alice* was at fault. A second enquiry (and the court of public opinion) found that the *Bywell Castle* was to blame. The Admiralty Court shared the blame between both ships. This confusion made it difficult to find a scapegoat; though Captain Harrison never went to sea again.

However, the public inquiries did have one useful outcome. It was decided that ships should always pass each other on the port side (in contrast to cars, which drive on the left and pass on the starboard side!). Had this rule been in effect, the accident never would have occurred.

The sinking of the *Princess Alice* deeply touched the sentimental Victorians, and a memorial to the victims — a marble Celtic cross — was erected at Woolwich Old Cemetery, King's Highway, Plumstead. It was paid for by public subscription, and 23,000 people donated sixpence each. A hundred and twenty victims are buried in a mass grave close by, including Captain Grinsted. Both the memorial and the grave can still be seen today.

FAMILIES OF VICTIMS

Captain William Grinsted (47) was not alone on the *Princess Alice* that day. Several of his relatives made the trip with him — and died by his side. They included his son John J. Grinsted. Aged just fourteen, he was employed as an apprentice engineer on ship. Captain Grinsted's brother Charles (56), and Charles's wife Jane (53), were also lost. All four are buried in Woolwich Old Cemetery. Luckily, the captain's wife, Eliza, and his other son, William, were not on board. William Junior was a waterman and spent the three days after the sinking helping the rescue operation, and searching for his brother and father.

The General Manager of the London Steamship Company was also on board that fateful evening. William Towse was on a trip with his parents, his wife, and his sons. All were killed, wiping out three generations of the family.

THE RIPPER CONNECTION

Elizabeth Stride was born in Sweden in 1843. She had picked up convictions for prostitution in Gothenburg at a young age and came to London at the age of twenty-three. She married Thomas Stride, but separated from him in 1877.

Like many Londoners, she was touched by the *Princess Alice* tragedy — but she saw it as a chance to explain her lack of a husband. She told acquaintances that Thomas and two of her nine children were on board the ship with her and were drowned. She had managed to swim to safety — but in the mêlée, she had been kicked in the mouth by another of the victims, which caused her to stutter ever afterwards.

She may well have been on board that day. But the rest of her story is pure fabrication.

In fact, she reunited briefly with her husband in 1881, and separated permanently afterwards. He died of tuberculosis in 1884, six years after the sinking. And the couple had no children.

Elizabeth Stride was murdered on 30 September 1888, the third victim of Jack the Ripper.

Many of the other survivors also did not do well. Sixteen died within a fortnight of being rescued, probably as a result of the highly toxic effects of the river water.

The pollution was so bad that most of the corpses decomposed at twice the normal rate. Special coffins had to be built to accommodate the badly swollen bodies.

I Did See Some People Bobbing About, But…
The Tragedy of the *Albion* Launch

According to some of the newspaper reports, it was a launch where nothing went right. When the Duke and Duchess of York (later King George V and Queen Mary) tried to give the

Albion a good send-off on 21 June 1898, the champagne magnum bounced off the iron sides of the mighty war ship. Three times the Duchess tried to break the bottle to give the ship its official blessing, and three times she failed.

So the ship slid into the water without that ceremony, a thing which many journalists on board gleefully reported the following morning. But what a lot of them missed was that the launch caused a swell on the river, which swept a temporary bridge, and thirty-eight people on it, to the bottom of the Thames.

The launch of the HMS *Albion* remains one of the least successful boat launches of all time.

The *Albion* was built at the Thames Ironworks in Blackwall, Canning Town. The shipyard occupied both banks of the Bow Creek as it flowed into the Thames. Because of the width of the river, larger vessels were built parallel to the shore and launched sideways into the river. At 390 foot long, 74 foot wide and weighing in at 6,000 tonnes, the *Albion* was large.

The local schools were all given the day off for the launch, as the future king and his consort were very popular. The shipwrights printed 20,000 tickets for the event. 8,000 would sit in prepared wooden stages, while the remainder would have to accommodate themselves as best they could around the shipyard. Anticipating huge crowds, the gatekeepers were instructed to admit people without tickets, provided they were "respectably dressed".

On the day, between 25,000 and 30,000 people thronged the yard at Blackwall. They scrambled for the best vantage points, and 200 crowded onto a temporary wooden bridge that had been put up to allow workmen access to a Japanese warship that was being worked on. The bridge was clearly marked as off limits because it was in an area that would be flooded by the launch, but no one was enforcing the rules. As one policeman said: "People about here are not like a west-end crowd. Tell a west-end crowd to stand back and they do so, but these people, you would have to chuck them off before they would move."

The bridge was occupied mainly by the families of workers in the yard. More experienced hands joked that those on the bridge would soon get their annual bath.

At 2.50 p.m., the Duchess swung the bottle against the hull for the third and final time. When it didn't smash, she just cut the ribbon and the large battleship began to slide sideways into the river. As it did so, a large swell was pushed in front of it, striking the far side of the creek and sloshing back around the boat. The tidal wave swept through the yard, engulfing the small creek that the temporary bridge spanned.

No one knows what caused the calamity — whether it was the weight of 200 people on a bridge designed for a handful, or the concussive power of the wave, or whether floating debris struck the supports, but within seconds, the bridge collapsed and over a hundred people found themselves floundering in 10 feet of water.

Such was the roar of the cheering crowd that many people did not realise what was happening. The cries of panic were drowned out by the cheers of the main crowd applauding the launch. Some spotted the danger and did their best to help. Several civilians helped the police and the dock workers.

As one man said afterwards (in an interview with the *London Times*): "My brother and I took off our coats and waistcoats and jumped into the struggling mass. I am a good swimmer, and was too excited to think of the danger. I kept diving underneath the spars and anywhere where I thought a body might be found, and my brother and I brought up five people, three alive and two dead. There were about ten of us in the water diving to save people.

"I am afraid that beyond the satisfaction of endeavouring to save life, I have gained little by the affair. My waistcoat, containing my watch and chain, was stolen."

Many were saved that day, but thirty-eight were drowned. They included twenty-three women and children, mainly the families of employees of the Thames Ironworks who had access to the bridge, which was not opened to the public. The first corpse plucked from the water was that of a little baby.

Mr Wilson, an electrician at the works, found his mother and his sister among the dead laid out in the sheds that evening. His sister was just back in London from her honeymoon.

More would have been lost had some brave spectators not jumped in. One, Thomas Cook of Percy Road, Canning Town, was praised for rescuing five people from a watery grave.

As *The Times* reported, with stoic understatement, the following morning: "A tragic accident yesterday marred the interesting and picturesque ceremony of launching the new battleship *Albion* at Blackwall Deeply as we must all sympathise with the unfortunate people who fell victims … it does not appear that blame can fairly attach to any but themselves."

The *Daily Mail*, on the other hand, missed the story entirely. Their reporter, Duncombe Jewell, rasped lyrical on the launch and missed the real drama. When his furious editor confronted him about the deaths reported in the other papers, he said: "Well, I did see some people bobbing about in the water as I came away, but…"

There is no memorial to those who died on the day of the *Albion* launch. But there is a memorial to the Thames Ironworks itself. You can find it at Canning Town Underground Station.

Sunken Ship Threatens Biblical Flood

A tidal wave of huge proportions could hit central London at any time, causing untold loss of life and property. Authorities are worried that the threat is getting closer and closer. The danger does not come from freak weather conditions or outlandish earth movements. It is far more mundane — and immediate.

The wreck of the SS *Richard Montgomery* lies in the Thames Estuary, filled with enough explosives to bring down the city.

The American cargo ship was carrying over six thousand tonnes of explosives when it grounded and broke in two off Sheerness in 1944. Much of that ordinance is still on the wreck, and the coastguard have warned that there is a serious and growing threat of significant structural collapse of the shipwreck.

If she blows, it will send a tidal wave sweeping up the Thames, which will overwhelm the Thames Barrier. The port of Sheerness would be wiped out within minutes.

The 420-foot long cargo ship was built during the Second World War, and launched in June 1943. A little over a year later — August 1944 — she left Philadelphia with 6,127 tonnes of munitions. She was bound for the Thames Estuary, where she would join a convoy heading for Normandy to restock the troops who had carried out the D-Day landings.

The *Montgomery* anchored off the north edge of Sheerness middle sands. But on 20 August, she dragged anchor and began to drift. Several ships spotted the danger and tried to signal an alert by sounding their sirens. But Captain Wilkie slept through the racket, and his chief officer unaccountably did not try to wake him. So the ship ran aground on a sandbank around 250 metres from the Medway Approach

Channel in 7.3 metres (24 feet) of water. The ship broke her back on the sandbank.

A salvage company tried to remove the cargo and got much of it off before the hull cracked open and the holds flooded. The ship broke in two and the wreck was abandoned — with half the cargo still on board. This included 1,400 tonnes of high explosive.

As the *Richard Montgomery* poses a real danger to shipping, the wreck is constantly monitored and a warning buoy marks the site. Part of the superstructure of the vessel remains visible above the water. In 1973, the site was the first wreck designated as dangerous, and there is a constantly policed exclusion zone around it.

A risk assessment is carried out periodically. After one in 1999 (unpublished), the port authorities said that: "Doing nothing is not an option for much longer."

According to a survey conducted in 2000 by the Maritime and Coastguard Agency, the wreck still contains 3,173 tonnes of munitions. Removing the explosives would be dangerous. An attempt was made to salvage a similar cargo ship off Folkestone in 1967. The explosion on that occasion had the force equivalent to an earthquake of 4.5 on the Richter scale, punching a 6 metre crater into the seabed, and bringing "panic and chaos" to Folkestone. Thankfully, no one was hurt.

But the *Richard Montgomery* lies in the estuary rather than in open water. Experts agree that if she blows, it would throw a 300 metre (1,000 feet) wide column of water, mud, metal and munitions nearly 3,000 metres (10,000 feet) into the air. It would generate a wave 5 metres (16 feet) high, which would sweep up the estuary.

As the river narrows near the capital, the wave would grow in size. Couple that with a spring tide, and London could become the Venice of the north in minutes. The initial blast would blow out almost every window in Sheerness and the wave, a few minutes later, would level much of the town.

How likely is the catastrophe? Some experts say a fuse in one of the fragmentation devices could become unstable as its lead azide reacts with water vapour to form hydrazoic acid. This could then react with copper in the detonating cap, forming extremely sensitive copper azide. A knock, perhaps caused by the ship breaking up further, or a collision with a passing boat, could cause the copper azide to explode, triggering a chain reaction resulting in the detonation of the bulk of the explosives.

But the government feels the danger is exaggerated, and that much of the dangerous chemicals in the fuses will have dissolved in the seawater by now. The truth is, no one knows.

Surveys in 2008 and 2009 show the ship continues to deteriorate, and is breaking up faster by the year. The Coastguard Agency said that a 2009 structural survey showed "accelerated deterioration". Its report concluded that collapse was "not imminent" but "getting closer". It went on to say: "At some point in the future, there could be a complete loss of structural integrity in hold number two, possibly leading to this section breaking into two."

If the ship explodes, it will be one of the biggest non-nuclear blasts ever — the equivalent of a one kiloton nuclear bomb — and will devastate the port of Sheerness. It will do more damage to London than even the Great Fire of 1666.

The Cargo of Death
The *Richard Montgomery* carries the explosive equivalent of a small 1.4 kiloton nuclear device, and it lies in the Thames Estuary, menacing London. Its deadly cargo still includes

roughly 1,400 tonnes of TNT. It is made up of:
- 286 x 2,000 lb bombs
- 4,439 x 1,000 lb bombs
- 1,925 x 500 lb bombs
- 2,815 x fragmentation bombs and bomb clusters
- Various explosive booster charges
- Various smoke bombs, including white phosphorus bombs
- Various pyrotechnic signals.

Submarine Sinks

Few things are more frightening than being on a ship that is about to sink. Perhaps the only thing worse is to be trapped in a submarine. That was the fate that befell seven-nine men — including a number of civilians — when a navy submarine collided with a tanker in the Thames Estuary in 1950.

The HMS *Truculent* was just eight-years-old, having been commissioned during the Second World War. At 275 feet in length, she had a crew of sixty-one. But there were far more aboard her that wintery evening.

The submarine was doing trials around Sheerness on 12 January, and after the trials, a number of electricians, fitters, dock officials and others who had helped with a refit, came on board for a jaunt. There were eighteen civilians, bringing the muster up to seventy-nine. The submarine dived around Margate and Ramsgate, then came to the surface in the late afternoon and began heading for port at a steady ten knots.

Unknown to the sub crew, the SS *Divina*, with a river pilot on board, was coming against them, en route from the Port of London to Ipswich. The *Divina* had a reinforced hull for sailing through ice. Shortly after 7 p.m. both boats reached the vicinity of the West Oaze Buoy, a narrow part of the Thames Estuary. The sub navigator and captain spotted the lights of the *Divina*, and thought they were a bit peculiar. So the captain sent down for a navigation book, the Manuel of Seamanship. Torpedo officer Frederick Henley came up the coning tower with the book.

The Board of Enquiry report says that the *Truculent* entered the estuary through Princes Channel, then passed between Red Sand Shoal and Shivering Sand Fort at 9 knots, then altered course by 20 degrees. She collided with the *Divina* a mile from Red Sand Tower.

Fredrick Henley told *Weekend Magazine* some years later: "It was a cold, dark night, the sky pricked with brightly shining stars. I didn't see the tanker ploughing inexorably towards us. I took a last gulp of fresh air and turned to go down the ladder from the conning tower.

"I had hardly grasped the rungs when I heard the Captain issue a stream of urgent orders. There was an almighty crash and I was pinned to the side of the conning tower as *Truculent* keeled over at a crazy angle. There was a sickening lurch and, in seconds, we sank like a stone to the seabed 80 feet below. The conning tower was flooded, and I knew that somehow I had to get clear.

"I managed to squirm round the periscope standards and breathed out as hard as I could. I found myself on the surface, swimming aimlessly in the darkness."

He was rescued an hour later, but most of those on board were not so lucky. Over fifty of her crew were swept away in the current after a premature escape attempt, while twenty were picked up by nearby boats. Most of the crew managed to survive the initial collision, but then perished in the dark and freezing waters of the Thames. Some scrambled onto mud islands in the estuary, where they froze to death.

In all, sixty-four men died that night, including two air force rescue crew members. The subsequent enquiry found the crew of the submarine to bear most responsibility for the tragedy.

Party Boat Marchioness Sank Like Toy

In the Great Nave of Southwark Cathedral is a memorial to one of the great shipping tragedies of the Thames. The circular memorial, occupying the spot once filled by the baptismal font, is a grisly reminder that a century after the sinking of the *Princess Alice*, poor shipping practices still cost lives.

The pleasure boat *Marchioness* was sunk in a collision with a dredger on a balmy summer evening in 1989, with the loss of fifty-one lives. There are eerie parallels with the sinking of the *Princess Alice*, just a hundred and one years earlier. Both were pleasure trips, both sank within minutes with massive loss of life. And both could have been prevented with proper seamanship.

The *Marchioness*, about the size of a double-decker bus, was a pleasure boat that did sightseeing trips down the Thames during the day, but was available for hire in the evenings. That night photographic agency boss Jonathan Phang had hired it to celebrate the 26th birthday of his friend and business partner, Antonio de Vasconcellos, a merchant banker and co-owner of the photographic agency.

It was a lavish party. Eight friends met for a dinner — little knowing it was a last supper for six of them. Following the dinner, they were joined by about twenty more people for cake and champagne. Then they set off for the pier at Charing Cross (now replaced by The Embankment Pier), where they joined another hundred guests. There were 113 guests, as well as crew and catering staff, making a total of 131 on board as they set off, looking forward to a night of drinking, dining and dancing. It was already past 1 a.m.

Many of those at the party were in their twenties. Some were former student friends of the birthday boy, and others worked in the fashion and music industry. There were also colleagues from the world of finance.

Twenty minutes into the trip, the *Marchioness* prepared to pass eastwards through the central arch of Southwark Bridge, heading towards Canon Street Railway Bridge. They were going downstream, sticking to the centre. Conditions were reasonable, but there was a fog on the river, reducing visibility. And it was the darkest part of the night. On the *Marchioness*, the party was warming up. In the disco area revellers were hooked together, dancing to The Hues Corporation's "Rock the Boat, Don't Tip the Boat Over".

But unknown to the partygoers, a much larger ship, the dredger *Bowbelle*, was also coming down the centre of the river and aiming for the central arch of Southwark Pier. Some crew of the *Marchioness* spotted the larger boat seconds before they collided, but no one on the larger boat saw the danger. The skipper of the *Marchioness* applied full throttle, but it was too late. The *Bowbelle*, at 8.5 knots, was moving twice as fast as the *Marchioness*. There was also a huge disparity in size; the *Marchioness* was a 90-tonne cruiser, while the *Bowbelle* was almost 1,800 tonnes, several times longer and three times higher. The skipper, Douglas Henderson, was not at the helm, and he had consumed six pints of beer that afternoon.

At 1.46 a.m., they passed under the arch and the *Bowbelle* struck the *Marchioness* on the stern, hard. The *Marchioness* began to spin to the left as the *Bowbelle* ploughed on, pushing her forward. The anchor of the *Bowbelle* ripped into the side of the *Marchioness*, letting water pour in. Within seconds, the

Marchioness began to roll over and the bigger boat rose up, her bow mounting the pleasure boat. As the *Marchioness* rolled, she filled with water and her entire superstructure became detached. Within half a minute of the initial impact, the *Bowbelle* had rode over the *Marchioness*, pushing her to the bottom.

One witness said: "The *Bowbelle* hit it in about its centre, then mounted it and pushed it under the water like a toy boat."

A survivor said: "I looked up and saw a monster. The boat that hit us was a big black shape above me and it looked like it had eyes. Then the deck was tilting, and I stepped into the water."

The *Marchioness* came to a rest on the bottom of the river, about halfway between Southwark Bridge and the Canon Street railway bridge.

Those on the upper decks were thrown into the river, and many were saved. But those trapped inside had no chance, the sinking happened so fast. Fifty-one of the 131 on board lost their lives, and almost half were recovered from the sunken hull. The majority of the survivors came from the upper decks.

The alarm was raised instantly, but the initial rescue effort was hampered by the fact that rescue vessels were sent to Battersea Bridge by mistake. Most of the survivors owe their lives to the *Hurlingham*, a pleasure cruiser which was a little behind the *Marchioness* and which had been overtaken by the *Bowbelle* a few minutes earlier. The *Bowbelle* docked downstream and never launched its lifeboats.

Twenty-four of the drowned victims were found below decks, and the remaining twenty-seven recovered from various parts of the Thames over the coming days. They included the birthday boy, Antonio de Vasconcellos, the last body to be recovered eleven days after the sinking.

Officially, the accident was blamed on poor visibility from each of the ships' wheelhouses, the fact that both vessels were using the centre of the river, and the lack of clear instructions to the lookout at the bow of the *Bowbelle*. The *Bowbelle's* skipper, Douglas Henderson, was tried for failing to keep a proper lookout, but was formally acquitted after two juries failed to reach a decision. A Coroner's Inquest six years after the accident found that the victims had been unlawfully killed.

Following pressure from the Marchioness Action Group, a formal investigation chaired by Lord Justice Clarke in 2000, blamed poor lookouts on both vessels for the collision, and criticised the owners of both vessels for failing to instruct and monitor their crews in a proper fashion.

The one positive thing to emerge from the tragedy is that four lifeboat stations have been put on the river. Since 2002, there are stations at Gravesend, Tower Pier, Chiswick Pier and Teddington.

In an ironic twist, the *Bowbelle* was herself lost seven years after the accident. After the Thames collision, she was sold to a Madeiran dredging company and was operating off the coast of Madeira when she split in half and sank on 25 March 1996.

You can visit the memorial to the victims at Southwark Cathedral, not far from the site of the disaster. Every year, a service of remembrance is held there for those who lost their lives.

The Victims

The birthday boy, Antonio de Vasconcellos, and five of the seven people who had joined him for an intimate celebratory dinner earlier in the evening were among the dead. De Vasconcellos was a Portuguese aristocrat and a rising name in the city. In the cut-throat world of banking, he was on a salary of close to a million a year. Young and carefree, he had a very active social life outside of banking. One of his interests was the photographic agency he was a partner in.

Because of this, the guest list included many of the bright and beautiful of the capital, including models and people from the fashion and music industries. The youngest person on board was nineteen-year-old Francesca Dallaglio, sister of the future England rugby captain, Lawrence. Another of the victims was the skipper of the *Marchioness*, Stephen Faldo. His son is Jeff Brazier, presenter and reality TV star.

Parallels with the *Princess Alice*

Although separated by a century, there are eerie parallels between the sinking of the *Princess Alice* and the *Marchioness*.

Both were pleasure cruises run over by vastly larger ships. The collisions occurred at night in late summer. Both ships sank very rapidly — the *Princess Alice* in four minutes, the *Marchioness* in half a minute.

The sinkings were preventable. Had proper rules been in place for passing on waterways, the 1878 disaster would not have happened. Had proper watches been maintained, the 1979 collision would have been avoided.

The big difference was that the *Bywell Castle* rescued many from the *Princess Alice*, whereas the *Bowbelle* docked and did not get involved in the rescue effort a century later.

CHAPTER THREE: RIVERSIDE BUILDINGS GIVE A VIEW OF HISTORY

A stroll along the banks of the Thames is a stroll through a thousand years of history. All the beautiful old buildings you pass — and the modern shiny chrome and glass structures — are part of a rich tapestry of human experience. They tell the history of London — and some fascinating anecdotes! While I can't tell every story, let's take a look at some of the more interesting.

Hell on Earth — The Marshalsea Prison

Nothing remains of it now but a single wall adjoining a graveyard. But, for much of the history of London, the Marshalsea Prison, on the banks of the river at Southwark, was the most notorious of London's eighteen hellholes used to incarcerate miscreants.

Second in importance only to the Tower of London, it housed debtors, those under court martial for offences at sea (including "unnatural" acts) and treasonous Catholics. Over the centuries, thousands died under the appalling conditions in which they were held.

Marshalsea operated from the fourteenth century until 1842 and was privately run, like most prisons of the time. As one wag put it, the prison looked like an Oxbridge college, but operated as an extortion racket. For prisoners who could pay, there was a bar, shop and restaurant, as well as the privilege of being let out during the day to earn money to repay their debts. But most debtors could not pay, and conditions for them were hellish.

The unlucky were crammed into nine rooms with dozens of others, sometimes for decades at the whim of their creditors. A parliamentary committee in 1729 was shocked to discover that 300 inmates had died of starvation within a three-month period. Eight to ten prisoners a day died during the warm days of summer. It was a charnel house.

Debtors made up most of the population. Before the Bankruptcy Act of 1869, men and women were routinely imprisoned for debt at the pleasure of their creditors, sometimes for decades. They would often take their families into prison with them, so that entire communities sprang up behind bars, with children being born and raised in prison. Prison keepers charged rent, bailiffs charged for food and clothing and attorneys creamed the rest off in legal fees. So once in the prison, the debtor was trapped in a vicious cycle that often ended with the grave.

In 1641, there were 10,000 people in prison for debt. Jailers found novel ways of extracting money from them. One was the "trade of chains", where prisoners were fettered in many iron links. Jailers removed one link every time a payment was made. Those who could not pay were often chained to the floor on their backs, with a spiked collar around their neck and heavy iron bars over their legs, until their family coughed up.

The Marshalsea occupied two buildings on what is now Borough High Street, and by the late fifteenth century, was in a state of decay. It operated from 1329 to 1811.

There were two sides to the prison. In the Master's Side, there were about fifty rooms rented to the well-off prisoners. On the Common Side were nine rooms, which housed 300 prisoners. The Master's Side contained a bar, shop and coffee shop, as well as a chop-house called Titty Doll's, run by a prisoner. There was also a tailor and a barber.

There were no such luxuries on the Common Side. Living conditions were horrific. In 1639, there were twenty-three women held in one small room. They were regularly beaten with a "bull's pizzle", a whip made from the penis of a bull. Men were tortured with thumbscrews and a skullcap, a heavy vice for the head.

Worst of all was confinement in the Strong Room. This was a windowless shed near the main sewer, next to the cadavers awaiting burial (sometimes up to a dozen a day). The room was awash in excrement, and was a haven for rats. One diabetic army officer was moved from the Common Side to the Strong Room, where he died within days. A few hours after his death, his face had been eaten off by the rats. Another prisoner got gangrene from lying on the wet floor, and a rat ate the nose, ear, cheek and left eye of another — while he was still alive.

A parliamentary committee was convened in 1729 after the death of a prisoner. They were shocked to find that prisoners were being routinely starved to death. One prisoner, Baronet Sir William Rich, was in irons. He had been burned with a red-hot poker, hit with a stick and kept in a dungeon for ten days. His offence was that he was unable to pay the prison fee. You had to pay for the privilege of being jailed back then.

Daily rations were an ounce and a half of beef, with a quarter of a half-penny loaf. But prisoners only got the rations three days a week.

"When the miserable wretch has worn out the charity of his friends, and consumed the money which he has raised upon his clothes and bedding, and has eaten his last allowance of provisions, he usually in a few days grows weak for want of food, with the symptoms of a hectic fever," reported the committee. "When he is no longer able to stand, if he can raise 3d to pay the fee of the common nurse of the prison, he obtains the liberty of being carried into the sick ward, and lingers on for about a month or two, by the assistance of the prison portion of provision, and then dies."

The sick wards were stacked like shelves as there were so many people in them. A committee member, taking pity on the wretches, shared some food with a prisoner. The man promptly died; his stomach was so distorted and contracted from starvation that he went into convulsions and passed away.

As a result of the committee, several staff members were tried for murder. But they were all acquitted.

By the start of the 1800s, the prison was in complete decay. One man made his escape by pushing the loose bricks of the wall down and walking through the gap. Numbers of inmates had dwindled after the damning parliamentary committee investigation. In 1812, Marshalsea Prison was closed and moved to a new location a little up the road. The new prison operated for forty years, and is most famous as the setting for much of the action in Charles Dickens' "Little Dorrit". The book gives a fairly accurate account of the life of a debtor in those times; a life that Dickens knew all too well, as his father had spent three months in the Marshalsea. His family lived in the prison, but twelve-year-old Charles, as the eldest, found lodgings outside and worked in a blacking factory to help out.

But the prison also held Admiralty prisoners. Those facing court martial for mutiny, desertion and piracy, as well as "unnatural crimes", were held there while awaiting trial or execution. Admiralty prisoners were often housed in the infirmary, chained to bolts in the floor. But the most notorious pirates were frequently held in the Strong Room, festering amongst the rats and the corpses.

The Marshalsea was finally closed in 1842, its remaining inmates moved to King's Bench Prison, or to Bethlem Royal Hospital if they were mentally unstable.

All that remains today of the most horrific of London's many prisons is the brick wall that marked its southern boundary. It now separates the Local Studies library from a small public garden that used to be a graveyard. The boundary wall is marked by a plaque from the local council. But if the story interests you, you can visit the Cuming Museum on Walworth Road, where you can see one of the pumps from the old prison. The Dickens House Museum on Doughty Street in Holborn houses one of the prison windows. Nothing else remains except the ghosts.

The Butcher of Southwark

William Acton was a butcher in Southwark when he paid the governor of The Marshalsea, John Darby, an annual free of the equivalent of £20,000 in today's money to be allowed to act as warden in the prison. During his brutal regimen, prisoners were routinely fleeced of everything they had, or killed in the process.

Following the Parliamentary Committee report of 1729, he was charged with multiple murders. The first case against him was for the murder of Thomas Bliss, a debtor in the Common Side of the prison.

Bliss was unable to pay the prison fees, so he was left with so little to eat that he was dying of starvation. He tried to escape over the wall, but the wardens cut his rope, dropping him 20 feet to the stone cobbles of the prison yard. Acton beat him with a whip, stomped on him, then placed him in "the hole", a small damp space under the stairs, too small to lie down or stand up in.

From there, he was moved to the infamous Strong Room. Bliss spent three weeks in the Strong Room, wearing a vice on his head, thumbscrews, iron collar and leg irons. One witness said the swelling in his legs was so bad that the irons could not be seen under the swollen flesh. His wife, who could see him through a small hole in the door, testified that he was bleeding from the mouth and thumbs. He was given a small amount of food, but the skullcap prevented him chewing; another prisoner had to chew his allowance and spit it into his mouth.

He was removed to the sick ward after three weeks, where he died.

Acton was also implicated in three other murders. Captain John Bromfield, Robert Newton and James Thompson all died after similar treatment to Bliss's — beatings, followed by spells in the hole or Strong Room. All three died in leg irons in the sick ward.

But the government did not want the public to know just how bad the prisons were, and Acton produced a string of witnesses who spoke of his good character. He was acquitted on all charges. The Parliamentary Committee could draw attention to the conditions of London's jails, but it was powerless to do anything more.

Prisoners of Note

As well as debtors and sailors, The Marshalsea also held several political figures, mostly for sedition and other kinds of inappropriate behaviour. Victorian historian William Hepworth Dixon said it "was full of poets, pirates, parsons, plotters, coiners, libellers, defaulters, Jesuits, and vagabonds of every class."

In Elizabethan times, it was the main prison for Catholics suspected of stirring up discontent against the government.

The last Catholic Bishop of London, Edmund Bonner, spent the final decade of his life there.

Playwright Ben Johnson, a friend of Shakespeare, was jailed in 1597 after his play, "The Isle of Dogs", was banned for being "inappropriate". He had satirised the queen. He was in good company; the poet Christopher Brook was jailed four years later for helping seventeen-year-old Ann More marry fellow poet John Donne.

Political satirist George Wither wrote his poem "The Shepherd's Hunting" while imprisoned for libel.

Eton College headmaster Nicholas Udall was sent to The Marshalsea for buggery and theft — but he went on to become headmaster of Westminster School, so it did his career no harm.

When Sir John Eliot, Vice-Admiral of Devon, questioned the king's right to levy taxes in 1632, he was jailed. So was John Seldon, the jurist, in 1629, for drafting a Petition of Right for Parliament, questioning the king's powers.

The most notorious prisoners in the riverside jail were pirates, but the most famous of them, Captain Kidd, managed to get sent to the most pleasant surroundings of Newgate. He escaped the hellish Strong Room, but he still did the Marshal's Dance on the end of a noose in 1701.

Women of the Marshalsea
The prison contained an eclectic mix of wives, lovers, daughters and prostitutes, who all had free access to the prisoners. Visitors could come and go freely, and even live with the prisoners without being challenged. And female prisoners were allowed to mix freely with the male ones.

In line with the commercial exploitation of every opportunity, some rooms were even kept aside and hired out to prostitutes. The only real rule was that when the prison closed its gates at ten, they had to leave with the other visitors. A warning bell was struck and an officer did the rounds calling: "Strangers, women and children, all out!"

The Marshalsea was not a safe place for women. Rape was common, as was the temptation to turn to prostitution to survive. As a result — and because debtors frequently brought their families inside to live with them — a number of women gave birth within the prison walls.

But the prison doctor was under strict orders — the women were off limits. He would visit prisoners and their children, but to protect his reputation, he would not attend their wives. So the women had to bear the pain of confinement and birth unaided.

One doctor told a Parliamentary Committee that he had assisted at one birth, but only as a matter of courtesy because it was not included in his salary.

The First Poll Tax Protests and the Storming of the Savoy Palace

The poll tax protests of the 1980s had nothing on The Peasant's Revolt of 1381, which almost saw a rabble of commoners overthrow King Richard II and the system of serfdom. In the moment of their greatest triumph, the rebels even managed to storm London Bridge and take over the Tower of London. It looked as if victory was in their grasp.

The rebellion had its roots thirty years earlier, when the Black Death had swept through England, wiping out a third of the population. This had an unexpected side-effect. The poorest of the poor, the farm labourers, now found that they were in demand because of their scarcity. But the monarchy imposed severe restrictions on their wages, so they never benefited from their new worth.

Walter (known as Wat) Tyler was a roofer from Kent, and a former soldier. Born in 1341, he lived through the Black Death and saw family, friends and relatives fall to the plague. By 1381, he had moved from his native Essex to Kent. Richard II was on the throne, but was only fourteen-years-old, and the country was being run by the Dukes of Lancaster, York and Gloucester. They levied taxes for unsuccessful expeditions against France, but the final straw came when they imposed a poll tax of three groats (one shilling) on everyone. This outraged the peasantry, because the tax was the same for the rich and the poor.

The method of collection also caused outrage. Everyone over fifteen was liable, and collectors, backed up by soldiers, insisted on checking pretty young girls for age by making them strip from the waist down. If they were not virgins, they were liable for the shilling.

Many who refused to pay were arrested, including one who was held in Rochester Castle, Kent. Wat Tyler led a group who stormed the castle and freed him. Then, as his group grew, widespread rebellion broke out. His men marched on London, taking Canterbury as they went. A second mob, led by Jack Straw, marched on the capital from Essex. They arrived at the city and marched across Deptford Bridge, merging with Wat Tyler's group at Blackheath.

Though it is known as the Peasant's Rebellion, the rabble included village craftsmen and tradesmen as well as labourers. From Blackheath, they marched back on the city, Wat Tyler at the head of 50,000 men. They were armed with sticks, swords, hammers, scythes, pitchforks, axes, and whatever they could lay their hands on. Many in the city welcomed their opposition to the poll tax and the gates were opened to them.

The group crossed the narrow confines of London Bridge without resistance. People leant from windows on the crowded structure and cheered them on. They rushed to the Savoy Palace, sandwiched between The Strand and the Thames. This magnificent dwelling was one of the most lavish palaces in the kingdom, and the home of John of Gaunt, son of the previous King Edward III. Along with the Archbishop of Canterbury Simon Sudbury, he was seen as responsible for the poll tax. The richest man in England, his home was the most magnificent nobleman's mansion in the country, stretching for hundreds of feet along the river bank. It was famous for its impressive collection of tapestries, jewels and ornaments. The poet Geoffrey Chaucer, author of "The Canterbury Tales" worked as an official at the palace.

The rebels stormed the Savoy Palace, swiftly taking possession. They went on a rage-fuelled rampage, systematically destroying everything. The rich tapestries were torn from the walls and ripped asunder, the jewellery pulverised and pounded with hammers. What could not be smashed or burnt was thrown into the river.

One of the rioters saw an opportunity to improve his situation, and he slipped a silver goblet under his tunic. He was spotted and his fellows turned on him, beating him badly and throwing him into the river to drown for his troubles.

Many of the rebels smashed open casks in the wine cellar and got drunk. They perished when the palace was torched. The rebels left the mansion, once a jewel on the Thames, as a smouldering hulk no longer inhabitable.

Their blood-lust unsatiated, the rebels stormed the Tower of London. The Archbishop of Canterbury, the unpopular Simon

Sudbury, had fled to the Tower after the rebels had taken Canterbury. Sudbury was seen as a close ally of the Duke of Lancaster and an architect of the poll tax. He was one of the most hated figures in the kingdom. When the rebels arrived at the Tower on 14 June, Sudbury's guards stood aside and let them take the Archbishop.

He was dragged to Tower Hill, where he was set upon by the mob and beheaded. His head was stuck on a long pole and hoisted over London Bridge. This continued a tradition began by King Edward I seventy-six years earlier, when he displayed the head of Scottish rebel William Wallace over the bridge. After the rebellion was quashed, Sudbury's body was buried in Canterbury Cathedral, but his head was removed to the Church of St Gregory at Sudbury in Suffolk. Mummified with age, it is still there in a glass case, but can only be viewed by appointment.

The Prior of St John's, Clerkenwell, another political heavyweight, was also beheaded.

The king was forced to come to terms with Wat Tyler and his peasant army. The Constable of Wallingford Castle, Richard of Wallingford, was one of the organisers of the rebellion, and he presented King Richard with a charter of demands on behalf of Tyler. The king met rebel representatives at Mile End and promised to address their grievances, including the poll tax.

Twenty thousand people assembled at Smithfield for the negotiations. Wat Tyler rode out alone to meet the king. Little is known about what was said, but it clearly did not go Tyler's way. Ignoring the white flag of truce and the rules of war, Tyler was suddenly jumped from behind by the Lord Mayor of London, Sir William Walworth, and slashed across the neck with a knife. He fell to the ground, badly injured. John

Cavendish, the son of the Chief Justice, stepped forward and applied the killing blow. The rebellion was over. Wat Tyler's body was removed to St Bart's Hospital, where it was beheaded.

Seeing their leader cut down — but with the young king still promising to address their grievances — the mob quickly disbanded, running to safety. Over the coming weeks, the king reversed all his concessions to the peasants and arrested the leaders. One hundred and fifty were executed. However, it was not all one-sided. Some of the king's men did not survive the rebellion. The Chief Justice, seeing what his son had done, knew that the rebels would be baying for his blood. So he fled to his home, Cavendish in Suffolk. He was pursued the whole way by some of the rabble, barely making it to the village.

As he reached home, he knew his only hope was to plead sanctuary in a church. At the time, this was a recognised and effective way of avoiding capture. He jumped from his horse and ran to the church door, grasping the handle in triumph. But just as the king had violated the white flag of truce, the Chief Justice's pursuers violated the rule of sanctuary. Rough hands seized him and he was pulled from the churchyard.

He was taken to nearby Bury St Edmunds and beheaded by rebel leader Jack Straw on 15 June 1381. It was the last hurrah of the rising, and within weeks, the country had returned to business as usual — the king and the nobility in charge profiting from the labours of the serfs and peasants. But the poll tax was removed, and no monarch tried to impose one on the English for another three hundred years.

All that remains now of the peasant rebellion is a street on Blackheath Common named after Wat Tyler — and the knife that killed him. The Mayor, Sir William Walworth, was a fishmonger by trade and a member of the Fishmonger's Guild.

The headquarters of the Worshipful Company of Fishmongers is still in an ancient Guildhall close to Southwark Bridge, where the knife is still located.

Fireworks Celebrate a Damp Squib

The most widely commemorated and remembered incident on the Thames is one that did not happen — the destruction of the Houses of Parliament in 1605. The Gunpowder Plot, a Catholic conspiracy against James I, failed from the start. But it made one of its protagonists, Guy Fawkes, a household name.

Fawkes wasn't even the leader of the conspiracy. The English Catholics were led by Robert Catesby. The plan was audacious: the House of Lords would be blown up during the State Opening of Parliament by the king. A popular revolt would break out in the midlands and the king's nine-year-old daughter, Princess Elizabeth, would be put on the throne in his place.

The cause of the discontent was simple. Since Henry VIII installed himself as head of the Church of England, there was an uneasy relationship between Protestants (in power) and Catholics. The Catholic nobility expected more tolerance when James I came to the throne, but in this they were disappointed. Catesby was joined by John Wright, Thomas Wintour, Thomas Percy, Guy Fawkes, Robert Keyes, Thomas Bates, Robert Wintour, Christopher Wright, John Grant, Sir Ambrose Rookwood, Sir Everard Digby and Francis Tresham. Fawkes, with ten years military experience, was in charge of the explosives.

There were many false starts, with five initial conspirators meeting at the Drake and Duck Inn on the Strand in May 1604, over a year before the final curtain fell on their plans. Parliament adjourned and they returned to their homes in the country, believing that they would strike in February 1605. They wanted to kill the king, but also senior figures in his government, and judges who enforced the anti-Catholic laws. Many of the judges would be present for the opening of Parliament.

Thomas Percy rented a room near the Prince's Chamber close by Westminster, where he installed Fawkes, posing as his servant. From here, they were in a good position to overhear discussions about the unification of England and Scotland. Explosives were stockpiled in Percy's residence at Lambeth, on the opposite bank of the river. Folklore has it they began tunnelling from their lodgings to the House of Lords, but no evidence has been found to support this.

In any case, by Christmas, they had their plans in place and the gunpowder ready. But, because of the plague, it was announced at the end of 1604 that Parliament would not sit in February as planned, but would be postponed to October. This threw the conspirators, leaving them fretting with no target for their explosives.

By March, the plot was growing unwieldy, with more conspirators coming on board. They leased a cellar under the Palace of Westminster, where they hoped to store their gunpowder. The palace back then was a warren of buildings clustered around the medieval chambers, chapels and halls of the former Royal palace that housed both Parliament and the various law courts. Many people lived and worked within its precincts. The undercroft, or cellar, that the conspirators leased was on the ground floor, directly beneath the first-floor House of Lords, and may once have been part of the palace's medieval kitchen. Unused and filthy, its location was ideal for what the group planned to do.

Twenty barrels of gunpowder were stored there initially, then a further sixteen barrels were brought in on 20 July. Gunpowder was supposedly strictly controlled by the government, but the conspirators had no difficulty getting their hands on large supplies.

Fawkes went away to Europe for a few weeks and was dismayed to find, when he returned, that the explosives had decayed. He purchased more gunpowder, hiding it behind stacks of lumber. Details of the plot were finalised in a series of meetings at various London taverns. Fawkes would light the fuse, then slip onto the river and make his escape by boat. He was to flee to Europe, to drum up support for the rebellion. Meanwhile, a rising against the Crown would happen in the midlands to coincide with the explosion.

The opening of Parliament was delayed another month, to November. Then Baron Monteagle (brother-in-law of Tresham, one of the conspirators) got a note warning him to make an excuse to miss the big event. The letter read: "My Lord, out of the love I bear to some of your friends, I have a care of your preservation. Therefore I would advise you, as you tender your life, to devise some excuse to shift your attendance at this parliament; for God and man hath concurred to punish the wickedness of this time."

Instead of heeding the warning, he went to the authorities. On 4 November, the House of Lords was searched by Monteagle and others. In the undercroft, they found a big pile of firewood. A servant was there, who told them he was John Johnson and the firewood belonged to his master, Thomas Percy. They left to report to the king, and Johnson — who was really Guy Fawkes — also left. Later that night, more searchers returned. They came across Fawkes once more, now dressed in a cloak and hat, and wearing boots and spurs, not normal clothing for a servant. He was searched and found to have a pocket watch, several slow matches and touchwood — the equipment needed to detonate the huge stock of gunpowder they found under the wood. There was enough gunpowder concealed to reduce the House of Lords, and all within, to rubble.

Fawkes was also carrying a lantern. This has been preserved and is on display at the Ashmolean Museum, Oxford. Fawkes was taken to the king on the morning of 5 November. His co-conspirators fled London, but were caught by the Sheriff of Worcester, who killed leader Robert Catesby during the stand-off.

They were held and tortured until their trial on 27 January 1606. Eight of the conspirators, including Fawkes, were convicted of treason, and sentenced to be hung, drawn and quartered, a particularly brutal form of Royal revenge. Most of the conspirators met their end on the banks of the Thames. On a cold 30 January, Everard Digby, Robert Wintour, John Grant and Thomas Bates were tied to wooden panels and dragged through the streets from the Tower to St Paul's Churchyard. Digby was stripped. Wearing only a shirt — not even breeches — he climbed a ladder and placed his head through the noose. The ladder was quickly pulled away and he did the Newgate Jig for a few moments, before being cut down, fully conscious.

Then the real punishment began. He was castrated, disembowelled and then cut in quarters. The other three followed in quick succession, much to the delight of the cheering mob.

The following day, Thomas Wintour, Ambrose Rookwood, Robert Keyes and Guy Fawkes faced the same punishment opposite the building they planned to blow up. They were executed at the Old Palace Yard, Westminster. Keyes tried to jump onto the noose and speed up his death, but was prevented. Fawkes succeeded in jumping from the scaffold, breaking his neck and sparing himself the experience of being castrated, disembowelled and quartered.

Steven Littleton was executed at Stafford. His cousin Humphrey co-operated with the authorities but was still executed near Worcester. Henry Garnet, a Jesuit who may have known about the plot but who was not involved, was also executed. Then the bodies of Robert Catesby and Thomas Percy, who had died fighting their capture, were exhumed and beheaded, their heads displayed on pikes outside the House of Lords.

Although anti-Catholic legislation was introduced soon after the plot's discovery, many important and loyal Catholics retained high office during King James I's reign. The thwarting of the Gunpowder Plot was commemorated for many years afterwards by special sermons and other public events such as the ringing of church bells. Today we celebrate with Guy Fawkes Night, where bonfires are lit across the city and fireworks displays, both formal and impromptu, light up the night sky. The burning of an effigy of Guy Fawkes is also quite a common feature of the annual 5 November celebrations, which have replaced Halloween for British children.

Cannon Sets the Globe Ablaze

By modern standards, the special effects used in theatres in Tudor times were primitive. But on a night in 1613, the cannons fired in the Globe Theatre, and patrons saw action that would have looked good in a modern Hollywood blockbuster. It was the night that Shakespeare's Globe Theatre burnt down.

Theatre was a very popular diversion in medieval London. And Southwark was the place to go. Southwark was outside the City of London, and was known for all things lawless. In the Liberty of the Clink (near modern Bankside), normal rules did not apply and entertainment of all sorts flourished — from dog fighting and bear-baiting, to brothels and wild taverns.

The bear pits were particularly popular, and several of them have been excavated on the banks of the river. But more high-brow entertainment was also available. In 1599, a group of actors — the Lord Chamberlain's Men — purchased a plot of land where there had once been a theatre. Records showed that the plot was somewhere between Southwark Bridge Road and Porter Street. The exact location of the theatre was not known until 1989, when part of the foundation was found beneath the car park at the rear of Anchor Terrace on Park Street. The majority of the foundations lie beneath 67-70 Anchor Terrace.

Those foundations mark the last remains of the Globe Theatre. The Lord Chamberlain's Men and their playhouse might have faded into obscurity, except that one of the six partners dabbled in a bit of writing. William Shakespeare owned a one-eighth share of The Globe. The partners were Richard and Cuthbert Burbage (who owned half), William Shakespeare, John Heminges, Augustine Philips and Thomas Pope, who owned an eighth each.

They were all actors, and Shakespeare and Pope also wrote plays. There is some doubt about what play was first performed at the Globe, but it may have been "Julius Caesar" by Shakespeare on 21 September. The Globe was an impressive building, dwarfing nearby theatres such as The Rose and The Swan. It was not circular, as is often thought, but had twenty sides and was cylindrical in shape.

There was a thatched gallery roof, three storeys tall, with a 30 metre (100 foot) wide open air amphitheatre that could house around 3,000 spectators. Under the stage was a trapdoor where supernatural beings, like the ghost in "Hamlet", could make their appearance. A balcony housed the musicians and the more wealthy patrons. This balcony could also be used for scenes requiring an elevated stage, such as the balcony scene in "Romeo and Juliet".

The Chamberlain's Men (later The King's Men) was one of the two most important acting companies in London, and the Globe was the cultural heart of the city. But competition was fierce, and productions became more elaborate. In an effort to keep ahead of their rivals, the company introduced real cannons to the stage. The cannons were kept close to the roof and fired gunpowder and wadding to herald the arrival of important characters, such as kings, or to provide battle noises.

On 29 June 1613, the play was "Henry VIII" by Shakespeare and John Fletcher, who later replaced him as house playwright for The King's Men. Although it was not called that at the time; the original name of the play was "All Is True". Today we regard it as one of his historic plays, but back then it was almost contemporary.

During the scene where Henry arrives at a masque in the residence of Cardinal Wolsey, the cannons were fired to signal the king's entrance. Some of the paper wadding shot out onto the thatched roof, and embers began to smoulder. At first, the audience assumed the smoke was a result of the cannon shot and ignored it. They continued to watch the play.

According to one eyewitness, Sir Henry Wooten: "The King's Players had a new play representing some principal pieces of the reign of Henry the Eight, which set forth with many extraordinary circumstances of pomp and majesty, even to the matting of the stage; the knights of the order with their Georges and Garter, the guards with their embroidered coats, and the like.

"Now King Henry making a Masque at the Cardinal Wolsey's house, and certain cannons being shot off at his entry, some of the paper or other stuff, wherewith one of them was stopped, did light on the thatch, where being thought at first but idle smoke, and their eyes more attentive to the show, it kindled inwardly, and ran round like a train, consuming within less than an hour the whole house to the very ground."

When the 1,500 patrons in attendance realised the theatre was on fire, panic ensued among them. The theatre had only two exits, but by extraordinary luck there were no fatalities, and only one casualty of any note — a man whose trousers caught fire.

As Wooten said: "Nothing did perish but wood and straw, and a few forsaken cloaks; only one man had his breeches set on fire. That would perhaps have broiled him, if he had not by the benefit of a provident wit, put it out with a bottle of ale."

The fire was spectacular, consuming the building in a little over an hour, and destroying one adjoining house. But the show must go on — within a year, a new Globe theatre had risen from the ashes, and continued to host plays for another three decades.

But then, the Puritans came to power, and like all other theatres in London, the Globe was closed down in 1642. It was pulled down two years later to make way for tenements. Little remains of that glorious flowering of the English language and drama. But if you walk down Park Street to the rear of Anchor Terrace, you can see an information board commemorating the site.

Better still, why not visit the new Globe Theatre. Constructed as faithfully as possible to the original, the new theatre is just 230 yards away from the original location, and has many interesting exhibitions and tours, bringing the history of Shakespeare's London alive. They also regularly stage his plays. More details on www.sheakspearesglobe.com.

Bloody Diversions

Though the age gave us the crowning glory of English culture and literature, the Tudors and Medieval Londoners had a coarse and bloody side; they liked a bit of gore in their entertainment. Bear-baiting was a perennial favourite, and the best place to go for the bears was the theatre district around Southwark. Bankside was a popular venue.

There had been bear gardens, or bear pits, along the river banks since the time of Henry II (1154-89). A bear would have its teeth and claws removed and would be chained to a post. Specially trained dogs were then set on it. The events were patronised by the most powerful and respectable; Queen Elizabeth attended one event in Bankside in 1575, in which thirteen bears were harried to death.

Among the guests was Richard Laneham, who wrote: "It was a very pleasant sport to see. To see the bear, with his pink eyes, tearing after his enemies; the nimbleness and cunning of the dog against the strength and experience of the bear. If he were bitten then see him get free with biting, with clawing, with roaring, with tossing and tumbling; and when he was loose to shake his ears two or three times with the blood and the slaver hanging about his face."

Bulls were also baited, and occasionally horses or ponies. John Evelyn, in his diary, was disapproving: "I went with some friends to the bear-garden, where there was cock-fighting, bear and bull-baiting, it being a famous day for all these butcherly sports, or rather barbarous cruelties.

"The bulls did exceedingly well, but the Irish wolf-dog was best when it beat a cruel mastiff. One of the bulls tossed a dog into a lady's lap, as she sat in one of the boxes quite high above the arena. Two poor dogs were killed, and it all ended with the ape on horseback. I am most heartily weary of these crude and dirty pastimes."

The Spanish Garden in Southwark was the best known of the bear pits. A Spanish visitor in 1580 wrote of seeing pony-baiting: "The animal was kicking amongst the dogs, while the ape clung to its back and screamed. The dogs hung from the ears and neck of the pony. It was most laughable."

On at least one occasion, in 1790, a pony was trained to kill sheep for the amusement of the mob.

By the nineteenth century, these pastimes had lost favour but not quite died out. When Tsar Nicholas I visited London in 1844, he was brought to see the bull-baiting (despite the fact it had been outlawed in 1835!) Bear-baiting gradually died out in the eighteen hundreds; bull-baiting went on until 1870. Cock-fighting and dog-fighting still go on, but are very much underground activities.

The Fatal Vespers

It was divine retribution on the Catholics when a building collapsed, throwing nearly a hundred of them to their doom in 1623. At least, that is how it was seen by the anti-Popish population of the city in those troubled times.

After Henry VIII established himself as head of the Church of England — to facilitate his unique form of wife-swapping — there was huge tension between Catholics and the established church. Most disasters and plots were blamed on the old religion, and anti-Catholic bigotry grew intense.

On the afternoon of Sunday, 5 November 1623, the French Ambassador allowed his home to be used by two Jesuit priests for a religious service. Three hundred people assembled in an upper room of his residence, Hunsdon House, Blackfriars, near the Thames. The priests, Robert Drury and William Whittingham, were renowned as powerful preachers.

Fr. Drury was in the middle of an impassioned sermon when the weight of the crowd caused the main beam holding up the floor to snap, plunging over a hundred people straight down to the floor below. Their weight suddenly falling on the floor, it too collapsed, and everyone went straight through, crashing into the ambassador's drawing room over the gatehouse, a drop of nearly 7 metres (22 feet).

The two Jesuits were killed instantly. Altogether, ninety-five people lost their lives, while several others suffered serious injuries.

Three floors above, a number of people had been on the edges of the room, and had not fallen through the collapsed floor. But they were trapped, unable to get to the door of the room. They had to break through the plaster into a neighbouring house to escape.

The bigotry of the times led many to regard the deaths as a divine judgement on the Catholics "for their idolatry". What reinforced that idea was the date of the Fatal Vespers. The building collapsed on 5 November, the anniversary of the Gunpowder Plot.

Hulks on the River

Even the name evoked terror — the Hulks. The big prison ships looming out of the fog with their cargo of the desperate and the doomed, were a sordid feature of the Victorian world. Their ghostly forms struck terror into the hearts of those dwelling near the Thames.

Strictly speaking, the hulks were not buildings. They were decommissioned ships that the authorities converted into floating prisons in the eighteenth and nineteenth centuries. But for the people incarcerated in them, they had all the solidity of stone.

The practice began in 1776, when a prison shortage forced Parliament to come up with innovative alternatives. Initially the hulks were authorised for two years, as a stop-gap solution. Although many deplored them, those two years stretched to eighty.

Parliament later extended the use of the hulks "for the more severe and effectual punishment of atrocious and daring offenders." The American and French revolutions and the Napoleonic Wars led to the availability of many retired ships suitable for conversion to floating prisons. Because of their size, they had accommodation for hundreds.

Converting the ships to prison hulks was easy. Rigging, masts and rudders were removed or rendered useless. The internal structure was altered to include cells. Then they were anchored offshore, ready to receive their human cargo.

They were typically anchored in harbours, making them convenient for holding convicts about to be transported to Australia and other penal colonies. In 1798, the hulks held more than 1,400 of the 1,900 prisoners scheduled for transportation.

Conditions inside were cramped, and sickness and fever were rife in the hulks. Convicts were taken in chains to work on shore during the day, then returned to their dingy quarters. New prisoners were kept in the lower decks, among the vermin and the smells and sounds of the river. Older convicts got to stay closer to the air. Many of the convicts never saw the gangplank leading to their release.

List of Hulks on the Thames

HMS *Ceres* (1787-1797), a 32-gun fifth-rate warship, anchored at Woolwich.

HMS *Dasher* (1832-1838), an 18-gun sloop launched in 1797, and anchored at Woolwich.

HMS *Defence* (1850-1857), a 74-gun third-rate ship of the line, anchored at Woolwich and Portsmouth.

HMS *Discovery* (1818-1834), a 10-gun sloop, famously captained by George Vancouver on his voyage of discovery. It was anchored at Woolwich and Deptford.

HMS *Dromedary* (1825-1864), an East Indiaman purchased by the navy, but converted to a hulk after only twenty years. Anchored at Woolwich and Bermuda.

HMS *Ganymede* (1819-1838), a French frigate captured in 1809. She was docked at Woolwich and Chatham.

HMS *Hebe* (1839-1852), a 46-gun fifth-rate warship anchored at Woolwich.

HMS *Justitia* (1830-1855), an East Indiaman converted to a gunboat by the navy, then used as a hulk at Woolwich.

HMS *Leven* (1827-1848), a hospital ship converted to a hulk at Woolwich and Deptford.

HMS *Prudent* (1779-1814), anchored at Woolwich.

HMS *Retribution* (11814-1835), a converted 74-gun third-rate warship anchored at Woolwich and Sheerness.

HMS *Savage* (1804-1815), a 14-gun sloop anchored at Woolwich.

HMS *Sulphur* (1843-1857), a 10-gun bomb vessel anchored at Woolwich.

HMS *Thames* (1841-1863), a 46-gun fifth-rate warship anchored at Deptford and Bermuda. This hulk sank at her moorings in 1863.

HMS *Unite* (1832-1858), a 40-gun fifth-rate warship captured from the French and anchored at Woolwich.

HMS *Warrior* (1840-1857), a 74-gun third-rate ship of the line, anchored at Woolwich.

Power Station Blacks Out Television Station

The opening of a new television station is a matter of great excitement. Back in 1964, when the BBC began broadcasting its second channel — and the country's third — it was an event of national importance. Unfortunately, the birth of one station was almost scuppered by the temporary demise of another.

The new station got off to a stuttering start, with the first evening's output disappearing into the ether as power outages almost closed the television studio.

The problem was a fire in the iconic Battersea Power Station, which ensured that the launch of BBC2 was a very tame affair.

Battersea Power Station was a large, coal-fired station on the south bank of the Thames at Battersea. The station was built in the 1930s, and a second plant was added in the fifties. The two plants were side by side and joined in one big building, which is still a familiar landmark to river users today. Plant A and Plant B were built to an identical pattern. There is a large, orange-red cathedral-style building topped by two towers and chimneys pointing to the river. Beside this are the two towers and chimneys of the later plant.

It is the largest brick building in Europe and has a distinctive, very lavish, art deco façade, which is also the theme of the interior. The four chimney layout made it one of the most distinctive buildings in London, and it featured in the Beatles movie "Help!" and on the cover of Pink Floyd's album "Animals". It is a Grade II Listed Building.

The station was built on fifteen acres at Battersea, formerly owned by the Southwark and Vauxhall Waterworks. The site was chosen because it was on the river bank, which made bringing in coal easy — and the river also supplied a source of cooling water for the plant. It was also in the heart of London, where the customers were.

Construction began in 1929, and took four years. During that time, a number of accidents plagued the work. Answering a question in Parliament on that issue in 1933, Home Secretary Sir John Gilmore revealed: "Since work began in July 1929, there have been reported to the Factory Department six fatal and 201 non-fatal accidents as having occurred on this site, and in addition a few very minor accidents, the exact number of which cannot be readily ascertained, but which are estimated at three or four per annum."

Plant A continued to provide power for the capital until it was joined, after the Second World War, by Plant B. Both continued in operation until 1983. But there was a temporary interruption on a very important night in 1964.

BBC had been operating as a radio station since the 1927, and had begun experimenting with television in the early 1930s. ITV had offered some competition from 1955, but there was great excitement in the Corporation when the government awarded them a second station. BBC2 was due to begin broadcasting on 20 April 1964.

But that afternoon, a serious electrical fault developed at the Battersea Power Station, five miles south of the BBC Television Centre. Technicians threw the switches to isolate the problem, but the switches burst into flame. The fire quickly swept through cable ducts and spread to other parts of the plant, eventually destroying eighty high-tension cable connections. By unhappy chance, the fire coincided with a breakdown in the 60,000 volt cable that carried electricity south from stations in the midlands. The two catastrophes, coming so close together, resulted in extensive blackouts throughout London.

Staff at the power station tried to raise the alarm, but the phone system was destroyed in the initial stages of the blaze, so it was nearly an hour before the fire service was alerted. A worker had to drive to a phone box and dial 999. More than sixty firefighters responded to the call, but it took them two hours to bring the inferno under control. London ground to a standstill. Trains stopped, a first division soccer game was abandoned and the streets went dark.

Hospitals were affected, as was Buckingham Palace, the House of Commons and thousands of homes. Some were inconvenienced: the Prime Minister had to eat by candlelight at the National Liberal Club dinner at the Café Royal. But there were more serious incidents. A man working on the new underground Victoria Line fell down a 30-foot shaft and was seriously injured.

Darkness lasted more than six hours before the power station was back on line. But those six hours coincided with the launch of BBC2. The Television Centre was plunged into darkness. Candles flickered, and emergency generators supplied dim light on the corridors and over emergency exits. But there was no power to drive the transmitters. Virtually all programming on BBC2 that night failed to transmit — with the exception of a few snippets of news broadcast from a different studio.

BBC1 was also badly hit, with live studio-based programmes scrapped, and replaced with a test card and an American western.

Michael Peacock, the BBC2 Chief of Programmes, took the decision that if power was not back on by 9.45 p.m., the launch would be abandoned. Power was not restored. The assembled press ran off gleefully to file their reports on the fiasco. BBC2 launched with a whimper the following morning, with the children's programme *Play School*.

But it was not all bad. As Michael Peacock recalled: "The moral of the power failure was: 'no mistake, no publicity; big mistake, big publicity'. Had it not happened, the nation may not have known that BBC2 had gone on the air. As it was, everybody knew that we hadn't!"

Battersea Power Station continued to provide electricity for a further twenty years, finally being decommissioned in 1983. In the past two decades, it has deteriorated greatly, and several parts of it are in a dangerous condition. The building has not been used regularly since power production ceased.

It was used for the Red Bull X Fighters Series, as well as being the site of the Conservative Party Election Manifesto launch in 2010. Numerous plans were proposed over the years — including an ambitious idea to turn it into a theme park. The site is now owned by an Irish company, Real Estate Opportunities (REO), who bought it in 2006 for £400 million. In 2010, REO was granted permission to refurbish the station for public use — and to build 3,400 homes across the site. But the company went into administration in 2011, throwing the future of the Battersea Power Station site into further doubt.

Whatever the future holds, it remains one of the most distinctive buildings on the Thames in London, and a cultural landmark.

Ronan Point Gas Explosion

Ronan Point was a glorious failure of the sixties housing policies. The twenty-three storey block of flats on Clever Road, Newham, in the East End docklands, was one of dozens of tower blocks built to house the poorer people in the city. The tower blocks were not universally welcomed — especially by the people who were expected to move into them.

At dawn on the morning of 16 May 1968, a gas explosion destroyed much of the tower block. It happened in the apartment of Ivy Hodge on the eighteenth floor, and ripped through four flats above, and sent all the floors below crashing down like dominoes.

Two women and a man were reported killed on the spot, and a third woman was missing. Her body was later found in the rubble. Eleven of the 260 residents were injured, one of whom later died from her injuries.

About eighty families were forced to flee, many in their night clothes. The lifts were not working in the building and they had to run down several flights of stairs, some holding their screaming children. The tower block was one of four, and had been occupied just two months.

Ivy Hodge, a fifty-six-year-old cake decorator, suffered burns. She said she put the kettle on: "Then I found myself on the floor."

Ronan Point had an enormous impact on housing policy in the city, giving ammunition to those who objected to the high-rise council blocks. The tower blocks did not disappear overnight, but it woke planners up to the need for a better solution to the housing problem.

CHAPTER FOUR: LAST JOURNEYS AND SAD FAREWELLS

London has a horrible history of bloody executions. Many people made their last journey along the Thames to keep an appointment with the hangman or the axe. These included the notorious — Pirate Captain James Kidd — to the pillars of society. Two queens were taken from the Tower of London to have their pretty heads chopped off. In this chapter, we will look at two of the most notorious places of execution — the Tower of London, and the execution dock at Wapping.

Eight Seconds of Hell

Here is an unusual, and rather grisly, fact: when you are beheaded, death is not instantaneous. Loss of consciousness is not even instantaneous. When the blade slices through your neck, everything from there down fairly much expires in a heartbeat. But the brain will remain conscious until loss of oxygen or the sudden drop in blood pressure causes it to faint. Medical experts estimate that this takes at least eight seconds.

When the head of an executed convict is raised aloft by the axeman, it is not just to show the gathered crowd that the sentence of the court has been carried out. It is a final taunt to the victim. He feels his hair being gripped by the executioner. He feels the sway as his head is swung out over the crowd. He sees and hears the jeering masses in front of him. He may even be still conscious to feel the bump as his head is tossed into the waiting basket.

Not all victims experience the full horror. Sometimes the executioner is inexperienced, or using a dull blade. In that case, a number of blows might be needed to sever the head. If one goes astray and hits the back of the head, merciful unconsciousness may be the result.

Beheading is a brutal punishment. Perhaps that is why it has always been a popular public spectacle.

Many of London's most famous beheadings took place at the Tower of London, on the north bank of the Thames, or at nearby Tower Hill. Although brutal, beheading was considered more humane than some of the alternatives — burning, hanging, drawing and quartering, for instance. So it was a punishment reserved for the elite — important state prisoners, or people of noble birth.

There were many crimes that led to beheading, but perhaps the most high profile, at least in Tudor times, was the crime of being married to King Henry VIII. The rotund ruler had a very direct way of ending romances that no longer interested him.

Henry VIII executed more nobles than any other monarch in Britain's history. The roll of heads included two wives, four leading public servants and six of his close attendants and friends — as well as one cardinal, and various heads of monasteries.

The Tower of London, and nearby Tower Hill, became notorious during his reign as places of execution.

The Tower of London

On the north bank of the River Thames in central London is a building as iconic and distinctive as the Houses of Parliament, and as important in the history of London and England. The Tower was built as a fortress by William the Conqueror in 1066, to consolidate the Norman hold on the capital. It is a chunky, large square stone fortress within a double-walled enclosure just outside the eastern edge of the City of London;

separated from it by an open space, Tower Hill. Each corner of the inner castle has a large tower which dominates the view for miles around. The White Tower, built by William in 1078, gives the entire castle its name. Almost from the beginning, the Tower was a prison, though that was never its primary purpose.

One of the grandest palaces in London when it was built, it served as a royal residence. It was expanded several times, mainly under Richard the Lionheart, Henry III, and Edward I, in the twelfth and thirteenth centuries. The layout remains relatively the same today as it did at the end of the thirteenth century. There are two outer walls and a moat protecting the castle.

The Tower has always been at the heart of England's history. It was besieged several times, and controlling it has been important to controlling the country. At various times, the Tower has been an armoury, a treasury, a Royal Mint, a public records office and the home of the Crown Jewels. The explosives stored in the Tower during the Great Fire of 1666 proved vital in creating the fire blocks that stopped that blaze.

By the time of the Tudors, the Tower was used less as a royal residence. It was an old building, not suited to defence against the canons that had been introduced since the time of the Norman conquest. But it became more important as a prison. The peak period for its use as a prison was in the sixteenth and seventeenth century, and it held many prominent prisoners. These included Elizabeth before she became queen. Being "sent to the Tower" became a euphemism for falling out of favour and being imprisoned. Some, like Elizabeth, were released. Others took their final walk from the Tower to their execution.

Only seven people were beheaded within the Tower itself, but 112 were executed on nearby Tower Hill over a four hundred year period. Executions went out of fashion as the world moved into the modern era, but three members of the Black Watch regiment were executed in the Tower by firing squad in 1743 for mutiny. And during the First and Second World War, the Tower was once again pressed into service as a prison. Beheadings were no longer carried out, but twelve men were executed by firing squad during the wars for espionage. Eleven were shot during the First World War, and one during the Second.

Ironically, the Tower saw more people executed within its medieval walls during ten years in the twentieth century than it did during four hundred of the most turbulent years in Britain's history.

Aside from the war years, the Tower had gradually slipped into disuse. The Royal Mint moved out in the late nineteenth century, leaving much of the buildings inside empty. Architects Anthony Salvin and John Taylor then undertook the task of restoring the Tower to its medieval glory. It was opened to the public as an attraction, and as a museum to display the Crown Jewels.

The Tower was closed to the public during the war years, and suffered damage in the Blitz. But it was repaired and reopened after the war. Today it is one of London's must-see attractions. It is maintained by the charity Historic Royal Palaces, and protected as a World Heritage Site. No visit to the capital is complete without spending some time at the Tower.

But don't go there at night: it is said to be haunted by the many people who spent their last, frightened weeks within its dour walls.

The Two Princes

When Edward IV died in 1483, the crown passed to his elder son, twelve-year-old Edward V. He was too young to rule, so power actually went to Richard, Duke of Gloucester, his uncle.

King Edward was sent to the Tower of London in May, and he was joined by his younger brother, nine-year-old Richard, Duke of York, in June. Both young princes were spotted occasionally playing in the grounds of the Tower in early summer. On 25 June, Parliament declared that Edward IV's marriage was illegitimate, making his children illegitimate. So Edward IV could not be crowned. The following day, Richard took the throne as Richard III.

But with the two princes still in the Tower as a rallying point for opponents, the crown sat uneasy on his head. Then, sometime in the summer of that year, both princes mysteriously disappeared. No one saw the two boys out playing any more, and the rumour quickly spread that they had been murdered.

No bodies were found, and the boys just faded out of history. Richard III protested his innocence and even offered a reward for information about the missing children. But the suspicion remained. Some believed that a loyal servant of Richard, Sir James Tyrell, snuck into the room where the princes were being held and smothered them both.

He confessed as much in 1502, but as the confession was taken under torture, it is sometimes disputed. He said that he killed the boys with two accomplices, and buried their bodies under a pile of rocks under one of the stairs of the castle.

Corroboration of a sort was found in 1674, when a wooden box containing the skeletons of two young children was found under rocks at the foot of a stairs in the Tower during renovations. The remains were interred in the wall of the

Henry VII Lady Chapel in Westminster Abbey. They were dug out in 1933 and examined, but the examination was inconclusive.

No one knows for certain the fate of the two princes in the Tower, but their ghosts are said to haunt the lonely corridors late at night.

Executions in the Tower

Only seven people were executed in the Tower itself, aside from the war executions in the twentieth century. All seven were beheaded on Tower Green.

13 June 1483: William Hastings, First Baron Hastings. He was beheaded after the Lord Proctor, later King Richard III, accused him of conspiring against him.

19 May 1536. Anne Boleyn, Queen of England. Anne Boleyn committed the terrible crime of marrying Henry VIII — and failing to bear him a male heir. She was condemned on trumped-up charges of adultery, treason and incest.

27 May 1541. Margaret Pole, Countess of Salisbury. This frail sixty-seven-year-old was accused of treason by King Henry VIII, supposedly for backing a Catholic rebellion in the north of England.

13 February 1542. Catherine Howard, Queen of England. The eighteen-year-old was no match for her husband, Henry VIII, who accused her of adultery and ended another marriage the quick way.

13 February 1542. Jane Boleyn, Viscountess Rochford. The sister-in-law of Anne Boleyn. Her actions led to the executions of two queens. Her time had to come.

12 February 1553. Lady Jane Grey, Queen of England. She was the nine day queen who lost her head because the nobility backed Mary ahead of her as a successor to Edward VI.

25 February 1601. Robert Devereux, Second Earl of Essex. He was a favourite of Queen Elizabeth I, until he led a rebellion against the Virgin Queen.

The Wives of Henry VIII

Everyone knows Henry VIII. He was a big, corpulent man with heavy jowls, thick legs and a scruffy beard, with small, pig-like eyes glaring from under heavy brows. The image comes to us from the famous portrait by Hans Holbein the Younger. But that was Henry in his declining days, when accidents and health issues had ravaged his body. In his youth, he was a handsome and dashing young prince, a jewel of the Renaissance. A scholar, musician and a writer, he showed early promise. But his flaws outweighed his greatness, and he is remembered now as the man who married six times and killed two wives.

Henry was born on 28 June 1491, and was crowned King on 21 April 1509. He held power for the next three decades, dying on 28 January 1597 of complications caused by obesity. He was the second Tudor on the throne, and is best known for his role in separating the Church of England from the Roman Catholic Church. His struggles with Rome led to the separation of the churches, the dissolution of the monasteries and the monarch assuming the position of Supreme Head of the Church of England. Despite this — and his excommunication — he remained at heart a Catholic.

He was considered an attractive, educated and accomplished king in his prime, and "one of the most charismatic rulers to sit on the English throne". He exercised absolute power, backing it up with a penchant for beheading opponents. But his downfall was that he became obsessed with producing a male heir. This stemmed partly from male vanity, and partly because he believed a daughter would not be strong enough to consolidate the Tudor Dynasty, and the fragile peace that existed following the War of the Roses.

Little did he understand the character of his little girl Elizabeth!

It was this obsession that led to his succession of marriages — and his idiosyncratic methods of dissolving those marriages.

Henry was first engaged as a thirteen-year-old boy; a political arrangement. In 1505, his older brother Arthur died, leaving a widow, Catherine of Aragon, daughter of King Ferdinand of Aragon and Queen Isabella of Castile. The couple had been married only five months when Arthur died, and King Henry VII was anxious that the Spanish connection be maintained. So an agreement was made that his second son, Henry, would marry Catherine when he came of age.

They married when he was seventeen, on 11 June 1509. Two weeks later he was crowned King at Westminster Abbey. His reign began well — he had been highly educated because, as the second son, he had not been expected to rule. He was a true Renaissance man.

But a year into the marriage, Catherine disappointed him by producing a daughter, who died within three days. Three more children followed, all dying in infancy, before Mary (the future queen) arrived. She was followed by one more sickly child who died within a week of birth. After eight years of marriage and six pregnancies, Henry was getting worried he would not produce a male heir.

His eye began to wander. He did produce a male heir by a mistress, Elizabeth Blount, in 1519, but of course the child was illegitimate. Henry changed the rules to allow him to name his successor — thus letting his son inherit the crown. But the point was moot: the boy died in 1536 at the age of seventeen.

In 1526, Henry was believed to have had a son by another mistress, Mary Boleyn. But he had become besotted with her sister, Anne. And Anne, a fiery and independent young woman, would not let him have his wicked way with her, unless he put a ring on her finger. To do that, he had to have his marriage to Catherine annulled. There lay the rub.

The Pope might have been willing to grant an annulment, but he was being held captive by Catherine's brother, so he stalled. It was the start of the split between the Crown and the church, which eventually led to the establishment of the Church of England. Henry continued to apply pressure and the Pope continued to oppose a new marriage. By 1531, Henry's patience was running out, and Catherine was banned from the palace, her rooms being given to Anne Boleyn.

In late 1532, he secretly married Anne Boleyn. She immediately became pregnant, so there was a public marriage in January 1533. Henry was excommunicated by the Pope, completing the schism. Anne produced a daughter, who went on to become Queen Elizabeth I. But this was followed by two stillborn male babies. Again, Henry began to lose patience. In 1536 he moved his new favourite, Jane Seymour, into the palace. She was a lady-in-waiting to the queen.

Thomas Cromwell, a close associate of Henry, began to conspire against the queen, building up a case of adultery with a number of courtiers. Perhaps the most damaging was a charge of adultery and incest with her own brother, George. The queen was also charged with treason.

One can only imagine the terror she felt when she was arrested on 2 May and taken to the Tower. She reportedly demanded to know where her father and brother were, then collapsed. Four days later she wrote to the king, acknowledging that she knew he intended to convict and execute her, but asking him to at least not condemn anyone else in the travesty of a trial. The plea fell on deaf ears; five men, including her brother, were convicted and executed.

Henry showed one bit of mercy. The punishment for treason in a woman was to be burnt to death. He commuted the sentence to beheading. And rather than having his wife beheaded with a common axe, he brought in an expert swordsman, Jean Rombaud from France, to perform the execution.

On the morning of her execution, 18 May, she told the Constable of the Tower, Anthony Kingston: "I heard say the executioner was very good, and I have a little neck." She seemed calm and resigned to her fate. In fact, Kingston found her in good humour.

Before dawn, she attended mass with Kingston and swore she had never been unfaithful to the king. Then at 8 a.m., she was brought to a special scaffold erected on the north side of the White Tower, in front of what is now the Waterloo Barracks. She was dressed in a red petticoat, under a loose grey gown of damask trimmed in fur, and a mantle of ermine. She smiled and put a brave face on it; she could have been walking to a dance. From the scaffold she made a short speech to the crowd of 150 onlookers, concluding: "I pray God save the King and send him long to reign over you, for a gentler nor a more merciful prince was there never; and to me he was ever a good, a gentle and sovereign lord."

The extraordinary speech had a purpose; she wanted to avoid criticising Henry in order to save her daughter Elizabeth, and her family, from further consequences.

Anne knelt upright, in the French style of executions. Her attending ladies removed her headdress and necklaces, and tied a blindfold over her eyes. Even the executioner seemed moved, but he did his job impeccably. A single stroke severed the head in an instance, freeing Henry to move on to his next conquest.

He moved on quickly; he didn't even organise a proper funeral or provide a proper coffin for Anne. Her body lay on the scaffold for some hours, before a Tower employee found an empty arrow chest and placed the head and body inside it. Anne Boleyn was buried in an unmarked grave in the Chapel of St Peter ad Vincula within the tower complex.

Henry became engaged to Jane Seymour the day after Anne's execution. Ten days later they were married. This marriage worked out, at least for Henry. In 1537, he finally had his male heir, Edward. But the birth was a difficult one and Jane suffered a serious infection, dying two weeks later.

Henry was devastated — he considered Jane his true partner. But in 1540, he decided to marry again, and Anne of Cleves, a German princess, was chosen as a suitable mate. She was reputed to be a beauty, but when Henry saw her, he was less than pleased with her looks. Despite this, the marriage went ahead. However, when Henry lost interest Anne was sensible enough to step aside gracefully. She admitted that the marriage had never been consummated and agreed to an annulment.

On 28 July 1540, Henry married Catherine Howard, the lady-in-waiting of Anne of Cleves, and also a cousin of Anne Boleyn. She was far younger than her new husband. No date of birth has been recorded for her, but she was no older than twenty-two, and may have been as young as seventeen. She was a lively girl, sexually experienced, with many admirers, and was quickly embroiled in an affair with a courtier. When the king found out, he had no choice. Catherine Howard became his second wife to face the axeman.

When charged initially with an affair with Francis Dereham, she had a way out. If she had admitted that the affair had begun long before her marriage (which it had) she would have paved the way for an annulment. She would have been disgraced, but would have lived. Instead, she denied it, claiming she had been raped by Dereham. There was also another affair, with young courtier Thomas Culpeper.

Catherine quickly realised the seriousness of the situation. She was under house arrest at Hampton Court. She managed to break free one morning while the king was at mass. She banged on the doors of the chapel and called Henry's name, but was quickly taken back to her rooms. In November 1541, she was stripped of the title of Queen and removed to Syon Abbey, Middlesex.

Meanwhile, her two lovers were tried, condemned and executed. Culpeper was beheaded, whereas Dereham was hung, drawn and quartered. Both men had their heads displayed on London Bridge, as was the custom at the time.

Catherine was removed to the Tower on 10 February 1542. Her execution was scheduled for 13 February. She did not take the news well. Younger and less mature than Anne Boleyn, she was terrified but determined to put up a good final show. On the night before her death, she asked for a block to be brought to her cell so that she could prepare for the morrow. She spent several hours practicing how to lay her head on the block.

The following morning she met her fate with relative composure. She looked pale and terrified, and required assistance to mount the scaffold on Tower Green. As she surveyed the crowd of court officials, she would have seen that Henry was not there. He had moved on. She made a brief speech, asking for mercy for her family and prayers for her soul.

Then she ended on a note of sincerity. There is a poignant version (possibly untrue) that gives her last words as: "I die a queen, but I would rather have died the wife of Culpeper."

Her preparation of the night before paid off: she did not waver. A single stroke of the axe was all that was required. Catherine Howard's body was buried in an unmarked grave in the Chapel of St Peter ad Vincula, alongside her cousins Anne and George Boleyn.

Henry married just once more. In 1543, he wed wealthy widow Catherine Parr. She bore him no children, but did manage to help him reconcile with daughters Mary and Elizabeth. Through her influence, he changed the rules yet again, to allow them succeed to the throne. Catherine outlived Henry, who died in 1547.

Anne Boleyn's Last Thoughts in Verse

A few days before her execution, while in the Tower, Anne Boleyn wrote a poem about her impending death. "O Death, Rock me Asleep" is a heart-felt plea for a swift end to her suffering:

O Death! rock me asleep;
Bring me to quiet rest;
let pass my weary, guiltless ghost
out of my careful breast.
Toll on, the passing bell;
ring out my doleful knell;
let thy sound my death tell.
Death doth draw neigh;
there is no remedy.
My pain, who can express?
Alas! they are so strong
my dolour will not suffer strength

my life for to prolong.
Toll on, the passing-bell;
ring out my doleful knell;
let thy sound my death tell.
For I must die;
there is no remedy.
Alone, in prison strong,
I wait my destiny.
Woe worth this cruel hap, that I
should taste this misery!
Toll on, the passing-bell;
ring out my doleful knell;
let thy sound my death tell.
Death doth draw neigh;
there is no remedy.
Farewell! my pleasures past;
Welcome! my present pain.
I feel my torments so increase
that life cannot remain.
Toll on, the passing-bell;
wrong is my doleful knell;
for the sound my death doth tell.
Death doth draw neigh;
there is no remedy.
Sound my end dolefully
for now I die.

The Nine Day Queen

Although Henry VIII made a habit of beheading queens, being married to him was not the only way a monarch could come to a grisly end. Lady Jane Grey was Queen of England for nine days — and ended her life on the scaffold.

Lady Jane (1536/37 – 12 February 1554) was the great-granddaughter of Henry VII, by his younger daughter Mary, and first cousin once removed of Edward VI. A highly educated and intelligent young woman, she was married to Lord Guildford Dudley, son of Edward VI's chief minister John Dudley, Duke of Northumberland. When the fifteen-year-old king lay dying in June 1553, he nominated Jane as his successor. His half-sisters Mary and Elizabeth also had claims on the throne.

Lady Jane resided in the Tower during her short reign, which began on 10 July. But on 19 July, the Privy Council abruptly changed sides and proclaimed Mary Queen. Lady Jane then became a prisoner in the Tower. She was charged with High Treason, and convicted in November 1553, and sentenced to be either burned alive or beheaded, at the new queen's pleasure. But initially, her life was spared.

Then Wyatt's Rebellion broke out against Queen Mary and her plans to marry a Spanish Royal. This had nothing to do with Lady Jane, who was still being held in the Tower. But her father joined in the rebellion, and this sealed her fate. The date of her execution, and that of her husband, was set for 9 February. It was then deferred three days to allow her to convert from Protestantism to Catholicism. This she refused to do.

On the morning of 12 February 1554, Guilford was taken from his rooms at the Tower to Tower Hill, where he was beheaded before a large crowd. A horse and cart brought his remains back to the Tower, past the rooms in Beauchamp Tower where Lady Jane was being held. Seeing her husband's mangled corpse, she screamed: "Oh Guildford, Guildford!"

A short while later, she was marched from her tower to a scaffold that had been erected at Tower Green, in front of the

Chapel of St Peter ad Vincula. Before a select crowd of officials, she met her end with dignity. She made a brief speech proclaiming her innocence, then recited Psalm 51 ("Have mercy upon me, O God") in English — a slap in the face to the now Catholic court of Queen Mary.

She handed her gloves and handkerchief to a maid, then said to the executioner: "I pray you dispatch me quickly."

He placed a blindfold over her and she fumbled to find the block, saying: "What shall I do? Where is it?" Sir Thomas Brydges, Deputy Lieutenant of the Tower, pushed her head down, then speedily removed his hands. Lady Jane spoke the last words of Jesus: "Lord, into thy hands I commend my spirit." Then the axe came down.

Lady Jane and her husband Guildford were buried in the Chapel of St Peter ad Vincula, with the other victims of the Tower chopper. Jane's father was executed a week later, but her mother was given a full pardon by Queen Mary.

Eleven Strokes of the Axe

Margaret Pole, Countess of Salisbury (14 August 1473 – 27 May 1541), was a remarkable woman. She was one of only two women in sixteenth century England to be a peeress in her own right, with no titled husband. She was among the few surviving members of the Plantagenet dynasty after their defeat in the War of the Roses, so she was always going to be a thorn in the side of the new Tudor dynasty.

Despite this, she was appointed lady-in-waiting to Henry VIII's first wife, Catherine of Aragon. She was at one point the fifth richest peer in the realm. But her relationship with Henry was always fraught, with lots of setbacks and clashes.

A widow, she devoted herself to the fortunes of her five children. Her middle son Reginald eventually became a cardinal and Archbishop of Canterbury. But it was a dangerous time to be a Catholic figurehead, as Henry was trying to break the power of the church.

By 1536 there was complete opposition between Henry and Cardinal Reginald Pole. The fallout would affect the cardinal's mother. Margaret Pole was imprisoned in the Tower for the final two and a half years of her life.

A frail woman in her sixties, she was treated well initially. She was held with two grandsons and supported by the king. She had servants and received an extensive grant for clothing in March 1541. But the charge of treason — and the ultimate sanction — hung over her. She struggled against the knowledge of her ultimate fate. A verse was found carved on the wall of her cell:

For traitors on the block should die;
I am no traitor, no, not I!
My faithfulness stands fast and so,
Towards the block I shall not go! Nor make one step, as you shall see;
Christ in thy mercy, save thou me!

The lines could have been prophetic. On the morning of 27 May 1541 — just two months after receiving her generous clothing allowance — she received news of a different timbre. She was to be executed within the hour. She protested her innocence, but was immediately taken from her cell to a small block that had been erected on Tower Green. About 150 witnesses — city and court officials — were waiting for her. The frail and thin widow between the burly guards made an incongruous sight.

She was dragged to the block but refused to lay her head on it. Like she had scribbled on the wall, she was not going down easily. Hasty hands forced her head down and held her by the shoulders. But she continued to struggle. The inexperienced executioner brought down his blade quickly, but her struggle and his haste sent the blow astray. Instead of hitting her squarely on the neck and ending her misery, he struck the old lady across the shoulder.

She screamed in agony and jumped from the low platform, running wildly towards the crowd. The executioner followed her, striking the running woman again on the shoulder with his axe. As she stumbled, she was caught and forced back to the block. This time there would be no mistakes. She was held firmly in place. But the crush of people prevented the executioner getting the clean stroke he needed. It took eleven blows before he could put the Countess out of her misery and end the bloody farce.

It was a horrific spectacle, made more so by the age and frailty of the victim.

Margaret Pole is regarded by the Catholic Church as a martyr, and was beautified by Pope Leo XIII in 1886.

The Taming of the Shrew

By all contemporary accounts, Jane Boleyn, Viscountess Rochford (1505-42), was a spiteful, jealous woman, whose intrigues led to the death of two of Henry's wives. Born Jane Parker, she was the wife of George Boleyn, brother of the queen. But it was an arranged marriage, and not a happy one.

So she was more than happy to help the king's chief minister Thomas Cromwell when he needed evidence to rid Henry of another wife. Jane had been married for eleven miserable years. There is some doubt about the nature of her marriage. Some sources say her husband was homosexual; other sources suggest he was a notorious womaniser with insatiable and depraved appetites. But it is equally possible they were just not in love. And Jane was jealous of her husband's sister, the queen.

So she made up a charge that Anne and George had been engaged in an incestuous affair since 1535, and that George, not the king, was the father of a child Anne had miscarried in the spring of 1536. It was all the king needed, and Anne went to the block, along with her brother.

Now Jane was a free woman, but impoverished by the death of her husband, as property never remained with the widow. She eventually returned to favour at the court, and became a lady-in-waiting to another of Henry's wives, Lady Jane Seymour. She provided evidence for the annulment of Henry's next wife, Anne of Cleves, and was a lady-in-waiting to the new queen, Catherine Howard. She quickly wheedled herself into the favours of the new queen, and that was her downfall.

She helped Catherine in her intrigues and romances, and facilitated meetings with her lover, Thomas Culpeper. When the king found out, Jane Boleyn took up permanent residence in the Tower. Although as an aristocrat she could not be tortured, prison had a very damaging effect on her, and she gradually lost her mind, suffering periods of insanity. This presented Henry with a problem, because it was not legal to execute the insane. So he had parliament change the law. The way was paved for another beheading.

Jane Boleyn was executed on the same morning as seventeen-year-old Queen Catherine Howard. The queen died first, weak but not hysterical. Jane watched from the scaffold as the axe fell and severed the royal head, blood spurting out in a final gush on the block. Then she had to kneel and lay her head on the fresh blood.

Despite her nervous breakdown over the previous months, she met her end in a calm and dignified fashion. One witness to the double executions, merchant Ottwell Johnson, said: "Their souls must be with God, for they made the most godly and Christian end."

One version has it that her final words were: "God has permitted me to suffer this shameful doom as punishment for having contributed to my husband's death. I falsely accused him of loving in an incestuous manner his sister, Queen Anne Boleyn. For this I deserve to die."

Jane was buried alongside Catherine Howard, and close to the husband and sister-in-law she had betrayed, George and Anne Boleyn.

Famous Executions on Tower Hill

Most executions were done at Tower Hill, just outside the Tower complex, and were public spectacles. Only a few very notable victims were allowed the privilege of a more discrete execution within the Tower walls. One hundred and twelve were executed on Tower Hill.

Some of the most notable who made the solemn procession through the Traitors' Gate to their doom were:

King Baliol of Scotland (1296)
William Wallace (1305)
Sir Thomas More (1535)
Thomas Cromwell (1540)
Guy Fawkes (1606)
Sir Walter Raleigh (1618)

Cigar Salesmen were Spies

When the SS *Estrom* arrived in Hull on 12 May 1915, she carried an unusual passenger. Haicke Petrus Marinus Janssen was a cigar salesman. But he was trying to peddle cigars around ports, and everyone knew that sailors favoured pipes or cigarettes. On top of that, he didn't seem to know a great deal about cigars. He moved down to Southampton, where the British Security Services began to suspect he might be more interested in information than sales.

Janssen was arrested on 30 May under suspicion of espionage. His order book was empty, and his telegrams to his office seemed to be couched in suspicious jargon.

Another Dutch man, Willem Johannes Roos, arrived from Amsterdam on 13 May, and he also claimed to be a cigar salesman. He went to Newcastle then Edinburgh, staying near Leith Port, which was used by the Royal Navy. His telegrams were also intercepted. Quickly, the security service realised both men were sending information about British ports and shipping to the enemy.

Under questioning, Ross admitted he knew Janssen, but then he tried to break a window and slash his wrist. He was taken to Brixton Prison. Both men were court-martialled at the Guildhall, Westminster, and condemned to death by shooting.

The executions took place just after dawn on 30 July. A detachment of Scots Guards carried out the sentence at the Tower ditch. What follows is a contemporary account of one of the few executions carried out at the Tower in the last century: "On July 30 there was a scene in the Tower of London which for grimness was never surpassed during the war. In the early dawn Janssen was led forth to face the firing party. His iron nerve, which had not deserted him throughout, held good to the finish and he died as he had lived, a brave man.

"Ross eyed the fatal chair, from which the bleeding body of his accomplice had just been removed, with a fair show of indifference, begging leave to finish the cigarette he had requested as a last favour. That ended, he took one last look at it, then threw it away with a gesture which represented utter contempt for all the failings of this world. With apparently no more interest in the proceedings, he seated himself in the chair. There was a momentary twinging of the face as they fastened the bandage around his face, but that was all. He too died bravely, and met his fate with a courage which could evoke nothing but admiration."

List of Spies Executed in the Tower During World War One

Karl Lody, 6 November 1914.

C. F. Muller, 23 June 1915.

W. J. Roos, 30 July 1915.

H. P. M. Janssen, 30 July 1915.

E. W. Melin, 10 September 1915.

A. A. Roggin, 17 September 1915.

F. Buschman, 19 September 1915.

G. T. Breeckow, 26 October 1915.

I. G. Ries, 27 October 1915.

A. Meyer, 2 December 1915.

L. H. Zender, 11 April 1916.

Wartime Spy is Last to be Executed

The last execution in the Tower of London was in living memory. A German spy faced the firing squad in 1941 for espionage. Corporal Josef Jakobs (30 June 1898 – 15 August 1941) was a German spy who parachuted into Ramsey in Huntingdonshire on 31 January 1941. The Home Guard saw him drifting to earth and captured him easily, as he had broken an ankle in his fall. When arrested, he was still wearing his flying suit and carrying British currency, forged papers, a radio and a German sausage.

He was tried in camera and condemned to death. He was held in the Tower, which was used as a prison during the war. Rudolf Hess was the most famous inmate, but many Germans were held there on a temporary basis.

On the morning of his execution, a rickety Windsor chair was placed against a wall at the old miniature rifle range in the Tower. The chair was used because of his broken ankle, which had not healed properly. A squad of eight Scots Guards, armed with Lee Enfield rifles, took aim at the white cotton target pinned over his heart. A silent signal was given by Lieutenant-Colonel C. R. Gerard, and all eight guns sounded simultaneously. Seven bullets struck the prisoner in the heart. The eighth shot went astray, hitting him in the head. He died instantly.

Jakobs was buried in an unmarked grave at St Mary's Roman Catholic Church, Kensal Green. All other German spies condemned to death during the war were executed by hanging at Wandsworth Prison in south London.

Ghosts of the Tower

The Tower of London is said to be haunted. The ghosts of five of the seven people executed on Tower Green wander the corridors at night, some with their heads tucked neatly under their arms.

All five are women. The two men beheaded on Tower Green apparently rest in peace. The five ghosts include three queens: Anne Boleyn, Catherine Howard and Lady Jane Grey. The sixty-eight-year-old Countess of Salisbury, hacked eleven times in a botched execution, and Jane Boleyn, also haunt the Tower.

Guy Fawkes and Sir Walter Raleigh also haunt the complex, along with Thomas Becket, King Henry VI and the Princes Edward and Richard, murdered in mysterious circumstances.

(Thomas Beckett had no connection to the Tower, but during construction work by Henry III, a small tower collapsed twice and the spirit of Beckett was seen. They called the tower St Thomas's Tower, and the problem ended.) Henry VI was also murdered in mysterious circumstances in 1471. It is said that on the anniversary of Henry's death (May 23), as the clock ticks towards midnight, the spectral shade of the mad king paces fitfully across the room. He continues to pace until the clock strikes midnight, when he fades slowly into the stones and rests for another year.

The Bloody Tower is the one haunted by the tragic two princes. Edward V, thirteen, and Richard of Shrewsbury, ten, disappeared from the Tower in July 1483, probably murdered. Their whimpering ghosts, wearing white nightgowns and clinging to each other in terror, are seen quite often in the rooms where they spent their last days.

That is quite a collection of spooks, making the Tower one of the most haunted locations in Britain. And there are more — there are several anonymous ghosts flitting through the ancient rooms. The Grey Lady and the White Lady have been spotted regularly by workers in the Tower.

The ghost of the Grey Lady has been described as a woman in mourning garments, but there is a black void where her face should be.

A phantom squad of soldiers in ancient uniform has also been seen patrolling the grounds. The Tower is one of the most popular tourist attractions in London. Just don't go there after dark…

The Ripper Connection

The Whitechapel area near the Tower was the stomping ground of one of the world's most notorious serial killers, Jack the Ripper. He preyed on prostitutes, of which there were many. The average East End prostitute in the late nineteenth century was middle-aged, skinny from hunger and often had teeth missing from poor diet and hygiene. Her face was puffy from drink, she stank and she wore all her clothing layered on top of each other because she was typically homeless.

It was a far cry from the glamour depicted in the movies.

Jack killed within walking distance of the river, but none of the killings or the victims was connected with the Thames. However there is a connection to the Tower.

On the evening of 6/7 August, two prostitutes, Martha Tabram and Mary Ann Connelly (Pearly Poll) were drinking and met up with two clients, both soldiers. When they left the tavern, the couples split to transact their business.

Martha was found a few hours later. She had been stabbed thirty-nine times. It was the second vicious slaying of a prostitute that year, though modern researchers believe they were not related to Jack the Ripper, whose reign of terror did not begin officially for another month.

Quickly, witnesses were found, who said Martha had been seen with a soldier. Four identity parades were held in the Tower over the following week, with all soldiers being asked to parade bare-headed. No clear suspect emerged and the murder went unsolved. Police treated Tabram's murder, and an earlier killing, as part of the Ripper investigation, though there were differences in the MO which suggests they were unrelated.

Martha's killer was never found.

Traitor's Gate

The Thames once lapped against the walls of the Tower of London. Now some land has been reclaimed, and the Tower stands fifty yards from the river, but in medieval times, you could enter the Tower via the water. Edward I built a stout wooden gate under one of the towers, St Thomas's Tower, and this provided an entrance for the Royal Barge.

In the sixteenth century, it became the custom to bring prisoners to the Tower along the river. A barge would bring them under London Bridge, where the heads of recently executed traitors were displayed on pikes. Among the most famous victims to pass through the Traitor's Gate were Queen Anne Boleyn, Sir Thomas More, and Queen Catherine Howard.

The Last Man Beheaded Does not Go Alone

Beheadings continued on Tower Hill until 1747. The last man to face the axe was an eighty-year-old Scottish peer, Lord Lovat. He made the mistake of choosing the wrong side in the uprising of 1745 and paid the ultimate price. But his execution was one of the most memorable in London history.

Bear-baiting had slipped out of fashion, so Londoners satiated their blood lust at hangings and executions. And Lord Lovat had been one of the leaders of the Jacobite rising, so everyone wanted a prime seat at his end. Knowing how many would be there, the authorities had built a number of grandstands so that everyone would have a better view of the executioner's block.

But the crowds were even bigger than expected, and the grandstands were groaning under the weight. One of the stands became so crowded that it collapsed, throwing hundreds of people to the ground. In the crush, twenty people lost their lives.

Lord Lovat, waiting to approach the block, saw the whole disaster unfolding. It caused him some wry amusement. He was heard to mutter, in a thick Scottish brogue: "The mair mischief, the mair sport." He then went to his death with a smile on his face.

Doing the Marshal's Dance at Execution Dock

A hanging was a wonderful day out for our forebears. It was as good as a football game today, and drew huge crowds to see the job done right — or botched, if they were lucky. London had two notorious execution spots that provided great sport for the citizens until the end of the seventeenth century, when executions were moved to the prisons themselves.

Tyburn, near the modern Marble Arch, was the chief execution spot, used since 1196. The unique, three-sided gallows allowed up to twenty-four prisoners to be hung simultaneously, as happened on 23 June 1649. Twenty-three men and one woman were dropped to their doom that day, having been conveyed there through the baying masses in eight carts.

But the more picturesque and gruesome location was Execution Dock, on the Thames near Wapping. This was reserved, in the main, for smugglers, pirates, mutineers and those guilty of capital crime on the high seas. And the executions were frequently more horrific than those at Tyburn. It continued in use up to 1830.

The site was reserved for the justice of the British Admiralty, responsible for prosecuting all crimes committed at sea. The dock symbolised that jurisdiction by its location; just beyond the low-tide mark of the river at Wapping, where the great ship yards were located.

Anyone who committed crime on the high seas eventually made their way back to London in chains, where they were tried by the High Court of the Admiralty. Capital offences included mutiny that resulted in death, murder on the high seas, piracy and smuggling.

Those found guilty were brought to the notorious Marshalsea Prison, on the banks of the river at Southwark. Conditions inside were dreadful and many did not survive their imprisonment. The worst treatment was reserved for pirates, who were held in the Strong Room instead of the main prison. The Strong Room was a bare, empty room near where the sewage discharged into the Thames. It was frequently rancid with raw excrement, and the rats did not wait until sleep or death before commencing gnawing. One man lost an eye and half his face while awaiting the gallows.

When the day of execution came — normally within a week or so of conviction — the prisoner was placed on a cart and paraded through the city, from Southwark to Wapping. There was an elaborate procession so that no one would miss the spectacle. The procession was led by the High Court Marshal on horseback, or occasionally his deputy. He carried a silver oar that represented the authority of the Admiralty. Other officials fell in line behind.

At the tail of the procession was the prisoner, flanked by his guards. The procession left Marshalsea Prison, then crossed London Bridge, proceeding past the Tower of London. Last meals are a modern indulgence, but the prisoner was allowed a last drink. The procession stopped at a public house, where the condemned man was allowed a quart of ale. This unusual clemency in a hard age probably served a practical purpose — it was easier to hang a man who was a little tipsy. He would struggle less than a fully sober man.

Once in Wapping, the prisoner was seen by a chaplain who attempted to extract a dying confession. They would profess their sins to go to their maker shriven.

It all provided great spectacle for the huge crowds that invariably gathered. They lined the river banks, often several deep. Those who could afford it, hired boats and moored them in the river for a better view. A Wapping execution was always worth catching.

There was no dedicated hangman: the job fell to one of the executioners at Tyburn or Newgate Prison. But there was one important difference: the length of the rope used.

Hanging is a precise science. The height and weight of the prisoner are taken into account, and the correct drop calculated. It should be long enough to snap the neck, resulting in immediate death, but not long enough to snap off the head. This was considered too gruesome, even for the London public.

However, when it came to hanging in Wapping, there was a distinct change of policy. A short rope was used on pirates. This resulted in prisoners being slowly strangled to death, rather than dying of a broken neck. They would dangle on the end of the rope, slowly spinning, their legs kicking ineffectually for up to five minutes before becoming still. It was known as the Marshal's Dance.

There was another difference. Those executed at Tyburn were cut down and buried in a nearby unmarked plot, often with quicklime to help decomposition. Sometimes, they were donated to medical students who were crying out for cadavers to practice on. But not at Execution Dock. The pirates were left dangling after they had died. The gallows was on the foreshore, at the low water mark, and the bodies were left there until three high tides had covered and revealed them. It served as a deterrent to others.

For some particularly notorious offenders, that was not enough. The Admiralty would order that their bodies be tarred then hung in chains, either at Cuckold's Point (a sharp bend on the river on the Rotherhithe Peninsula, opposite the West India Docks) or at Blackwell Point, the tip of Greenwich Peninsula. The bodies could be left on the gibbet for months.

The *Gentleman's Magazine* of 4 February 1796, gives a vivid account of a typical execution day: "This morning, a little after ten o'clock, Colley, Cole and Blanche, the three sailors convicted of the murder of Captain Little, were brought out of Newgate, and conveyed in solemn procession to Execution Dock, there to receive the punishment awarded by law. On the cart on which they rode was an elevated stage. On this were seated Colley, the principal instigator in the murder, and his two wretched instruments; and behind, on another seat, two executioners. Colley seemed in a state resembling that of a man stupidly intoxicated, and scarcely awake, and the two discovered little sensibility on this occasion, nor to the last moment of their existence did they, as we hear, make any confession.

"They were turned off about a quarter before twelve in the midst of an immense crowd of spectators. On the way to the place of execution they were preceded by the Marshall of the Admiralty in his carriage, the Deputy Marshall, bearing the silver oar, and the two City Marshalls on horseback, Sheriff's officers, etc. The whole cavalcade was conducted with great solemnity."

Hangings continued at Execution Dock until 1830. Sailors George Davis and William Watts, convicted of murdering their captain, were the last to do the Marshal's Dance.

There is some controversy about the exact position of the gallows at Execution Dock. As it was a moveable one, unlike Tyburn (which was not affected by tides!), there is no permanent structure to visit. Also, it was not always located at

Wapping. It was originally situated by the river at St Katherine's Dock, just downstream from the Tower of London. In the sixteenth century, it was moved downstream to Wapping. It was on the western end of Wapping for a period, then was moved to the eastern end, leading to confusion as to its exact location.

There is a large "E" on the Thames side of a building at Swan Wharf (80 Wapping High Street) which some maintain marks the location of the gallows. It is close to the new apartment development, Execution Dock House. Others say that the gallows stood roughly where the small Underground station now stands, about two-thirds of the way along Wapping High Street.

Captain Kidd

One of the most notorious pirates executed at Wapping was Captain William Kidd (1654-1701). A Scottish sailor, he began as a privateer, or semi-official pirate, preying on the enemies of Britain. Many pirates began that way and got a taste for the rich pickings available at sea. William Kidd got his first ship in 1689, when he was on the crew of a French-English pirate ship in the Caribbean. After a mutiny, he was elected captain. He began working for the British in the Caribbean, defending the island of Nevis against the French.

He ranged the seven seas, making friends of influence in London and America. He was even rewarded by the government for his work as a privateer. But a few years later, a rival pirate stole Kidd's ship while he was enjoying R&R on shore at Antigua in the West Indies.

In 1696, a number of investors put up the money to reship Kidd, and he set out on his final voyage, tasked with rooting out pirates and enemy French ships. The King was among the investors. The new ship, *Adventure Galley*, was a massive 284 tonnes, equipped with thirty-four cannon, and 150 men. It also had oars, making it more manoeuvrable in combat.

But the enterprise was doomed from the start. As Kidd sailed down the Thames, he arrogantly failed to salute a navy yacht at Greenwich, as custom dictated. When the yacht fired a shot to make him show respect, the crew responded by dropping their breeches and mooning the naval vessel.

It was an unpardonable insult, and Kidd was punished. The navy came on board and press-ganged many of his crew. He had to sail to America shorthanded. He recrewed with hardened criminals and former pirates in the colonies, but failed to capture any ships in the Indian Ocean.

The crew became mutinous and, in an angry confrontation, Kidd struck one over the head with an iron-bound bucket, killing him. Even by pirate standards, this was out of line. Kidd became crueller as discipline dwindled. He did capture one Armenian ship in 1698, but her captain was English, so Kidd was back in trouble with the authorities. The Royal Navy declared him a pirate and the hunt was on for him.

He was eventually captured in Boston and returned to London to face trial. He believed his rich backers would come to his aid: he was mistaken. He was convicted of both piracy and murder, and sentenced to hang.

Kidd escaped the Strong Room at Marshalsea, instead being held in Newgate. He was brought from there, in great procession, to Execution Dock on the morning of 23 May 1701. He had a notorious reputation, probably unwarranted, and his execution drew record crowds. The blood-thirsty onlookers were not let down.

Kidd stood on the platform and the noose was put around his neck. The trap was pulled and Kidd plunged down — but the rope snapped and he fell to the mud underneath the gallows. But when death beckons, no man escapes. The pirate captain was hauled back to the platform and the noose was put around him again. This time there were no mistakes; Kidd fell the short distance and began his convulsions, much to the delight of the crowd.

After his death, and the passing of three high tides, Kidd's body was taken down and tarred. He was then placed in an iron gibbet, and his remains hung by the river at Tilbury. It hung there for more than twenty years, as a warning to all those leaving the Thames and heading to sea: step out of line, and the Execution Dock awaits.

CHAPTER FIVE: SPANNING THE THAMES

Before roads, rivers were the transport infrastructure of the world. If a river was navigable by boat and could be forded or bridged, a settlement would spring up. That is how London began. There was a stretch of the river that was narrow enough to bridge, yet deep enough to allow ships to dock, and Roman traders built their homes. They also built the first bridge. Some of the wooden foundation posts still survive, buried in the mud of the river bank.

For many years, one bridge sufficed. But as the centuries passed, the bridge took more and more traffic. So other bridges were added, then tunnels. Some are private, owned by utility companies or rail networks. Most are open to the public. The Thames is no longer a barrier between the north bank and the south bank.

The most famous bridge is London Bridge — which is not, as some tourists think, the bridge with the two towers. That is Tower Bridge — which is not named after the two towers, but after the nearby Tower of London. Confused? You have reason to be; today there are sixty-two bridges or tunnels spanning the Thames in London alone. But a few of them have a history that makes them special.

London Bridge — Two Thousand Years of History
London Bridge is falling down, falling down, falling down…

Bridges have been erected and have fallen at the site of London Bridge since ancient times. The current bridge was finished in 1973. But it was over two thousand years earlier that the first bridge went up at the site. And in the two millennia since, the bridge has gone up and down more times than a child's yo-yo.

London Bridge is 860 feet long, and carries five lanes of the A3 through the city. It spans the river downstream of the more picturesque Tower Bridge, and forms the western end of the Pool of London. On the south side of the bridge are Southwark Cathedral and London Bridge Station; on the north is a monument to the Great Fire.

The current bridge is the largest to have spanned this stretch of the river, and was the most downstream bridge on the Thames until Putney Bridge opened in 1729. There has been a bridge of some sort on the site for more than 2,000 years.

The first bridge was a wooden pontoon put in place by the Romans in AD 50. A more permanent structure went up five years later, and a small trading settlement grew around it — Londinium. Five years later, that second bridge also came down, as Queen Boudicca swept through the settlement. But her victory was short-lived, and soon the Romans were back in charge. The bridge went up for a third time.

But this bridge fell into disrepair after the Romans left — and Londinium was also abandoned. Centuries later, around AD 990, King Ethelred built another bridge — but he left out an important part of the construction. He forgot to sacrifice a child.

The Celts held sway over much of Britain before the Roman invasion, and human sacrifice was an important part of Celtic religious life. It was also important to the Picts. This persisted into early medieval times, with human sacrifices being discreetly made during the construction of many large public buildings. St Columba reputedly buried St Oran under the foundations of his great monastery in Iona, Scotland, in the sixth century; legend has it he then dug him up, very much alive, three days later.

Tradition dictated that a child should have been sacrificed and buried under the foundations of a bridge to placate the spirits of the river, but there is no archaeological evidence that King Ethelred conducted the sacrifice when his bridge went up.

So in 1014, Prince Olaf of Norway, a Viking who was assisting Ethelred to divide the Danes in London from the Danes in Southwark, pulled down the new bridge. The event might be the inspiration for the rhyme "London Bridge is Falling Down".

Two years later, the wooden bridge had been re-erected, but was destroyed in turn by the worst tornado ever to hit Britain, in 1091. William II used forced labour to replace London Bridge (as well as building the Tower of London). But a fire in 1135 destroyed the Norman construction. The fire broke out on the bridge on Pentecost, on the seventh Sunday after Easter. It was so severe it destroyed most of the city between St Paul's and St Clement Danes in Westminster.

The replacement bridge was controlled by a warden, Peter de Colechurch, who quickly realised that it was carrying too much traffic for the wooden structure. Thomas Becket had been murdered in Canterbury in 1170, and the cathedral there quickly became a major pilgrimage site for Londoners who needed to cross the bridge to begin their journey. So he recommended replacing the wooden structure with a stone one.

Construction of the eighth version of London Bridge began in 1176, and took thirty-three years. Opened in 1209, the bridge even featured a chapel near the centre, dedicated to Thomas Becket. The chapel was grander than many in the city and featured a river-level entrance for fishermen and water taxies.

King John licensed the building of shops along the bridge to pay for its upkeep. The medieval bridge had nineteen small arches and a drawbridge with a defensive gatehouse at the southern end. It was crowded with buildings, several reaching up to seven storeys in height. The narrowness of the arches obstructed the flow of the Thames, and made it liable to freezing in winter.

The buildings led to huge congestion on the bridge, with crossings often taking an hour. It also made the bridge a fire hazard — 3,000 people were reputedly burnt to death in the first Great Fire, in 1212. The bridge also saw large loss of life in a fire in 1633.

In 1756, parliament ordered that all the buildings on the bridge should be removed, and the two centre arches replaced by a single, wider one, to aid navigation on the river. The uncongested bridge was still too narrow for the volume of traffic at the end of the eighteenth century, so in 1799 a competition was held to commission a new structure. The new bridge, began in 1824 and completed six years later, had five stone arches. The cost, factoring in new approach roads and other infrastructure work, was around £2.5 million (or £186 billion in today's money).

It is not known whether engineer John Rennie, who designed it, and his son John Rennie the Younger, who built it, included the sacrifice of a child in the plans, but it is probably safe to assume they didn't.

By 1896 the bridge was the busiest point in London, with 8,000 people and 900 vehicles crossing every hour. The bridge was widened in 1902-04 to cope with the volume, but the widening work proved too much for the bridge's foundations.

It began to sink at a rate of about an inch every eight years. And to compound the problem, the east side was sinking faster than the west side. By 1924 the east side was three or 4 inches lower than the west side. It became apparent that London needed London Bridge number ten.

The new bridge was built between 1967 and 1972, and opened by Queen Elizabeth II on 17 March 1973. It is a less ornate bridge than the others spanning the Thames, but does have its charms. The bridge's lights were made from cannons captured from Napoleon's fleet.

So far, it has stood up well, so perhaps the bad luck associated with earlier bridges has finally left the site. But in 1984, it had a close call. The warship HMS *Jupiter*, nearly 400 feet long and weighing 2,500 tonnes, was leaving the Pool of London, in the docklands, after a visit to the capital. But manoeuvring through the bridge proved a problem, and it collided, causing significant damage to both ship and bridge. The ship's captain, Commander Colin Hamilton, was court-martialled.

London Bridge is one of the most fascinating structures in the city, throwing light on two thousand years of history. A great place to start exploring that is the London Bridge Experience, at 2-4 Tooley Street on the south side of the bridge. This tourist attraction is in the vaults below the southern abutment of London Bridge, immediately outside London Bridge Station. Their website is www.thelondonbridgeexperience.com.

During the building of the London Bridge Experience, a collection of skeletons was unearthed in the crypt, and the building is supposed to be haunted. Can there be a better way of exploring history?

Admission to the London Bridge Experience also includes admission to its sister attraction, The London Tombs.

The Man Who Bought London Bridge

In 1967, it was time to take down bridge number nine and begin work on number ten. But London councillor Ivan Luckin had a bizarre idea — why not sell the old bridge?

It was sold to an entrepreneur from Missouri, Robert McColloch of McColloch Oil, for $2.46 million. Many people believe he thought he was purchasing the more picturesque Tower Bridge, but he knew what he was getting.

The bridge was dismantled carefully and rebuilt in Arizona, opening in 1971. It now spans the Bridgewater Channel canal from Lake Havasu to Thomson Bay, and is the second biggest tourist attraction in Arizona, behind the Grand Canyon. A whole English theme park, with a Tudor period shopping mall, has grown up around it.

London Bridge is Falling Down

London Bridge is falling down,
Falling down, falling down.
London Bridge is falling down,
My fair lady.

It's a nursery rhyme every child knows, and has been around several hundred years. It first appeared in print in 1744 (but was at least a hundred years old by then, and probably far more), and tells of the troubles in trying to keep the bridge from falling. The meaning is a bit ambiguous, but several possible interpretations have been put forward.

Some scholars claim the poem commemorates the Viking destruction of the bridge in 1014. But folklorist Alice Bertha Gomme (later Lady Gomme), at the end of the nineteenth century, put forward the idea that the song refers to the burying, perhaps alive, of children in the foundations of the bridge. This came from the idea that a bridge would collapse unless a human sacrifice was buried in its foundation.

Although there is no archaeological evidence of human remains in the foundations of the bridge, there is a tradition of human sacrifice in Britain, starting with the Celts and Picts.

As for the identity of the Fair Lady in the song, that also points towards the sinister possibility of a sacrifice. The Leigh family of Stoneleigh Park, Warwickshire, has a family tradition that a member of their family was buried under the foundations.

But other scholars have suggested that the Fair Lady may be Matilda of Scotland (1080-1118), or Eleanor of Provence (1223-91), both of whom had connections with the bridge.

Narrow Arches Cause Problems
The narrowness of the nineteen small arches under London Bridge brought many problems. They obstructed the flow of the Thames, making it sluggish. This meant that the river became prone to freezing during the hard winters of the medieval and late medieval period. This led to the famous Frost Fairs on the Thames — which brought great joy and revelry to the city, but which cost many lives when the ice broke up.

The current was also obstructed by waterwheels under the two north arches, which drove water pumps, and two under the south arches, which powered grain mills. This all led to ferocious rapids between the piers of the bridge, as the difference in water levels on both sides could be as much as 6 feet. Only a brave or a foolish waterman would attempt to "shoot the bridge" (steer a boat between the piers). Many were drowned in the attempt, making London Bridge one of the most dangerous on the Thames.

As an illustration, in one week in 1763, there were four accidental drownings under the arches. A boat with ten on board overturned shooting the arch, and three were drowned. A few days later, a barge carrying a cargo of timber, struck an arch, and one of the bargemen, John Herbert, fell overboard and was lost.

It was said that the bridge was: "For wise men to pass over, and fools to pass under."

The Expulsion of the Jews

Jews were seen as the money-men of medieval Europe. There was a Christian prohibition against usury (charging interest on loans), which meant that Jews had a great advantage in the world of banking and finance. The prohibition on usury did not apply to them.

Being seen as the money men did nothing to increase their popularity. There was always an uneasy relationship between Christians and Jews, and unsavoury rumours were rife in the twelfth and thirteenth century. Specifically, some believed that the Jews in Britain would select a Christian child, who would be kidnapped and crucified on the feast of the Passover, to ensure that the Jewish people eventually got back to Palestine.

It began when a young boy was murdered in Norwich in 1144. A number of years later, Thomas of Monmouth wrote a book, *The Life and Passion of St William the Martyr of Norwich*, which first made the allegation that the Jewish community was behind the killing. There was no evidence for the allegation, but nonetheless it stuck.

A number of boys died over the coming decades. Among the uneducated and unthinking populace, a belief began to grow that Jews were targeting Christian children and killing them for their blood — this despite the fact that Jewish law makes consumption of blood a taboo. There was never any evidence to back up rumours, and no Jewish people or groups were ever charged with any of the murders.

Over the next century, tensions between Christians and Jews increased, particularly during the Crusades. Also, as taxes increased to finance the Crusades and costly wars, the Jewish money-men began to suffer. Their goods were confiscated by the Crown, and their power in the financial world dwindled. They were no longer as useful to the king. Finally, in 1290, Edward I ordered the expulsion of the entire Jewish race from England.

One group of London Jews hired a ship to bring them to Europe. They boarded just upstream of London Bridge. But they timed their departure badly, and were caught by an ebb tide. They ended up stranded on a sandbank. The captain suggested they get off the boat and wait on the dry sandbank for the tide to turn. But the tide began to rise faster than they expected. Panicking, the captain ran to the boat and cast off, abandoning the passengers.

Their shouts and screams could be heard from the shore as the tide rose and engulfed them, drowning them all. The exact spot of the tragedy is not recorded, but tradition says that it happened under London Bridge, where the narrow arches caused silt and mud to pile high, forming banks. To this day, the curve of the river near the site of the old London Bridge is meant to be haunted and on lonely winter evenings, you can faintly hear the cries of the dying coming across the water.

King Causes Chaos and Congestion

Avaricious King John saw his new bridge as a cash cow and determined to milk it dry. He allowed so many shops, taverns and other businesses on the bridge, that traffic was reduced almost to a standstill. The bridge was 26 feet across, which was big for the day, but the buildings on each side reduced the central passageway to just 12 feet. Some of the buildings projected as much as 7 feet over the bridge, giving the whole structure a very topsy-turvy appearance. Nearly 200 places of business lined both sides of the narrow bridge — but there were a few gaps, where people could opt out of the throng and watch the river flow by.

With large crowds funnelled through the narrow passage, an accident with a cart, or a misbehaving animal, could back everything up, and it often took an hour to cross the bridge. Many pedestrians opted for the quicker but more expensive option of a water taxi to cross from London to Southwark. Dozens of small vessels operated the route.

Every sort of business, except pubs and ale houses, operated on the bridge. There were no pubs because of the lack of cellars. Merchants lived above their shops and sold goods from the ground floor, displaying them from upper floors. Several built floors connecting both sides of the street, giving London Bridge the feeling of a tunnel. It was guarded by a gatehouse and gate at either end, which were closed at night.

Over the years, the superstructure suffered blows and calamities. Some of the arches collapsed under the weight and had to be rebuilt. Houses on the bridge were burnt during fires and revolts, but were always replaced. But the bridge is remembered for a far more grisly reason than falling buildings and overcrowded streets.

The southern gatehouse became notorious as a site for displaying the heads of convicted traitors.

It began in 1305, when the head of executed Scottish rebel William Wallace was displayed on a stake at the southern entrance to the bridge, as a warning to all others that the Crown would not tolerate revolt. The tradition continued for another 355 years. The heads were dipped in tar to preserve them, then displayed on pikes. Famous heads included Jack Cade (revolutionary) in 1450, Thomas More (philosopher, adviser to Henry VIII, and martyr) in 1535, Bishop John Fisher the same year, and Thomas Cromwell (another adviser to Henry VIII — a dangerous job) in 1540.

In 1598, a German visitor to London, Paul Hentzner, counted over thirty heads on the bridge: "On the south is a bridge of stone eight hundred feet in length, of wonderful work; it is supported upon twenty piers of square stone. The whole is covered on each side with houses so disposed as to have the appearance of a continued street, not at all of a bridge. Upon this is built a tower, on whose top the heads of such as have been executed for high treason are placed on iron spikes. We counted above thirty."

The practice was finally stopped in 1660, following the Restoration of King Charles II.

Fires on London Bridge

The medieval London Bridge lasted longer than any of its predecessors, but it was not without incident. Congestion and the huge number of buildings meant the structure was a fire hazard. In 1212, the greatest of the early fires of London (there were several) broke out at Southwark and pushed across the bridge, trapping a huge number of people. The Guinness Book of Records says that 3,000 died on the bridge alone that day, but the number is almost certainly exaggerated and is not accepted by historians.

Whatever the true number of casualties, every building on the bridge was gutted, but the stone structure survived. The buildings went up again and the fire hazard remained.

In 1633, a fire broke out on the north side of the bridge, destroying forty-two buildings on that third of the bridge, and another eighty on Thames Street. Many of these buildings were not replaced, and ironically that is what saved the bridge in the Great Fire of London in 1666. The gaps acted as a natural firebreak.

Duke Takes a Ducking

The arches of London Bridge were no respecter of rank. People learnt to avoid them. It became common to pull in at one of the steps down-river of the bridge and let people disembark. Passengers would walk down the banks and rejoin the boat once the crew had "shot the bridge".

Sometimes, foolhardy passengers decided to remain on board for the thrill. James Boswell, the writer and diarist, was on the river with the Duke and Duchess of York, and the crew began pulling the barge to the shore. But the Duchess dismissed the danger and ordered them to "shoot the bridge" with everyone on board.

"She refused to get out of the barge, and insisted upon shooting the Bridge. But we shipped a good deal of water and all got very wet," grumbled Boswell. He didn't realise how lucky he had been.

A few centuries earlier, another Duke had taken the same decision. On a wintery November afternoon in 1429, the Duke of Norfolk took to the river on his barge with a number of companions. They boarded at St Mary Overie Dock, on the south side of the river, at 4 p.m., and decided to pass through London Bridge, rather than going to the trouble of getting off and walking.

But poor seamanship while they were "shooting the bridge" led to calamity. The barge, instead of popping through the arch, collided with one of the pillars and lurched dangerously, tossing many of the passengers overboard.

Some spotted the danger in time. Three or four, including the Duke, managed to leap onto the foot of the pillar, and clung to it despite the fast-flowing water. Passers-by on the bridge spotted the survivors and threw them a rope, pulling them to safety.

The barge battered its way through the arches, but those who took a ducking were swept away forever.

London's Yo-yo Bridge

The current London Bridge is at least the tenth to stand on the site. Like a yo-yo, it keeps going up and coming down again.

Bridge No 1: This was a pontoon, built by the Romans in AD 50.

Bridge No 2: This pile bridge replaced the pontoon in AD 55, but was destroyed by Queen Boudicca in AD 60.

Bridge No 3: In AD 60 or within a few years, the Romans had replaced the bridge destroyed by Queen Boudicca. It gradually fell into disuse after the Romans pulled out of Britain.

Bridge No 4: In AD 990, King Ethelred replaced the abandoned and collapsed Roman structure. But in AD 1014, Prince Olaf of Norway destroyed the bridge to split the Danes on both sides of the river.

Bridge No 5: In AD 1016, a wooden bridge replaced Ethelred's bridge, but was destroyed by the London Tornado of AD 1091.

Bridge No 6: This replaced the structure torn down by the tornado, but a fire in AD 1135 burnt it to a crisp.

Bridge No 7: A wooden bridge replaced the one destroyed by the fire of AD 1135.

Bridge No 8: In 1209, the wooden bridge was replaced by a stone bridge with several narrow stone arches.

Bridge No 9: The medieval London Bridge was replaced with a bigger one in 1830 to accommodate greater volumes of traffic.

Bridge No 10: In 1973, the modern London Bridge replaced the existing bridge as it was slowly sinking under its own weight.

First Witch Burning

Many societies burn those they consider to be witches. But nowhere was the practice of burning witches more prevalent than in England and Western Europe between 1480 and 1750, during the period of the great witch hunts. England even appointed a Witchfinder General, Mathew Hopkins. A sadistic puritan, he was responsible for almost half of the entire number of witch burnings carried out in the country.

Exaggerated accounts exist of how many died during the witch purges. Some claim the number is 9 million, but the actual figure is between 35,000 and 40,000, most of them women. Germany was the worst. But in England less than 1,500 witches were put to the torch.

England's only real distinction is that it had the first recorded witch execution in Western Europe. The event is noted in the Codex Diplomaticus Aevi Saxonici (963-975). A woman and her son were convicted of trying to take the life of a nobleman by witchcraft. They were accused of sticking pins into a waxen effigy of him.

The woman was sentenced to death and was taken to London Bridge, where she was publicly drowned. Her son managed to escape and became an outlaw. King Edgar the Peaceful ordered their land to be forfeited to the nobleman they had tried to bewitch.

A Model of Old London Bridge

Several etchings and woodcuts exist showing London Bridge in all its medieval splendour, with its narrow arches and the houses piled precariously on top. They give a flavour of what it must have looked like, but if you want to see the real thing, the closest you can come is a visit to the Church of St Magnus the Martyr on Lower Thames Street.

This is one of the lesser-known jewels in London, part of the fifty churches rebuilt by Sir Christopher Wren after the Great Fire. The building is stunningly beautiful inside, and no visit to London is complete without spending a few minutes in contemplation of its rich heritage. Among all the magnificence is a long, highly detailed model of the old bridge.

You can walk along and study the structure, seeing all the houses leaning inwards towards one another, the little impromptu bridges linking the upper floors of several. The detail is incredible, and little models of people, animals and carts go about their business. One figure is oddly out of place: among the medieval clothing, the modern Bobby stands out. But with good reason: this is a representation of the model-maker, David T. Aggett. He is a Liveryman of the Worshipful Company of Plumbers, and was formerly a policeman.

The church is open every day, and admission is free.

The Bombing of Hammersmith Bridge

The Irish Republican Army (IRA) tried on three separate occasions to destroy Hammersmith Bridge, with very mixed results.

Hammersmith Bridge was the first suspension bridge to span the Thames. It was built in the 1820s, and goes from just south of Hammersmith on the northern bank of the river, to Barnes in the borough of Richmond-upon-Thames on the south. But it wasn't particularly strong. By the 1870s, it was not strong enough to support the weight of the increasingly heavy traffic in the city.

Then authorities became alarmed at the annual University Boat Race in 1870, when between 11,000 and 12,000 people crowded the structure to watch the rowers pass under. The bridge creaked ominously. It was time to replace it with a more stable structure.

The current bridge was opened in 1887, to replace the original. It is a beautifully ornate structure, but it was also narrow and not very strong. In 1984 an overloaded lorry caused significant damage to the structure, requiring repairs. The weight of the lorry caused bearings to fail. In 1992, a weight limit was finally imposed, banning all heavy goods vehicles and double-decker buses from the bridge.

Perhaps it was the weakness of the bridge that caused the IRA to target it. Their first attempt was shortly before the start of the Second World War. The IRA began a bombing campaign that lasted nearly a year, but caused little real damage.

They planted two bombs on the bridge on the morning of 29 March 1939. However, a women's hairdresser from nearby Chiswick was walking home across the bridge after a late night out. He spotted a suitcase lying on the footpath, and noticed smoke and sparks coming from it. Curious, he opened the suitcase. He was shocked to see it contained a bomb. He quickly dragged the suitcase to the parapet and flung it into the river.

He was only just in time. As the case struck the river, it exploded, throwing a sixty-foot column of water into the air. Seconds later, the bridge was rocked by a second explosion from the other side, as the second bomb detonated. Some girders on the west side of the bridge collapsed, and windows in nearby houses shattered in the blast.

Two men, Eddie Connell and William Browne, were subsequently jailed for their involvement in the bombing. Connell got twenty years, while Browne was sentenced to ten years.

Maurice Childs, whose quick action prevented the damage being much worse, was awarded an MBE.

The next attempt to blow up the bridge did not come until 1996. The IRA planted the largest Semtex bomb ever found in mainland Britain. No one was injured when the 32 lb device went off, but the bridge structure was damaged.

In February 1997, the bridge was shut to all "non-essential" traffic. Only emergency vehicles, pedestrians, buses (single-decker), motorbikes and bicycles were allowed cross. After two years, the bridge reopened.

The IRA were on a ceasefire, but a new group, the Real IRA, were still very much active, and opposed to the Northern Ireland peace process. They decided to go for a familiar target, and have another go at destroying Hammersmith Bridge.

At 4.30 a.m. on 1 June, the Real IRA detonated a bomb under the Barnes span of the bridge (near the north side). No one was injured and the bridge only suffered minor damage. It was closed for repairs, and as part of the renovations, the bridge was repainted, restoring it to the original colour scheme of 1887. A new lighting system was also installed. The bridge was declared a Grade II listed structure in 2008, providing protection for its unique structure.

Good Samaritan Perishes

A Good Samaritan got a Christmas ducking in 1919. South African airman Lieutenant Charles Campbell Wood, RAF, was crossing the bridge around midnight when he saw a woman struggling in the water. He bravely threw off his jacket, mounted the upstream footway parapet, and dived into the Thames.

He reached the drowning woman and managed to bring her to shore, where they were both helped out of the water. But the story did not have a happy ending for the airman. He struck the bridge while diving into the water. The Thames is one of the most polluted rivers in the world, and Campbell Wood got tetanus from the wound. He died of the infection.

His act of bravery is commemorated to this day by a plaque on the handrail of the bridge.

Biker Gangs on Chelsea Bridge

The Joust to the Death on London Bridge in front of Richard the Lionheart (see Chapter Eight) was an unusual event, but not the only one of its kind to take place over the Thames. A similar event occurred as recently as 1970, but the horses were of steel and shiny chrome, and the crests of the knights were the one-percenter badges of the outlaw biker gangs.

Starting around 1950, Chelsea Bridge became a proving ground for the various biker gangs that sprang up across the UK after the war. On Friday nights, bikers would gather on the bridge and race each other across it on their powerful choppers. Rivalries were intense, because the gangs were not just concerned about the bikes. Some were fronts for major international criminal organisations, involved in drugs, prostitution and intimidation.

The Hells Angels were the most notorious gang. The FBI classify them as one of the "big four" motorcycle gangs involved in violence, drug dealing, trafficking stolen goods, extortion and murder. They proudly display their one-percenter badges — proclaiming that they are not among the 99% of bikers who are decent, honest people with an interest in motorcycles.

The Outlaws were a similar organisation, established in the USA, but spreading worldwide after the war. Most Hells Angels chose Harley-Davidsons. For Outlaws, a Harley was compulsory. The gangs met frequently on Chelsea Bridge, and macho posturing — as well as random violence — was common. Each gang had numerous local groups that affiliated to it and shared its hatred of the rival gang.

Clashes between the major gangs and their minor affiliates were common. The Friday night gatherings were fuelled by testosterone. As one biker recalls: "The burn-ups (informal races) were legendary. Edgware Road, Park Lane, Sloane Square — they were unreal. Every one of us was taking our lives in our hands. How most of us survived I don't know. The soldiers used to come out of the army barracks in Chelsea and sit on the wall to watch this lunacy. Imagine forty or fifty bikes all racing as hard as they could through the streets of London. There was no quarter asked or given either — we were on the wrong side of the road, scratching round corners, forcing cars onto the pavement. You just had to get back to Chelsea Bridge first. It was madness but it was fantastic."

But on 17 October 1970, things came to a head. The usual large crowd of bikers that night included members of the

Essex and Chelsea chapters of the Hells Angels, as well as rival gangs the Road Nuts, Nightingales, Windsor Angels and Jokers. Simmering tension erupted into a fight that evening. Quickly, it escalated as gang members joined in the fray.

Within minutes, fifty people were involved in a full-scale riot. Motorcycle chains were whipped off bikes to be used as impromptu but vicious weapons. Many of the bikers carried flick knives, inflicting horrible injuries when the fight went to close quarters. At least one spiked flail was recovered after the night of carnage.

In the midst of all the violence, one of the Hells Angels produced a sawn-off shotgun. A witness recalled: "The one that did the shooting got out of a car and walked across the road and shot this other bloke. There were a lot of bikes at the bridge that night and everyone took off before the police arrived."

The unknown gunman had fired at one of the Jokers, hitting him at point-blank range. The Joker died moments later.

Police eventually broke up the riot and dozens of arrests were made. Subsequently, twenty of those present were sentenced to between one and twelve years in prison.

The event had one positive outcome. Bikers meet peacefully under the crest of the bridge (an engraving of doves holding olive branches) every Friday night still, in tribute to their fallen comrade. However, not every local is pleased at this devotion.

Residents of luxury flats overlooking the bridge say their peace is being shattered by the bikers. Bikers counter by saying they have been meeting on the bridge for decades and were there before the exclusive flats went up. Police acknowledge they are aware of the problem and are committed to tackling it.

Putney Bridge

Putney Bridge has a unique distinction — it is the only bridge in London with a church on both ends. St Mary's Church, Putney, is on the south end, while All Saint's Church, Fulham, is on the north. It was built between 1726 and 1729 and was a toll bridge. Mary Wollstonecraft, the writer, women's rights campaigner and mother of Mary Shelley (author of *Frankenstein*), tried to commit suicide off Putney Bridge in 1795, but was rescued.

The bridge was badly damaged by a collision with a river barge in 1870. Part of the bridge had to be replaced.

The entire structure was replaced in 1886 by the five-arch stone structure that stands today. In March 1953, serial killer and necrophiliac John Christie was arrested on the bridge. He hung for his crimes.

Tower Bridge

This is the most distinctive bridge across the Thames and is often mistakenly called London Bridge by visitors. The combined bascule and suspension bridge was opened in 1894 and consists of two towers tied together at their upper level by two horizontal walkways. The centre of the bridge can open upwards to allow ships to pass through.

The bridge is called Tower Bridge not because of its distinctive twin towers, but because of its closeness to the Tower of London. One of its hidden features is a narrow tunnel on the north tower, which leads to the river. This was known as the Dead Man's Hole, and allowed dead bodies to be recovered from the river. The bodies were stored in a small mortuary under the tower.

The bridge is closed to traffic on average three times a day so that shipping can pass under. Ships need to give 24-hours' notice so that the closures can be planned. In December 1952, a double-decker bus was caught on the bridge when the central portion began to rise. The normal procedure was that a gateman would ring a warning bell and close the gates once the road was clear, but a relief watchman was on duty, and the procedure failed. The bus was near the edge of the southern bascule, or rising portion, when it began to rise up.

The bus driver, Albert Gunter, had only a split second to make a decision: try to stop and reverse, or put his foot to the floor and hope for the best. He accelerated. The bascule had risen 3 feet by the time he reached the edge, but the northern one had not begun to rise yet. The bus hit the edge at over thirty miles an hour, then shot over the gap and came down with a crash on the northern bascule. The passengers were tossed around and shook up, but there were no serious injuries.

Hawker Hunter

Another transport incident involved a more high-tech vehicle than a double-decker bus. In 1968, the RAF was celebrating its first fifty years. On 5 April, Flight Lieutenant Alan Pollock took off on a routine flight from RAF Tangmere, Sussex, to RAF West Raynham, Norfolk. His flight took him over London and he decided to make an informal protest against the government of Harold Wilson. He flew low over the Houses of Parliament, then went right down almost to street level. He circled Parliament three times slowly, then turned and flew along the Embankment, tipping his wings as he passed the RAF monument. Tower Bridge was ahead of him.

An experienced fighter pilot, the urge was too strong. He could have flown over the bridge, but decided instead to fly between the two towers, under the connecting walkways. His fly-through was completely unauthorised.

He was arrested within an hour of landing and was discharged from the RAF on medical grounds, without the chance to defend himself at a court martial.

Unusual Suicide

On Tuesday, 30 July 1973, the police got an unusual call: a hysterical woman told them that her husband planned on crashing his small plane into Tower Bridge. Paul Martin, 29, was in despair because he was on bail following accusations of stock market fraud.

Police, ambulance and fire-services rushed to the bridge, and rush-hour traffic was diverted to other bridges. Radar failed to pick up anything, then suddenly they heard the scream of the engine. The Beagle Pup came screaming down the river at a height of just 300 feet, then swung north and buzzed The City, the financial district where Martin worked. Then he came back and flew at the bridge. Cops and ambulance men scattered, but he did not crash — he flew between the towers, swung through the City again, then returned and flew between the towers for a second time. Then he rose into the air and disappeared.

Two hours later the plane flew into forest at the Lake District in northern England, killing Martin instantly.

The Big Drop

A number of tourists had a narrow escape on 11 May 2009, when the lift in the north tower of the bridge failed and fell 3 metres (10 feet). Four men and two women suffered leg injuries. They included Spanish tourists and one staff member. One broke a leg while another broke an ankle.

Another ten people escaped with bruises. The exhibition in Tower Bridge was closed for a number of weeks to check all the lifts. London Corporation's Director of Environmental Services Philip Everett said: "We are desperately sorry in causing this inconvenience. We clearly very much regret it and we wish the injured people well."

Waterloo Bridge

Waterloo Bridge became famous for suicides, and Thomas Hood wrote the poem "The Bridge of Signs" about the suicide of a desperate young woman, pregnant and abandoned, there (see Chapter Six). Built on a bend of the river between Hungerford Bridge and Blackfriars Bridge, it commands great views of the city.

It opened in 1817 as a toll bridge. Because of this, it was quieter than other bridges, and a good place for suicides. It was also the scene of the KGB assassination of Bulgarian dissident writer Georgi Markov. But one of the most dramatic incidents on the bridge was the death of American stuntman Samuel Gilbert Scott on 11 January 1841.

An ex-navy man, Gilbert was famous for his dramatic high-dives. He plummeted over the Niagara Falls in Canada, and in Cornwall he dived 240 feet into 8 feet of water. After each of these stunts, he would pass the hat.

Some of his stunts were quite dangerous. He liked to tie a rope to his feet then swing from it. But when he reached London, he began to get careless. He swung from the rigging of an American ship docked near Deptford in London and the rope accidentally slipped around his neck, nearly strangling him. Scott was saved by a quick-thinking sailor, who caught his feet and supported him, which allowed him to loosen the rope.

Scott grinned at the crowd after the accident, saying: "The hemp that is to hang me is not grown yet!"

He could not have been more wrong. On 11 January, a huge crowd gathered on Waterloo Bridge to see the twenty-eight-year-old's latest stunt. It was a bit of a challenge as well as a dive. Scott planned to run from the White Lion Pup in Drury Lane to Waterloo Bridge, climb a scaffold he had constructed high over the bridge, dive into the river, swim to shore, run back to the pub, and accomplish it all within an hour.

He left the White Lion at 1 p.m., with the crowd cheering him on. Arriving at the bridge, he scrambled up the scaffold then tied his ankles to a rope. He planned to swing out on the rope a few times, then do the dive. But when he swung out, the rope snagged around his neck, just like in Deptford. The noose tightened and he began to choke. As his body kicked convulsively in the air, doing the gibbet gig, the crowd roared their approval. They thought it was part of the act.

For about three minutes he kicked in the air, then his movements became more sporadic. Slowly, it dawned on the audience that something had gone tragically wrong. One man in the crowd began to scream for the American to be cut down. Someone scrambled onto the scaffolding with a knife, but it was too late.

According to a report in the newspapers the following morning: "Scott was immediately taken to Charing Cross Hospital, where every attention was paid to him, but unfortunately without effect, as life was quite extinct."

Battersea Bridge

Battersea Bridge is a five-span iron and granite bridge linking Chelsea on the north to Battersea on the south. But when it was built in 1771, the original bridge had nineteen arches. It was poorly designed and proved a danger to its users and to shipping. Collisions with ships were common, and eventually two arches were removed. It helped but did not solve the problem.

The bridge was damaged extensively by collision with an ice floe in the heavy frost of 1795 and had to be closed for repairs.

The modern five-span bridge was opened in 1890. Its construction was safer than the bridge it replaced, but its location was the same: on a bend in the river, which meant the problem with shipping was not solved.

In 1948, the MV *Delta* jammed under the bridge, and its master, Hendrikus Oostring, needed to be rescued from the smashed wheelhouse. He suffered two broken arms. On 23 March 1950, the collier *John Hopkinson* collided with the centre pier, causing massive damage to the bridge. The only thing holding the structure together was the tram tracks. The bridge was closed for almost a year.

On 21 September 2005, the *James Prior*, a 200 tonne barge, collided with the bridge, causing over half a million pounds damage. The bridge was closed for six months, causing severe traffic congestion. Brian King, the master of the *James Prior*, was charged with navigating without due care, but was acquitted when the judge in the case injured his back and was unable to hear all the evidence.

The bridge was reopened after the collision and was in the news again in 2006 when a 5.8 metre (19 foot) bottlenose whale became stranded at the bridge. Huge crowds flocked to see the whale transferred to a barge. The rescue was successful, but the whale died while being transported back to the sea. Its skeleton was put on display at the offices of *The Guardian* newspaper, before moving to the Natural History Museum, where it resides today.

Blackfriars Bridge

Built in 1869, Blackfriars Bridge links the Inns of Court and Temple Church on the north, with the Tate Modern art gallery and the Oxo Tower on the south. It became notorious after Italian banker Roberto Calvi, who had strong connections to the ailing Vatican Bank, was found hanging under it in June 1982. Initially, it was thought to be suicide, but now it is accepted that he was murdered. Why remains a mystery.

The Thames Tunnel

There is a whole world under the surface of London that you don't see. There are entire rivers (like the Fleet) that have been built upon and pushed under the streets. There are tunnels big enough to take a truck, bringing sewage through the city to the processing plants. There are pipes and cables for electricity, gas and water — and tunnels for their maintenance. There are cellars, often connected in bewildering patterns — remains of old excavations, mines from earlier eras, escape tunnels from buildings, hidden priest holes, layers of intrigue.

But most of us are familiar with London beneath the surface through the famous Underground, the rail network that can get you just about any place in the capital by travelling under the city.

Tunnelling such large passages through deep earth is a difficult engineering process, but to dig under a river is a huge undertaking. The first tunnel under the Thames was a mammoth task that lasted years, left many workers dead or seriously injured and nearly ended the career of the greatest engineer of the Victorian age, Isambard Kingdom Brunel.

Brunel was the son of a French immigrant, also an engineer, and the Thames Tunnel, built between 1825 and 1843, was his first blooding in the field of massive engineering. Even today the statistics are impressive. The tunnel measures 11 metres (35 feet) wide by 6 metres (20 feet) high, and is almost 400 metres (1,300 feet) long, running at a depth of 23 metres (75 feet) below the river's surface at high tide. It connects Rotherhithe and Wapping, and was the first tunnel to have been successfully constructed beneath a navigable river.

Originally designed for horse-drawn carriages, it never quite went to plan. But if you want to see the engineering wonder of the age, the good news is that it is still in daily use as part of the London Overground rail network.

The Thames Tunnel wasn't the first attempt to go under, rather than over, the river. In 1799, Ralph Dodd tried but failed to build a tunnel between Gravesend and Tilbury, to link the docks. Then, in 1805-09, a group of Cornish miners tried to go from Rotherhithe to Wapping/Limehouse, but even their expertise failed when they encountered soft clay and quicksand.

But Frenchman Marc Brunel was undaunted. He was a fan of tunnels. When he failed to interest the Tsar of Russia in a tunnel under the Neva in St Petersburg, he went to London, producing plans in 1823. Private funding was raised and work began in 1825.

The key to the work was his new invention, the Tunnelling Shield. This was a movable platform that allowed workers to tunnel, while those behind them removed the debris and built up a brick wall to seal the tunnel. The shield, in theory, kept water out of the works.

The plan was to drop a shaft, 5 metres wide by 7 metres deep, at Rotherhithe. The shield would be constructed at the bottom and pushed under the river. The biggest problem was the geology. There was a layer of clay and gravel under the river, then a small layer of more solid material. But under this was a layer of quicksand, with subterranean water under pressure. The Brunels had to keep the tunnel within the 10 metre (34 feet) layer of good earth. If they went up or down from that layer, the tunnel would flood.

Work was slow. The plan was to dig 2.6 metres (8 feet) a week, but it took a month to dig the first week's distance. The work was deeply unpleasant. Marc's son, Isambard Kingdom Brunel, was the chief engineer. Just out of his teens, he was a workaholic, once spending five full days underground, snatching brief naps on the dug-out debris.

For a thousand years, the Thames had been the sewer of southern England. Conditions were frequently horrific. The ground was a disgusting quagmire of mud and excrement, constantly wet, and miners worked initially by candlelight — though gas was eventually introduced. Periodically, filthy water poured through the boards of the shield and threatened to flood the tunnel. The air was foul, so much so that men frequently fainted at the shield face, and were carried away suffering from dizziness, chest pains and impaired vision. Cuts and wounds festered, becoming oozing ulcers.

Another constant danger was that the rotting sewage gave off methane gas, which could trigger an explosion when it came in contact with the miners' lamps. Then there were the health issues.

On 27 April 1827, a major leak struck the project, with thousands of gallons of freezing water pouring into the shaft. With it came coal, gravel — and human bones. What had happened to the three foot of protective clay that they thought they were under?

Isambard hired a diving bell to investigate, and found a small depression in the river bed. He could stretch through the porthole at the bottom of the diving bell and tap the top of the

160

mining shield. He pushed an iron tube through the shield and spoke to the miners in the tunnel. They did their best to shore up the damage, but on 27 May the clay turned to silt and "the ground seemed as though it were alive".

The river burst through and hundreds of tonnes of mud washed into the tunnel. Brunel dumped clay into the depression in the river bed, then they began pumping out the tunnel. It was October before work resumed. But on 7 October, Brunel fell into a water tank in the engineering works yard and nearly drowned. It was the first of his narrow escapes.

On 11 January 1828, the river burst through again. This time Brunel was among those trapped by the flood. He wrote in his journal afterwards: "Here I am in Bridge House (Brighton, where he convalesced). I have now been laid up useless since 12 January. I shan't forget that day in a hurry. Very near finished my journey then. When knocked down I certainly gave myself up, for I never expected we should get out. The roar of the water in a confined space was very grand, cannon can be nothing to it.

"Never felt so queer, could not bear the least shake, felt as if I should be broken into pieces."

The flood of fast-moving water had swept Brunel from the shield and back into the tunnel, knocking him unconscious. A fellow engineer dragged him from the water in the nick of time. But others were not so fortunate: six men died that night. Two of the most experienced miners on the project were among the dead.

Brunel, who took six months to recover, took a pragmatic view, writing: "Apart from the loss of those six poor fellows, the whole affair was well worth the risk."

It wasn't — the latest disaster drove the company to the brink of financial ruin. The tunnel was sealed and work suspended for eight years.

Tunnel Disease

Illness was a constant problem, and Isambard Brunel suffered as badly as any of his miners. As his father Marc recorded in his diary in May 1828: "16 May, inflammable gas. Men complain very much. 26 May. Heywood died this morning. Two more on the sick list. Page is evidently sinking very fast. The air is excessively offensive. It affects the eyes. I feel much debility after having been some time below. All complain of pain in the eyes. 28 May. Bower died today or yesterday. A good man."

A common complaint was stinging eyes and blindness — temporary and permanent — was not unknown. It was called "tunnel disease" and was caused by the noxious chemicals released by the disturbance of thousands of year of river detritus.

Marc Brunel suffered a stroke himself, perhaps brought on by the stress of working in the foul vapours. Isambard suffered pleurisy.

One worker fell down the entrance shaft while drunk and died. Many others died of fevers and dysentery, and a few were recorded to have suffocated in the "thick and impure air".

Tunnelling Begins Again

It was 1836 before tunnelling began again. Isambard Brunel had moved on to other projects, but his father Marc completed the work. There were floods in August 1837, and again in March and April of the following year. Leaks of methane and hydrogen sulphide (highly poisonous as well as flammable) gas were common, and there were fires which damaged the shield. But in late 1841, the tunnel reached Wapping. Access tunnels and stairs were built, and an engine house on the Rotherhithe side drained the structure. It was finally open to the public in March 1843.

Although it was a triumph of engineering, the tunnel was a financial disaster. It had overrun its budget substantially, and funds never stretched to allowing horses and carriages through it. So it remained a pedestrian crossing. It did become a major tourist attraction, with a million people a year paying a penny to walk under the river.

But it also became known as a haunt of prostitutes and thieves, who preyed on the tourists.

In 1865 the tunnel was purchased by the East London Railway Company, providing a link between Wapping (and later Liverpool Street) and the South London Line. The tunnel's disused entrance shafts at Wapping and Rotherhithe were converted into Wapping and Rotherhithe Stations. The East London Railway was later absorbed into the London Underground, and continued until 1962. The Thames Tunnel was the oldest piece of the Underground's infrastructure.

It is now part of the London Overground rail system, and some of the original architecture has been preserved. For those interested in finding out more, a visit to the original Brunel Engine House at Rotherhithe is essential. It is now open to visitors as the Brunel Museum, and incorporates part of the entrance shaft to the tunnel.

Brunel Dies Young

Marc Brunel, the man behind the Thames Tunnel, lived to a ripe old age of eighty. But his son was not so lucky. He died at the age of just fifty-three. Even in Victorian times, this was young. He was a heavy cigar smoker, but so were many of his contemporaries.

Near the end of his days he was diagnosed with Bright's Disease, a progressive failure of the kidneys. It was not very well understood back in those days, but was believed to be caused by a bacterial infection which affected the immune system. It could have been slowly working on his system for years.

Weakened, he suffered a stroke in 1859 and died ten days later.

There is every possibility that Isambard Kingdom Brunel was a victim of the "thick and impure air" that claimed so many of his workers on the Thames Tunnel.

Thames Archway

The Thames Archway Company was set up in 1805 to build a tunnel under the river between Rotherhithe and Limehouse which could accommodate pedestrians, and allow the passage of goods from the wharfs on both sides of the river.

Cornish mining engineer Robert Vazie was in charge. But he encountered serious problems with his tunnel leaking and got no further than sinking the end shafts of the tunnel. Cornish inventor and mining engineer Richard Trevithick (1771-1833) was brought in to finish the project. The company agreed to pay him £1,000 if he could successfully complete the tunnel, which would be 366 metres (1,220 feet) long.

In 1807, Trevithick began digging a small pilot tunnel, or driftway, through the earth. Once that was completed it would serve as a drainage tunnel and the main tunnel could be built alongside it. The driftway was most of the way under the river — 285 metres (950 feet) — when a sudden influx of water two days before Christmas flooded the works. The tunnel was shored up and work continued. But a month later, on 26 January 1808, a more serious leak occurred.

At that stage, the tunnel was 312 metres (1,040 feet) long and nearing the opposite bank. But water began gushing in at a very fast rate and the tunnel began flooding. As it was less than a metre high, and workers were on their bellies, it was a difficult task to get everyone out alive. Trevithick was the last man out, and nearly drowned.

Clay was dumped on the riverbed to seal the hole, and the tunnel drained. But the job was getting progressively more difficult. The project eventually petered out, uncompleted. The driftway had got from Rotherhithe to the low waterline at Limehouse, but no further. Officially, the reason the tunnel was abandoned was because the ground was more difficult than expected. Cornish miners were used to rock, not clay and quicksand.

Tunnelling Gets Easier

The Tower Subway was the second tunnel under the Thames, built in 1869 close to the Tower of London. It ran from Lower Thames Street on Tower Hill (north of the river) to Vine Lane (off Tooley Street) on the southern bank. The engineers improved on the tunnelling shield, making it smaller, lighter and stronger.

Work began in February 1869, with tunnelling starting in April. By December it was finished. It took less than a year, in sharp contrast to Brunel's eighteen year epic struggle with the clay and silt. The construction team was lucky in that it struck a stable bed of clay. The tunnel was also smaller than Thames Tunnel, a few miles further downstream.

The under-river section took just fourteen weeks, and the tunnel was lined with cast iron rather than brick. But like the original tunnel, it was a financial failure. Originally designed to carry a cable car, this was removed as uneconomic. The tunnel then became a pedestrian walkway, with 20,000 a week paying a halfpenny to cross under the Thames.

But when Tower Bridge was opened in 1894 — without a toll — the subway was doomed. It was closed in 1898 and sold to the London Hydraulic Company, who used it to carry hydraulic power lines and water mains.

The subway was badly damaged during the Blitz when a German bomb fell in the river near Tower Pier in December 1940. It exploded on the river bed close to the tower roof. The shock of the blast compressed the tunnel, reducing its diameter to only 1.2 metres (4 feet). But the tunnel lining was not breached.

Apart from that, the tunnel remains in excellent condition. It still carries water mains and telecommunication cables. But all that remains for the curious traveller to see is a small round entrance building at Tower Hill near the Tower of London ticket office, a short distance to the west of the main entrance to the Tower. This was not the original entrance, but was built in 1920 by the London Hydraulic Company.

The Ripper Connection

Like many parts of central London, the Thames Subway has a connection to Jack the Ripper, though it is a tenuous one. In September 1888, at the height of the Ripper murders in nearby Whitechapel, a man was seen brandishing a knife in the tunnel.

It caused widespread panic, but there is no suggestion that the sighting had any connection to the Whitechapel murders. The Ripper killed three times that September.

CHAPTER SIX: FOUL DEEDS DARKEN THE RIVER

Every city has a seedy underbelly. Behind the façade of the great buildings, the palaces and the pomp and glory, there lies an underclass who struggle to feed themselves and clothe their children. Urban life breeds crime and a great city like London breeds great evil. In this chapter, we will look at some of the most notorious murders along the Thames.

Law enforcement was arbitrary for centuries, and record-keeping scant. So we will start our examination with the Old Bailey, the London Law Courts. Once the courts began keeping records, a clear picture emerges of how common murder had become.

A Century of Suspicious Drownings

Although London did not get a police force until the establishment of the Thames River Police in 1798, the law was still enforced on and around the river with vigour. The late seventeenth and early eighteenth century saw great vigilance on the water, with several suspicious deaths resulting in watermen facing the wrath of the Old Bailey. At least ten deaths were the subject of trial in that austere old building in its first hundred years.

The Old Bailey, on Bailey Street adjacent to the old Newgate Prison, is a stone's throw from the river. It was first used in the late sixteenth century, but was destroyed in the Great Fire. Rebuilt (open to the elements to prevent the spread of diseases) in 1674, it is the Central Criminal Court of England and Wales.

It has handled some of the most notorious murder trials of all time — such as Dr Crippen — but it also concerns itself with more mundane matters, such as death on the river.

Over its first century the court showed remarkable lenience in an age of frequent hangings. Many were convicted of manslaughter rather than murder. Manslaughter back then rarely carried a prison sentence. The most common penalty was to be permanently branded (the mark of Cain) with a hot iron on the hand.

The first such recorded trial occurred on 11 July 1688. Edward Latish and Edward Ridge, both of St Ann's, Blackfriars, were charged with the murder of a waterman, Anthony Parker, on 21 June. Parker was ferrying the two men across the river when they decided to hop onto a passing boat and not pay Parker's fee. A row developed, and the men beat Parker over the head with an oar. He fell into the river and drowned.

Both men were convicted of manslaughter and were branded on the hand, a popular and painful punishment in those days.

The following year, a man, only identified in the court records as NC, was charged with killing James Baskerfield on 10 December. He was out shooting ducks on the river near Blackwall and accidentally shot Baskerfield when he stood up suddenly. NC was acquitted.

Another fight on the river led to James Scott, Southwark, being charged with the murder of John Barnes. Barnes was ferrying some women across the river to Southwark Cathedral. When they were in the middle of the river, Scott rowed up to them and caught hold of their boat. Apparently, he wanted to chat to the women. Barnes threatened to slap Scott unless he let go. Scott picked up a stick and struck the waterman on the head. He later died of the head injury.

The court found Scott guilty of manslaughter and he was branded.

On 2 August 1707, John Watkinson was in a litre near the Custom House Quay, when he was confronted by Peter Small on board a wherry. Both were common small boats on the river. Small told Watkinson he had no right to be where he was, and ordered him off, threatening to strike him if he didn't get his boat moving. Watkinson lifted a spike to protect himself, at which point Small grabbed his leg and pulled him into the river.

Small tried his best to pull Watkinson out again, but Watkinson drowned. Small was convicted of manslaughter and branded.

On 13 July 1715, it was fighting watermen that took up the courts time. William Ems went to the river for his boat, but it was missing. So he borrowed a nearby boat and set off to find his own. As he was returning, successful, the owner of the boat he had borrowed — Francis Barns of Stepney — confronted him "in a great passion" and hit him a number of times. Ems tried to step onto a nearby litre to save himself, but Barns pushed the litre away and Ems crashed into the water. Witnesses shouted to Barns to save the drowning man, but he replied: "Let him go and be damned."

He was found guilty of manslaughter and branded.

In 1721, Thomas Currey was convicted of manslaughter after throwing a shipmate, William Underwood, overboard from the deck of a ship into the Thames. Underwood was the ship's mate, and was in a temper because he had ordered a Cornish sailor to do something and the sailor had refused. Currey attacked the Cornish man, who was lame in one arm. But his wily opponent was an accomplished Cornish wrestler and beat off the mate, making a run for it. The mate chased him across the deck, picking up a stuck to strike him. Underwood, the ships boatswain, stepped in to restrain Currey, but the mate now turned on him, throwing him overboard into the stygian waters of the Thames. Currey tumbled over the railings with him, but was fished out. Underwood sank without trace. Currey was convicted of manslaughter and branded.

A collision under the arches of London Bridge in 1721 left one man mortally injured. John Miller was coming down river with the current, and was shooting through one of the narrow arches of the bridge. William Palmer was in a small boat coming the other way, and the two collided under the arch, with Miller's boat coming off worse. He tried to see the number on Palmer's boat, but Palmer struck out with a boathook to prevent him. Miller received a shallow cut near his thigh, but he never recovered from the wound and died a few days later.

Palmer told the Old Bailey that Miller had punched him and called him a "son of a bitch" when both boats collided, and he had struck out with the boathook in self-defence. A doctor testified that the wound was a slight one, but that the deceased was in poor health and that had probably killed him.

The court convicted Palmer of manslaughter and branded him.

In 1737, John Wharton was on board *The Dolphin* when he saw a lighter crossing the hawser of his ship, and tried to warn him off. He picked up a plant of wood and threw it at the man. He missed, but the man, John Strainer, jumped to avoid the plank, fell into the river and drowned. Wharton was acquitted of manslaughter.

There was a fight in 1761 between a man on a barge and a man on a neighbouring boat on the river. It was a trivial matter over who could tie-up where. It was resolved in the normal way on the water: one man threw a plank at the other.

William Platten picked up a heavy piece of wood and threw it at Richard Snow, knocking him off the gunnel of the boat and into the water. As he told the court, throwing bits of wood at other vessels was common, both as a way of warning them off and as a way of showing your annoyance when they were doing something wrong. Common as the practice might have been, Snow was struck on the head by the wood and fell into the river, where he drowned. Platten was acquitted of his manslaughter.

In 1768, nine men were in the dock following a fight between sailors and coal haulers on shore. The fight began when the haulers taunted the sailors and the sailors came on shore to respond to the taunt. The fight quickly spread onto boats as the sailors tried to make an escape from a mob armed with sticks, shovels and cutlasses. One of the coal haulers, James Murphy, struck sailor John Beattie on the head with a cutlass, then slashed him across the shoulder. Beattie was also beaten with a stick and died of his wounds.

Murphy and James Dogan were convicted of murder and hung two days later. The other seven, charged with aiding and abetting a murder, were acquitted.

Boisterous horseplay saw Thomas Cripps convicted of manslaughter in 1773. He was an apprentice waterman, as was Abraham Russley. Both men were in their small boats trying to reach an Indiaman (a cargo ship of the East India Company) and Cripps used his boathook to push Russley aside. He probably just intended to slow down the other man, but Russley toppled into the river. He rose once, but sank immediately and was never seen again. Cripps was convicted of manslaughter and branded.

With the establishment of the River Police at the end of the eighteenth century, and the regular police a few years later, it was no longer up to the magistrates to investigate and prosecute deaths on the river. That responsibility passed on to other authorities. But during the first hundred years of the Old Bailey, it meted out justice on the river with efficiency and compassion.

Drowned for Sleeping Rough

Somerset House is one of the gems of London architecture. A massive public building situated on the south side of the Strand in the centre of the city. It overlooks the Thames just east of Waterloo Bridge. The central block of the neo-classical building was designed by Sir William Chambers, and dates from 1776-96. Classical Victorian wings extend to the north and south. Today, Somerset House is used by government departments and holds archives, as well as being an arts and cultural centre. But in 1715, it was the scene of a particularly brutal and vicious killing.

Back then, an older version of the building occupied the site and the Thames flowed fast and deep beside it. Somerset House was a "grace and favour" residence owned by the Crown, with many royal associations. A Mr J. (unidentified by the Old Bailey), from the parish of St Mary le Savoy, was employed as night porter. Part of his duties was to keep the grounds clear of idlers and vagabonds. The city's homeless often tried to sleep rough in the grounds of the great public buildings.

On the night of 1 June 1715, he carried out his duties with zeal.

A witness told the Old Bailey that, at midnight that evening, he was coming on shore from his boat when he heard a boy cry out: "Pray, Mr J., don't throw me in. Indeed I can't swim." The frightened cry was followed by a splash and the porter was heard laughing: "The dog swims bravely."

But the boy, Richard Salisbury, did not swim bravely. He sank under the murky waters and drowned.

A girl, Elizabeth Murfet, said that the porter then took her up in his arms and held her over the water, saying he would drown her as he had done the boy, but she managed to escape. She clung to his clothing and he had to let her go. But he beat her as she ran off.

Two witnesses, living nearby, swore they heard someone shout: "Push him in." This was followed by a splash.

A coachman and a groom of the Marquis de Merimont told the trial that they had been with Mr J. on the evening of the killing, looking for idle persons. They separated and he went towards the Dunghill, while they searched other parts of the grounds. They did not hear a boy cry out, but did hear the girl struggling with him.

They said that the following morning, Mr J. sought them out and told them: "'Tis talked there is a boy drowned, and that I have drowned him. Pray don't say anything of it, for if you do, I am ruined."

In the end he wasn't ruined. He was convicted of manslaughter rather than murder, so escaped the gallows. The court went to some lengths to conceal his identity — not a common thing when a man was convicted of killing another. He was branded, then presumably resumed his duties driving the idle and the homeless from the grounds of Somerset House.

First Policeman Killed in the Line of Duty

As the West India Merchants and Planters Marine Police Institute was the first police force in the world, it is perhaps unsurprising that the first officer killed in the line of duty was drawn from their ranks. It happened during a riot just three months after they began patrolling the Thames.

Gabriel Franks was a Master Lumper in the police. That's not a recognised rank today, but back then the force was a little different. It was composed of surveyors (or inspectors), watermen (or constables) and lumpers, who supervised the "lumping", or unloading, of cargo on the river. At the time the shipping industry was losing £500,000 annually to dishonest lumpers.

The force was stationed at Wapping New Stairs. The lumpers supervised the unloading of the ships and ensured that theft was kept to a minimum. Other dock workers were in no doubt that men like Franks were part of the new police force, despite their lack of uniform and the physical nature of their work.

Coal was one of the chief targets of the cargo thieves, and illegal coal markets were openly held on the streets at Wapping. The police clamp-down was not well received locally, with many coal heavers feeling that theft was just a little harmless extra income, an unofficial perk of the job.

Things came to a head on the evening of 16 October 1798. Two coal heavers and a watchman's boy were convicted of theft at the Thames Magistrates Court and each fined forty shillings. Friends paid the fines, but the brother of one of the accused, James Eyers, was not happy. He dragged his brother Charles towards the police station, which adjoined the Magistrates Court, and said: "Damn your long eyes. Come

174

along and we shall have the money back, or else we shall have the house down."

The dockers agreed, and within a short while a hostile crowd had gathered outside the police office, and stones and rocks were being thrown at the windows by the shouting mob. Several constables were trapped inside, along with the magistrates. It was late, it was dark outside, and the situation was tense.

Gabriel Franks was not in the station when the riot began. He was in a nearby public house, The Rose and Crown, with friends. When he heard what was going on, he went to the police station with two other men (Bartholomew Peacock and John Webb, the pub landlord) and tried to get in. But he was told that no one was being allowed in or out because of the mob. So he went out onto the street to observe and gather evidence.

One rioter seemed particularly aggressive, and Franks instructed Peacock to keep an eye on him while he went to the station to fetch a cutlass for their protection. A warning shot was fired from the station and the crowd briefly retreated, some towards the Dung Wharf, about twenty yards away. Others went towards the Cooperage, in the other direction. The riot was getting more serious by the minute. Someone shouted: "Bring arms, and let us shoot all the bastards!" A large rock smashed through the window of the station. A constable, Perry, took a pistol and fired through the broken window at the mob, hitting one. As the crowd drew back, one of the rioters, concealed near the Dung Wharf, returned fire. There was a scream and Master Lumper Gabriel Franks fell to the ground.

In the few moments of quietness that followed the shooting of the two men, the supervising magistrate Patrick Colquhoun came out of the building and read the Riot Act to the mob, ordering them to disperse. One unnamed rioter was dead, and Franks was mortally wounded, though still conscious.

Franks lingered on for several hours, during which time he remained conscious and lucid. He was treated by surgeon William Blizzard at the London Hospital, but had no idea who fired the fatal shot. To this day, it is not known who fired the shot, and whether Franks was killed by a stray bullet, or deliberately targeted because he worked with the police. The latter is more likely.

Investigators quickly decided that James Eyers, whose behaviour after the Magistrates Court had triggered the riot, should be charged with murder. There was no evidence that he fired the shot — in fact he almost certainly didn't. Only one witness placed him anywhere near Gabriel Franks. But the feeling was that his actions led to the riot, and so he was, in law, responsible for Franks's death. And evidence was given that he had helped the dead rioter and urged on the others at the same time. He had threatened to stone anyone who walked away from the mob. One witness testified that he had heard Eyers shout: "Shoot the bastard."

On 9 January 1799, James Eyers was convicted of the murder of Gabriel Franks. He was sentenced to be hanged the following Monday morning. Justice was swift in those days. As the Judge pronounced the dreadful sentence, he said: "May the Lord have mercy upon your soul."

Eyers stoically replied: "Amen, I hope he will."

The Thames River Police Museum contains exhibits on the Wapping Coal Riot, and many other fascinating incidents. It is located in what was once the carpenters' workshop at Wapping Police Station on Wapping High Street, and offers visitors a unique insight into the world's first police force. Exhibits include uniforms and documents, as well as the everyday hardware of policing, from handcuffs to cutlasses. As the museum is in a working police station, visits must be arranged beforehand.

PM Gunned Down in Lobby

American presidents seem to be assassinated on a regular basis, but only one British Prime Minister has had that dubious honour. Spencer Perceval was shot in the Palace of Westminster in 1812, after just three years in office.

The Palace of Westminster is one of London's jewels, best viewed from the river. The London Eye Ferris wheel offers wonderful views of the Mother of Parliaments, sitting in state on the banks of the Thames. It is one of the most iconic sights of the city. Both houses — Lords and Commons — overlook the river, and the political dealings inside can often be as murky as the waters that flow outside the windows. Parliament has met at Westminster since 1265 — with occasional forays elsewhere. It began as a royal palace, with bits added as parliament became more important. By the start of the nineteenth century, it was a hodgepodge of different architectural styles and historical eras. The magnificent present building was only erected following the great fire of 1834, after Spencer Perceval's time.

Perceval was in power during a turbulent period. A former Attorney General and Solicitor General, he led the Tory government during the Napoleonic wars, and had been in office just three years. During those years, he had presided over an unstable government, dealt with a financial crisis and suffered a series of setbacks in the wars. But none of those controversies played a part in his death. He was shot by a bitter businessman settling a personal vendetta.

John Bellingham was an export trader who fell afoul of authorities in Czarist Russia, and was jailed for six years in Moscow. When he got home to the UK, he was very bitter, believing he had been let down by his government. He wanted compensation.

It was a cause he pursued vigorously, lobbying MPs and ministers. He even approached the Prime Minister for help. But none was forthcoming. Thirty-five years old and with three children to support, he was ruined and he was desperate. One final visit to the Foreign Office — where he was again rebuffed — tipped the balance of his mind. He purchased two pistols and concealed them in an inner pocket of his coat.

On 11 May 1812, he travelled to Westminster Palace and walked into the lobby of the parliament. It was not uncommon for people to enter the building, either on business, or simply to see and be seen. So no one took any notice of the dapper man in the frock coat and top hat.

He waited until Spencer Perceval walked from the House of Commons into the lobby, then stepped forward, drawing out one of the guns. He shot the Prime Minister in the chest at close range.

"I am murdered — I am murdered," Perceval groaned, as he collapsed to the ground. The bullet had gone straight to his heart, a fatal wound.

Bellingham simply sat down and waited for his inevitable arrest. Justice was rapid in those times, and four days later he found himself before the Central Criminal Court at the Old Bailey, further along the river. He pleaded not guilty, telling the jury that his actions should be a lesson to future Prime Ministers.

"Recollect what was my situation. Recollect that my family was ruined and myself destroyed, merely because it was Mr Perceval's pleasure that justice should not be granted," he said.

"I demand what is the birth right and privilege of every Englishman. When a minister sets himself above the laws, as Mr Perceval did, he does it at his own personal risk. If this were not so, the mere will of the minister would become the law, and what would then become of your liberties? I trust that this serious lesson will operate as a warning to all future ministers, and that they will henceforth do the thing that is right. Gentlemen, my life is in your hands. I rely confidently in your justice."

It was not a defence likely to produce sympathy with a country at war. The jury did not take long to find him guilty of murder, and he was sentenced to death.

The Lord Chief Justice said: "You have shed the blood of a man admired for every virtue which can adorn public or private life — a man whose suavity and meekness of manner was calculated to disarm all political rancour, and to deprive violence of its asperity.

"By his death, charity has lost one of its greatest promoters; religion, one of its firmest supporters; domestic society, one of its happiest and sweetest examples; and the country, one of its brightest ornaments — a man whose ability and worth was likely to produce lasting advantages to this empire, and ultimate benefit to the world."

On 18 May, Bellingham was removed from Newgate Prison and took the short journey along Deadman's Walk to the gallows. Just a short week after he took the life of a man innocent of any wrongs against him, John Bellingham did the dance macabre on the end of the noose.

In our own century, the tale of the only Prime Minister assassinated took a delightful twist when a descendant of the assassin, Henry Bellingham, ran for parliament and took his seat, for North West Norfolk, in the election of 2001.

"I have always avoided raising the murder myself, and I wouldn't bring it up in conversation that I am a descendant — or a near-descendant — of a murderer of a Prime Minister," he told the BBC. "But I don't try to deny it."

One Shilling for Christmas Murder

Joseph Hoyston and his brother John, apprentices to Captain Ellsworth of the Mariner, were sent on Christmas Eve, 1815, to bring a message to another ship on the river. They set off around four o'clock, rowing against the tide between the steps on the Middlesex side of the river and the boats moored further out. A scull, rowed by William Waithman, came against them. The brothers warned him to go left or right to avoid a collision. He kept rowing, ignoring their warning.

As the boats collided, Joseph Hoyston shouted at the sculler, who replied by striking out at the brothers with his scull. He used the scull to hook the woollen Guernsey frock of Joseph. As Joseph struggled to free himself, Waithman pulled him off balance and used the scull to push him into the freezing river. The heavy woollen garment did the rest, dragging Joseph Hoyston to the bottom.

Forty-seven-year-old Waithman was convicted of manslaughter. The days of branding were over. He was sentenced to three months in prison, and fined the princely sum of one shilling.

The Christmas Eve killing took place just yards from one of the hundreds of sets of steps that crowded both sides of the river bank up until a hundred and fifty years ago. Several thousand small craft plied the cold waters of the river, acting as water taxis and cargo vessels. Now the small craft are almost all gone from the Thames in central London, and few of the steps survive.

Amelia Dyer — Baby Farmer and Mass Murderer

One of the horrors of the Victorian age was baby farming. It was an age of upright morality, where women were the chattels of their menfolk. If a young woman found herself pregnant, she became an untouchable.

Many women fled to the anonymity of the city, losing themselves in the teeming mass of humanity. And when they had their child, they needed to be rid of it fast. The baby farmers stepped in. Proper adoption agencies and social services were a century away, but untrained and often unscrupulous women offered legal fostering and adoption services to unmarried mothers.

The poor young woman would hand over her baby and a fee of ten or fifteen pounds (a stretch in those days) in the hope that the child would be rehomed. Some baby farmers made a sincere effort to find adoptive parents for the babies. Others opted for casual neglect, letting nature take its course on the tiny foundlings. The death of countless thousands of innocents was brushed quietly under the carpet.

If a baby disappeared, the mother was often too frightened or ashamed to report it to the police. So it was not difficult for the unscrupulous baby farmers to kill off unwanted or hard to foster children. Some discovered it was the easiest way to run their business. Murder yielded a quick profit without the need for caring for the child for a number of weeks or months.

Many a tiny body was pulled out of the Thames in the nineteen-hundreds, and was buried unidentified. And four baby farmers were convicted of murder and hung in the capital. The most notorious was Amelia Dyer, thought to have drowned or strangled as many as four hundred babies.

Born in 1839, she began baby farming in her thirties and operated for twenty years or more all over southern England, moving frequently and changing her name to keep ahead of suspicion. Her modus operandi was simple. She would advertise in the papers as a respectable woman looking to adopt a foundling. Young mothers would put their babies in her care, pay over the hefty fee, and in a few months, the kindly benefactor and the baby would have moved on to a new town. Only, the baby never arrived at the new town.

Dyer developed her own method for disposing of the children. She would strangle them with a white tape, which she left around their necks. Then she would wrap them in paper or carpet and drop them in the Thames. A disturbed woman, she reputedly took pleasure in watching them choke to death.

When she was finally caught, Dyer told the police: "You'll know all mine by the tape around their necks."

She was tried at the Old Bailey on one charge of murder, that of four-month-old Doris Marmon. That was the practice back then. If the first trial failed, the police had a second charge ready to prosecute. But there was no need. The defence tried to plead insanity, but the jury was horrified by her crime — and by the suspicion that she could have killed as many as four hundred infants during her twenty years in business. She was convicted and sentenced to death.

She was hung by James Billington at Newgate on 10 June 1896, within sight of the majestic Thames that had not hidden her secrets. At fifty-seven, she was the oldest woman to be executed in more than half a century. Her ghost still haunts that stretch of road between the prison and the river.

The Ghost of Amelia

As Amelia Dyer was being led to the gallows on Deadman's Walk, she met a young warder, Mr Scott. Fixing her evil gaze on him, she sneered: "I'll meet you again someday, sir." Moments later she was dancing at the end of a noose.

He thought nothing more of it, but several years later, he was alone in the warders' room, his back to a grille that looked out on Deadman's Walk. He felt a shiver down his spine and had the distinct impression that someone was watching him. Then he heard a raspy voice: "Meet you again, meet you again…"

Turning, he saw an old woman's face leering in at him through the grille. He ran out onto the street, but it was empty. She had come back, as she promised, but she wasn't going to get caught a second time.

River Betrays Evil Baby Farmer

Ada Chard-Williams was a baby farmer at the start of her career when the treacherous Thames gave up her grisly secrets and sent her to the gallows.

She was just twenty-four when she put an advert in the local paper offering to find adoptive parents for unwanted children. Unmarried mother Florence Jones read the ad and met Chard-Williams at Charing Cross railway station on 31 August 1899. She handed over £3 of the £5 fee, and arranged to meet Mrs Chard-Williams a few weeks later with the balance. But Chard-Williams, and the twenty-one-month-old baby, had disappeared. Florence immediately went to the police.

They were unable to find Chard-Williams, but a week later, she wrote them a letter denying killing baby Selina, saying she had sold her to a couple in Croydon. She did admit to being a baby farmer.

Then the river threw up its secret. Waterman William Stokes was on a barge off Church Dock, Battersea, when he saw a brown paper package floating on the river. He pulled it towards him and was horrified to see a child's leg sticking out. He called Constable David Voice, who fished the parcel from the river and opened it, revealing a golden-haired toddler, dead about three days. The child was tied up, and a distinctive Fisherman's Bend knot had been used. This turned out to be a signature of Chard-Williams, as the white tape had been of Amelia Dyer.

A post-mortem revealed little Selina had been struck on the head to stun her, then suffocated.

Chard-Williams was tried for the murder of Selina Jones and hung in the yard of Newgate Prison on 17 February 1900 — the last woman to be executed there. She was suspected of killing several other children, although no other charges were proceeded with. Her husband, William, helped her with her grisly business, but he was acquitted on the murder charge.

Baby Farming in the Twentieth Century

Baby farming continued up to the early days of the twentieth century, only ending when the government stepped in with legislation in 1904. Annie Walters and Amelia Sachs were the last to be hung for killing the babies in their care, in 1903. They operated in Finchley but used the Thames to dispose of their victims.

Sachs, 27, ran a nursing home which offered a haven for unmarried mothers and their babies. For a fee, she would care for the babies afterwards and organise their adoption. But once the baby was left with Sachs, she would pass it over to her accomplice, fifty-four-year-old Annie Walters. Walters would either poison the baby with a morphine-based drug, or suffocate it. The body would then be buried or, more often, dumped in the Thames.

But Walters wasn't the brightest, and she liked babies. So she occasionally took them home to play with before killing them. Her landlord noticed she had a baby once, and she said she was minding it for friends. A few days later, she told him the baby had died in his sleep. A few months later, she had another baby. The landlord became suspicious when this one, too, died in its sleep. He called the police.

Walters was charged with murder and quickly implicated Sachs. The investigators were shocked to learn that the two women may have killed as many as twenty children. At the Old Bailey trial in January 1903, it took the jury only forty minutes to find them both guilty. They hung three weeks later, the first women to hang in Holloway Prison.

Hangman William Billington wrote in his diary: "These two women were baby farmers of the worst kind and they were both repulsive in type. Sachs had a long thin neck and Walters a short neck, points which I was bound to observe in the arrangement of the rope. Sachs had to be almost carried to the scaffold, while Annie Walters stayed quite calm."

Once the trap opened on the last double female hanging in Britain, it brought an end to the era of the Victorian baby farmers.

Ripper Suspect Kills Himself

When thirty-one-year-old Montague John Druitt jumped into the Thames at Hammersmith with his pockets loaded with stones, he immediately became a suspect in the Jack the Ripper investigation. The killings stopped after his death.

Druitt was a member of the upper classes, trying to establish himself at the bar. After graduating from Oxford, he took a position teaching at a London boarding school while he passed the Bar exams. Once he qualified as a barrister, he continued to teach at the George Anderson boarding school in Blackheath in parallel to his law work. The earning power of a junior barrister was not great, and the school was a prestigious one.

Druitt was also a talented cricketer, playing with many of the leading players of the age. A promising and productive life seemed to lie ahead of him.

But on Friday, 30 November 1888, Druitt was dismissed from his post at the school. The reason is not clear, but his brother told a newspaper that: "He had got into serious trouble." It was speculated that he might have been a homosexual, or that he succumbed to a family history of psychiatric problems (the more likely explanation). Whatever the reason, the day after his dismissal, he disappeared.

But on New Year's Eve, his body was found floating in the Thames off Thornycroft's torpedo works, Chiswick. Stones in his pockets had kept his body submerged for about a month. He was carrying a train ticket to Hammersmith, dated 1 December, a silver watch and cash and cheques equivalent to £5,400 in today's money.

By coincidence, the Jack the Ripper killings, which claimed at least five victims, came to an end around the time of Druitt's death. Quickly, the police formed the theory that the killer had died, emigrated or been imprisoned for some other offence. An MP announced in parliament that the Ripper was the son of a surgeon who had drowned in the Thames — a clear reference to Druitt.

In 1894, Chief Constable Sir Melville MacNaghten named Druitt as a suspect in a private memorandum, but MacNaghten had not worked on the Ripper investigation. There is no real evidence to link him to the killings, and he was playing cricket on the days of some of the murders, making it improbable that he could have been involved.

Most modern researchers do not believe Druitt could have been Jack the Ripper.

The Monster of Rillington Place

One of Britain's most notorious serial killers was finally hunted down and arrested on Putney Bridge in March 1953. Serial killer and necrophiliac John Christie killed at least eight women in the 1940s and 1950s. He may have killed many more.

Christie was born in 1899 and had a high IQ, but a spotty employment record. He was a petty criminal with an addiction to prostitutes. His favourite killing method, refined over the years, was to gas his victims in his kitchen at 10 Rillington Place, Notting Hill, then rape them as they passed out. He strangled the drowsy women, then boarded them up in an alcove in the kitchen, or buried them in his backyard when he was finished with them.

He first came to police attention when one woman, Beryl Evans, and her baby daughter Geraldine, were found strangled in a shed at the back of the property in 1949. Timothy Evans, the husband of the dead woman, was accused of murder. Unbelievably, the police investigating the crime failed to spot that one of the fence posts in Christie's back garden was actually a human thigh bone, from one of his earlier victims. Had any real investigation been carried out, the career of the serial killer would have been cut short and several lives saved.

Despite his criminal record, Christie was a witness for the prosecution in Timothy Evans's trial. Evans was convicted and sentenced to death.

Christie went on killing, with at least four more women losing their lives over the next six years. No thorough investigation was carried out subsequently, but Christie almost certainly killed more than the police officially credited him with. In the light of his eventual excesses, he may have killed several times and got away with it.

On 14 December 1952, Christie strangled his wife Ethel. This seems to have triggered the final killing spree. In the first few months of 1953, he killed three more women. He gassed them, raped them and boarded up their bodies in an alcove in the kitchen.

Then, broke, he sublet his flat and moved out. Another tenant of the building, using Christie's kitchen, found the three bodies and called the police. The citywide hunt for Christie began.

After leaving Rillington Place, Christie moved to King's Cross, but left within a week as news of the discovery of the bodies made national headlines. He wandered around London, spending much of his time in cafés, and sleeping rough. After a week on the run, a haggard man was spotted by an alert police officer moving from the embankment onto Putney Bridge. He followed the man onto the bridge and challenged him. The hunt for Christie was over.

When Christie was arrested, he had just a few coins left — and a newspaper clipping about Timothy Evans.

Christie confessed to seven murders and was sentenced to death. However, his conviction threw grave doubt on the conviction of Evans for the murder of Beryl Evans. Evans was eventually granted a posthumous pardon, and the miscarriage of justice in his case was one of the factors in Britain deciding to abolish the death penalty.

The Umbrella Murder

In a bizarre incident that would have done justice to the scriptwriters of a James Bond movie, a Bulgarian writer was killed while crossing Waterloo Bridge in 1978. His assassin used a pellet gun built into an umbrella, and disappeared into the crowd following his successful mission. Georgi Markov thus became the most famous victim of the Cold War.

Born in 1929, Markov trained as a chemical engineer in Bulgaria, but was also a successful playwright and novelist. He was highly respected in his home country, and also scripted a popular detective series for Bulgarian television. However, some of his plays were censored, and then one of his novels was banned before publication. His works were becoming highly critical of the communist government, and were increasingly being censored.

In 1969, Markov decided to visit his brother who was living in Italy. Initially, it was to be an extended holiday, but he decided to stay in the West until his reputation at home improved, and the censor got off his back. In 1971, the Bulgarian government refused to extend his passport, so Markov became a defector. He moved to London and began working for the BBC World Service and Radio Free Europe.

The Bulgarian government, in his absence, sentenced him to six years in prison — but was frustrated in its attempts to make that stick. And he was a thorn in its side with his radio broadcasts. They had to do something. They made two unsuccessful attempts to assassinate Markov, then enlisted the help of the Russian KGB.

The man allegedly chosen for the job was a Danish smuggler who had been arrested in Bulgaria. Francesco Gullino had been given a stark choice — jail behind the Iron Curtain, or become an agent against the West. He happily took assignments from his new masters.

On 7 September 1978, Markov was on his way into work at the BBC. He crossed Waterloo Bridge on foot and was just coming off the bridge to catch his bus when he felt a sharp pain on the back of his right calf.

He turned and saw a man (Gullino) bending down to pick up an umbrella. The man apologised profusely for accidentally clipping Markov's leg with his umbrella, then stepped into a cab and disappeared. Markov caught the bus to the BBC offices, but was feeling unwell when he arrived. He had a deep red mark on his calf, and was running a fever.

He was rushed to hospital, where he died four days later. At the post-mortem, doctors found a small platinum pellet in his leg. It contained traces of Ricin, a deadly poison made from castor beans. There is no known antidote. The pellet, which was 1.52 mm across, contained two small holes to deliver the poison. It was fired from the tip of the umbrella, a very high-tech and futuristic method of assassination.

Two weeks previously, the Bulgarian secret service had tried to murder a dissident in the Paris Metro with a similar pellet, this time fired from a biro. That attempt failed as the poison leaked out of the pellet before it entered the victim, and he survived. But when it came to assassinating Markov, they got everything right. The pellet was coated in sugar, which held in the ricin. But the sugar melted at 37C (body temperature) allowing the ricin to seep out into his bloodstream.

For those morbidly curious, the pellet is on display at the Black Museum at New Scotland Yard. However, the museum, which contains many relics of famous crimes over the past two centuries, is only open to police officers and others with a legitimate interest in crime.

Gullino (known by the codename Piccadilly) was never convicted of the assassination. He is still at liberty in Western Europe (exact whereabouts unknown).

Georgi Markov is buried at Saint Candida and Holy Cross Churchyard in a small village in Dorset, Whitechurch Canonicorum. The inscription on his gravestone reads: "In Memory of Georgi Ivanov Markov, Novelist and Playwright. Most dearly beloved by his wife Annabel, his daughter Sasha, his family and friends. Born Sofia 1-3-29, Died London 11-9-78. In The Cause of Freedom."

God's Banker

In a story as convoluted and improbable as a Dan Brown novel, a leading Italian banker brought down the second biggest financial institution in the country — and was then found hanging under a London Bridge. It was ruled as murder, and the chief suspects were the Mafia, the Vatican and a mysterious Masonic Lodge.

The story reached its climax on a mild and cloudy morning in the summer of 1982. A postman crossing Blackfriars Bridge at 7.30 a.m. on Friday, 18 June, spotted something under the bridge, and was shocked to see it was a middle-aged man.

God's Banker Robert Calvi was dangling under scaffolding, an orange rope tied in a lover's knot around his neck. When he was cut down, he was found to have building bricks in his pockets to weigh him down, along with £7,500 in cash. Back then, that was enough to buy him a good family car.

Calvi was known as God's Banker because of his strong links with the Vatican, the bureaucratic nerve centre of the Catholic world. He was chairman of Banco Ambrosiano, which was Italy's second largest bank. The Vatican Bank was the largest shareholder in Banco Ambrosiano.

In 1978, irregularities were discovered — the bank was exporting money illegally. In a country with a strong Mafia presence, that could not be ignored. In 1981, Calvi was given a four-year suspended sentence — though he did spend some weeks in jail during the trial, and attempted suicide while inside. Despite the sentence, he did not lose his position as chairman of the bank.

In 1982, Calvi saw another scandal coming down the line. The bank had debts of close to one billion dollars, and was on the verge of collapse. He wrote to Pope John Paul II, warning him that the Vatican was about to take a big hit unless it intervened to save the bank. Then he shaved off his moustache and flew to London in a private plane. The bank collapsed days later.

Within a week of the bank's collapse, Calvi was found dangling under Blackfriars Bridge. It was initially thought to be suicide, and the inquest in July concurred. But the family disputed the verdict and a second inquest returned an open verdict. Subsequent investigations have all found that Calvi was murdered, most probably to prevent him implicating major figures in Italy in the collapse of Banco Ambrosiano.

Adding to the suspicions was the fact that Calvi's private secretary had jumped to her death from a window in the bank the day before Calvi was found hung. Coincidence, or double murder?

A new post-mortem confirmed Calvi was murdered. The injuries on his neck were inconsistent with hanging. He had not touched the bricks in his pockets. His shoes were not scuffed, as they would have been had he scrambled over the bridge and onto the scaffolding. And the level of the Thames when he died (as opposed to when he was found) was high enough that he could have been placed on the scaffolding from a boat, rather than dropped from overhead.

Assuming it was murder, who had it in for Calvi? There were many candidates.

Calvi was a member of a controversial — and illegal — Italian Masonic Lodge, the Propaganda Duo, or P2. The Lodge had many prominent members, including forty-eight MPs (among them future Prime Minister Silvio Berlusconi), judges, journalists, industrialists, military leaders and the heads of all three Italian secret services. P2 was involved in a number of financial scandals, and implicated in a few murders, including that of a journalist. Members of the group called themselves Frati Neri, or black friars. Did they kill Calvi on Blackfriars Bridge as a message: threaten their security and they would reach you, no matter where you fled?

But another possibility was that Calvi was murdered by the Mafia, a huge organised crime network that thrives to this day in Italy. As well as owing money to P2, the collapsed bank owed millions to the Mafia. Was Calvi being punished for embezzling from the wise guys?

Conspiracy theorists have even speculated that the Vatican might have been behind the killing. They lost a fortune, and some of their dealings — such as their funding of the Polish Solidarity Trade Union — were questionable.

After two decades of extensive investigations by London and Italian police, five men were charged with murdering God's Banker. The picture painted by the prosecutors was that the Mafia was acting with P2, and Calvi was killed for losing their money, and to prevent him embarrassing establishment figures in Italy. The Vatican bank was also implicated in the conspiracy.

But after a high-profile trial that lasted twenty months (from 2005 to 2007), all five were acquitted due to lack of evidence. The truth will never be known about how one of Europe's leading bankers found himself dangling on a rope under Blackfriars Bridge, with the Thames flowing coldly beneath his feet.

Drowned in the River for Fun

Murder intrigues people. The Penny Dreadfuls — accounts of colourful Old Bailey trials — were bestsellers a 150 years ago. Today, a juicy murder will shift newspapers. But some murders are so cruel, no one can take a vicarious pleasure in reading about them.

Such was the case of six youths convicted of murdering law student Timothy Baxter, and attempting to murder his friend Gabriel Cornish on Hungerford Bridge, on the night of 18 June 1999.

The two friends, aged twenty-four and twenty-five, were walking home from an evening out in the West End. At 4 a.m., they began to cross the new pedestrian Hungerford Bridge in the centre of the city. But they were confronted by three youths, intent on robbing them. The youths had earlier robbed and beaten a man on The Embankment.

Sonni Reid (20), John Riches (22) and an underage teen accosted the two students and began to push them around, demanding their wallets. The two young men turned and tried to make their escape off the bridge. They saw three people coming towards them and appealed for help.

But the three — Cameron Cyrus (19) and a teenage couple — knew the attackers, and instead of helping the students, they joined in the attack. The five men beat the two unconscious, while the girl looked on and cheered encouragement at them. She also used a phone to take pictures of the attack.

At one point, a closed-circuit security camera shows her kissing her boyfriend while the others continued to kick their prone victims. Eventually, someone shouted that it would be "fun" to throw the students into the river.

So the attackers picked up the two unconscious young men and heaved them over the railing into the Thames. Gabriel Cornish revived on hitting the water, and he was rescued. But his friend Timothy drowned. His body was recovered the following day.

After the trial, Detective Chief Inspector David Shipperlee said: "It was the most callous of acts by a group of young people. They not only beat these two young people unconscious, but they — it would appear for fun — picked them up and threw them over the railings into the River Thames. Anyone in their right mind would have known it would cause someone's death."

The six were convicted of murder and attempted murder, and received the mandatory life sentences.

Adam — A Return to Human Sacrifice Under the Bridge

When pedestrians spotted an orange object floating under Tower Bridge, and saw that it was the mutilated body of a young child, they set in train an investigation that revealed possible large-scale human sacrifices in the heart of London.

But the case of "Adam" remains a mystery more than a decade after the torso was fished out of the river by the police. It is one of the few unsolved murder of a child in the history of the force.

It all began on a showery and cool autumn day in 2001. It was Friday, 21 September, and a number of people spotted a brightly-coloured object floating down the river past the Tower of London and under Tower Bridge. It passed under the bridge, and one of the people looking into the river realised it was a human torso, wearing bright orange shorts. He phoned the police.

Within minutes, the police Marine Search Unit was on the scene and the body was recovered downstream, near the Globe Theatre. Police knew they had been lucky: two more turns of the tide and the body would have been lost in the North Sea.

The torso was that of an African boy of between four and seven years of age. His arms, legs and head had been removed, making identification impossible. Forensic tests revealed that the boy came from Nigeria, and had been in London only a few days. The contents of his stomach included the ingredients of a traditional magic potion from Africa.

In the absence of any clues to the boy's identity, the police named him Adam. There was huge media interest in the story, but very slow progress was made. The police felt that it was not a typical sex crime and concentrated on the idea that Adam had been the victim of Muti, ritualistic murder, in which human body parts are harvested for native medicine.

They believed he had been paralysed with an extract from the Calabar bean before being ritualistically slain.

But without knowing who he was, it was difficult to make further progress. A huge reward was offered for information, and even former South African president, the late Nelson Mandela, threw his weight behind the campaign.

No substantial progress was made, but the huge investigation began to unravel a terrifying picture of a hidden community nestled in the civilisation of the capital. Linked cases were investigated. In July 2002, a Nigerian woman arrived in the UK from Germany, claiming to have fled from a Yoruba cult that practiced ritual murders. She said they attempted to kill her son, and she knew Adam was murdered in London by his parents. Police trawled her associates, and one man, Kinglsey Ojo, was jailed for four years for child trafficking.

Police also investigated the death of an eight-year-old African girl in 2000. She was beaten to death by relatives trying to exorcise evil spirits from her. There were many similar cases of children being beaten because of so-called demonic possession. The police began an extensive investigation into the practice. The resulting report was shocking: it concluded that boys from Africa were being murdered as human sacrifices in London churches.

There was progress of sorts a decade after Adam was recovered from the Thames. He has been tentatively identified as six-year-old Ikpomwosa, a Nigerian boy whose parents were deported back to Nigeria. He had been cared for by a woman in Germany, who handed him over to a man who took him to London.

Former Detective Inspector Will O'Reilly, who worked on the initial case, described the identification in 2011 as "a major breakthrough."

Whether that proves to be the case or not, one thing is certain, the publicity from the case has highlighted a very dark area of London life. Police believe the attention has deterred further ritualistic murders, and may have saved some lives.

Scotland Yard Report on Human Sacrifice in London

A Scotland Yard report following the death of mystery child Adam, found that some fundamentalist sects from West Africa, with congregations in London, believed that some powerful spells required the deaths of "unblemished" male children — young boys who had not yet been circumcised.

Police believed such boys were purchased on the streets of cities such as Kinshasa for as little as £10, and trafficked to the UK.

The report also cited cases of children being tortured and killed because of suspicion they were witches, or were possessed. It also highlighted a belief among some African communities that a cure for HIV was to have sex with a child.

The report was prepared after a series of workshops with members of the West African community in London. They revealed to shocked officers that powerful spells needed the sacrifice of an uncircumcised boy, and such boys were trafficked in for the purpose.

Scotland Yard also revealed that it had traced just two of three hundred black boys between the ages of four and seven who had gone missing in a three-month period. The true figure of missing black children could run to thousands. Those who were trafficked into the country illegally were never even reported missing.

The report concluded that children could be in "serious and possible life-threatening situations."

River of Despair — Suicide on the Thames

One of the most popular places for suicides in London is on the Underground. A dive under the spinning wheels of the trains is a quick ticket to oblivion for over a hundred people a year. But before the Underground, the dark ribbon of the Thames was the route of choice.

Access was easy — for centuries, you could walk to the banks and take any one of the hundreds of steps down to the black swirling water. Or, you could step off a bridge into the embrace of the river.

Suicides have been recorded on the river for nearly a thousand years. In *The London Eyre* of 1244, it is reported: "Alice de Wanewyck drowned herself in the port of Dowgate, being non compos mentis."

Many other deaths were recorded on the river, but some were murders, and others were drunks falling off the steps. The suicides tended to be unrecorded, or at best anonymous. No one wanted to admit that their loved ones had been driven to the ultimate desperation.

But some records do survive. Diarist Samuel Pepys noted on 24 February 1666: "My waterman told me how the mistress of the Beare Tavern, at the bridge foot, did lately fling herself into the Thames, and drown herself. It seems she has had long melancholy upon her and hath endeavoured to make away with herself often."

Two decades later, the son of the Secretary of War (Sir William Temple) hired a boatman to go under London Bridge at the turn of the tide. He wanted to "shoot the bridge". Because of the narrowness of the arches, there were ferocious rapids between both sides of the bridge. The drop could be as much as 2 metres (6 feet). Shooting the bridge was a sport for the brave, and many died in the attempt.

Just as the boatman steered through the arch, Temple stood and flung himself into the river. He was immediately sucked under by the current. He rose once, then sank again and drowned. His body was later recovered and his pockets were filled with stones. It was a needless precaution. The current would have pulled him under unaided. If he had escaped the current, the cold would have finished him within ten minutes. And if he survived the cold, the toxic water would have done for him.

Another notable suicide was the poet Stephen Duck (1705-56). A man from an undistinguished background (his father was a labourer), he was a natural, or country, poet, in contrast to the more studied poets such as his contemporary Alexander Pope. A devoutly religious man, he was roundly satirised by both Pope and Jonathan Swift. Perhaps this is what drove him to despair. Towards the end of April 1756, he walked behind a pub and threw himself into the river.

Records become more comprehensive as we move into the more modern era. In the nineteenth century, many suicides were reported. Some were reported in detail.

One young man became depressed after his brother drowned. So he threw himself into the river. But he thought of others: he changed into his bathing costume so that his relatives might have his clothes. Some filled their pockets with stones, but one man went further to ensure that he had no last minute change of heart. He tied a 56 lb weight around his neck. Another man managed to tie his hands and feet before stumbling into the river. He had recently lost his child.

Certain spots became associated with suicide. Researchers have long known of the cluster effect, whereby one suicide triggers a number of copycats. So once a spot became known as suitable, people were drawn to that spot.

There was a swing bridge near Old Gravel Lane in the Docks close to St Peter's Church, which was nicknamed the "Bridge of Sighs" because so many chose it as their final destination. When Waterloo Bridge opened in 1817, it became known by a number of names, including "Lover's Leap", "Arch of Suicide", "Bridge of Sighs", and "Bridge of Sorrow". At the time, it was an isolated enough spot, especially in the evenings. There was a penny toll to cross, and that kept pedestrians to a minimum. At one point, thirty people a year were jumping from Waterloo Bridge.

The problem became so bad that the authorities docked the Jumpers' Boat near the bridge. This was a boat with a special roller system at its stern which allowed crew to pluck people from the dark waters and pull them on board easily. The Jumpers' Boat was replaced with a special floating police station, the only one in the world. It was moored at Waterloo Pier on the Victoria Embankment, almost under the bridge. Now the river is policed by a number of ribs and speed boats — and special constables — based at Wapping. Suicide continues to be a major problem. In 2002, the Lifeboat, River Police and Coastguard dealt with 400 incidents.

Dead Houses

With so many suicides (not to mention accidental drowning, and the occasional shove!), bodies floating through the centre of the city were something the authorities have had to be prepared for. There were "dead houses" along the river where the bodies could be brought. Three to four bodies could be fished out in a typical week. Authorities on the Surrey side of the river paid five shillings (a crown) for every floater recovered, but if you brought the corpse to the Middlesex side, you only got half-a-crown. So most floaters — stripped of any valuables by the boatmen! — ended up on the Surrey side.

Instead of being brought to a police station, they were removed to the parish Dead House where they were photographed to aid identification. If they were not identified, they were buried in a communal plot, their clothes preserved to aid future identification.

Because of pollution, decomposition was accelerated. Bodies became bloated because of gasses produced in the first few days after death. Special coffins were made to accommodate the swollen corpses, twice the normal size.

Taking Inspiration from Suicide

William Cowper (1731-1800) was a great poet, but a poor suicide. He attempted to take his own life on at least three occasions, each time failing. But at least two of the suicide attempts were followed by very well received poems.

Cowper was born in Hertfordshire and trained for the law. But on the eve of his final exams, he had a breakdown and tried to commit suicide for the first time by poisoning himself (he balked at swallowing the poison), by driving a knife through his heart (the blade broke) and by hanging with a garter (the garter broke after he passed out).

After eighteen months recovering in an asylum, he moved from London to the country and switched to writing poetry and hymns, celebrating nature and everyday life. He was a forerunner of the Romantic poets and quickly made a name for himself. But the mental instability followed him, and he made two more attempts on his life.

On one occasion, in the early 1770s, he was in London for a visit. An attack of despair hit him, and he decided to end it all in the Thames. He hailed a cab and ordered the driver to take him to the river bank. Some reports suggest it was a dark night with very heavy fog — a typical London pea-souper — and that the driver was unable to find the river, so drove Cowper back to his house. The truth is less picturesque.

As Cowper reported: "Not knowing whether to poison myself, I resolved upon drowning. For that purpose I took a coach and ordered the man to drive to Tower Wharf, intending to throw myself into the river from the Custom House Quay. I left the coach upon the Tower Wharf, intending never to return to it; but upon coming to the quay I found the water low, and a porter seated upon some goods there, as if on purpose to prevent me. This passage to the bottomless pit being mercifully shut against me, I returned back to the coach."

Reflecting on his close brush with death, Cowper wrote the poem for which he is most famous: "Light Shining Out Of Darkness".

"*God moves in a mysterious way,*
His wonders to perform;
He plants His footsteps on the sea,
And rides upon the storm.
Blind unbelief is sure to err,
And scan His works in vain;
God is his own interpreter,
And He will make it plain.
Judge not the Lord by feeble sense,
But trust Him for His grace;
Behind a frowning providence
He hides a smiling face."

Cowper eventually settled in Norfolk and passed away from dropsy, or oedema, in 1800.

Frankenstein's Mother Plans her Death

Putney Bridge was the spot chosen by Mary Wollstonecraft to end her life, after the thirty-six-year-old writer and women's rights campaigner discovered that her affair with her lover Gilbert Imlay was over.

Wollstonecraft was a free thinker who went to France at the height of the revolution, and thrived in the frantic atmosphere. She fell in love with the American Imlay. She had a baby, but the relationship became strained. He returned to London.

She followed him in April 1795, but he rejected her. In May, she attempted to commit suicide with laudanum, but Imlay saved her life. She left for Scandinavia, but returned in October, knowing the relationship was over for good. In despair, she left Imlay a note: "Let my wrongs sleep with me! Soon, very soon, I shall be at peace. When you receive this, my burning head will be cold... I shall plunge into the Thames where there is least chance of my being snatched from the death I seek. God bless you! May you never know by experience what you have made me endure. Should your sensibility ever awake, remorse will find its way to your heart; and, in the midst of business and sensual pleasure, I shall appear before you, the victim of your deviation from rectitude."

She chose a night of heavy rain, to ensure her clothing was heavy with water. After spending half an hour walking up and down, she plucked up the courage and jumped off Putney Bridge into the Thames. But a man saw her jumping and managed to rescue her, causing her to later write: "I have only to lament that, when the bitterness of death was past, I was inhumanly brought back to life and misery."

Mary found love again with William Godwin. They married when she became pregnant. Their child, Mary Shelley, went on to fame with her gothic horror novel "Frankenstein". Her mother, however, did not live to see that. She died of complications in childbirth in 1797.

The Bridge of Sighs

The death of a young child, and the attempted suicide of his mother, was all that was needed to fuel the creative juices of the mawkishly sentimental Victorians. Thomas Hood wrote his best poem on the case of Mary Furley, while Charles Dickens featured the story in his Christmas tale "The Chimes". Others wrote about her, painted her, campaigned for clemency for her.

It all began on Regent's Canal, close to where it merges with the Thames at Limehouse Basin. Mary Furley was a woman of forty with a young child. Her husband deserted her, and she ended up in Bethnal Green workhouse. Her son got head lice and was shaved by a drunken barber, suffering severe cuts to his head. The wound festered, and Mary decided she would be better off leaving the workhouse.

Desperate, she obtained work sewing. But the meagre money she earned was stolen. That was the final straw. Rather than re-enter the workhouse, she decided to end their sufferings. "I preferred death for myself and my child," she said afterwards.

Mary took her young son and jumped into the canal. A waterman heard her in the water and managed to pull her to safety. But the child was never seen again, and in April 1844, Mary Furley was tried for infanticide. Convicted, she was sentenced to death and sent to Newgate Prison.

There was a public outcry. Leading writers of the day, including Dickens, led the campaign for clemency. Within a fortnight, Thomas Hood had published his poem, "Bridge of Sighs", but in an effort to ratchet up the tragedy, he moved the location to Waterloo Bridge. It was in the centre of the city and already had a reputation for suicides. Roughly thirty people threw themselves from the bridge every year, representing 15% of the annual city total of around two hundred. It was known as The Bridge of Sighs or the Arch of Suicide.

One reason the bridge was so popular was that there was a penny toll to cross it. So that made it a bit quieter, and gave some privacy to the desperate and the lonely. Hood extracted all the pathos out of the situation:

"...The bleak wind of March
Made her tremble and shiver;
But not the dark arch,
Or the black flowing river:
Mad from life's history,
Glad to death's mystery,
Swift to be hurl'd—
Anywhere, anywhere
Out of the world!

In she plunged boldly—
No matter how coldly
The rough river ran—
Over the brink of it,
Picture it—think of it,
Dissolute Man!"

At the end of April, the public campaign succeeded. Mary Furley's sentence was commuted to transportation to the penal colonies in Australia for seven years. It is unlikely she ever returned to London and the dreaded Thames.

CHAPTER SEVEN: LONDON AT WAR

Global conflicts are a new feature of the last hundred years. But Britain has always been a warlike nation, and London has been at the centre of planning military campaigns for more than a thousand years. Because Britain is an island, London has rarely been subjected to land attacks or invasions. The Romans did attack, and so did the Normans. The Germans tried, twice, with air attacks. In the last fifty years, terrorist attacks have replaced conventional battles. In this chapter, we will look at how London has coped with war and conflict.

Roman Londinium Sacked and Torched

The first recorded attack on the capital occurred when the soldiers of Queen Boudicca sacked the town of Londinium. Londinium was the Roman settlement formed around a section on the Thames that was deep enough to take boats, but narrow enough to bridge. The site was on the northern shore of the river, close to what is now London Bridge.

The remains of a Roman pier were found in 1981, fixing the exact location. It was not a military fortress, but a civilian trading centre. The entire settlement was about the size of modern Hyde Park.

In AD 60, Queen Boudicca led her Iceni warriors against the fledgling town, fresh from their victory at Colchester. They slaughtered those inhabitants who did not manage to flee, then put the town to the torch. To this day, the layer of red ash from that fire survives, and is used by archaeologists to date strata when they do digs near London Bridge. The layer of ash stretches down to the river on the northern bank.

The Romans swiftly defeated Boudicca at the Battle of Watling Street. The exact location of the battle is unclear, but it may have been at King's Cross, near the ford of the River Fleet, a short distance from where it joins the Thames.

The rebel forces were destroyed, with 70,000 killed. The victorious Romans rebuilt their trading town. London had risen from the ashes for the first time.

A monument to the rebel queen was commissioned by Prince Albert. The bronze statue of the queen riding into battle on her chariot, flanked by her two daughters, is at Westminster Pier, close to the underground station.

The Battle of London Bridge, 1014

The Vikings were the next to attack London, but in 1014, they were driven from the city. King Ethelred was an unpopular English ruler who had lost the throne to King Sweyn of Denmark in 1013, fleeing to Normandy in disgrace.

But when Sweyn died the following year, Ethelred the Unready returned to reclaim his throne. As part of the process, he had to attack Danish-occupied London. He was supported by his ally, Prince Olaf of Norway.

According to a Nordic saga, the Danes lined London Bridge and showered the forces of King Ethelred with spears. Undaunted, the king's soldiers pulled the roofs off nearby houses and held them over their heads as shields as the boats moved under the bridge.

They managed to manoeuvre their ships beneath the wooden arches of the bridge, then tied ropes around the supporting posts. They rowed furiously downstream, the force of the river helping. They managed to pull out the supports, bringing the bridge and its compliment of Viking defenders crashing into the Thames.

Many of the warriors, encumbered with heavy armour, were lost in the collapse.

This ended the Viking occupation of the city. It may also have been the original inspiration for the nursery rhyme "London Bridge is Falling Down".

London Bridge is broken down—
Gold is won, and bright renown.
Shields resounding,
War-horns sounding,
Hild is shouting in the din!
Arrows singing,
Mail-coats ringing—
Odin makes our Olaf win!

The Norman Invasion and the Battle of London

Bodies found during a recent excavation at Ludgate, close to the river, are thousand-year-old relics of one of the turning points of history.

London was the key to conquering Britain. The Romans knew it, the Danes knew it and the Normans knew it. So after defeating the British forces at the Battle of Hastings in 1066, (British King Harold was shot through the eye by a Norman archer), the French forces advanced on the capital.

William of Normandy moved through Kent, destroying Romney, then accepted a surrender at Dover, which gave him the important castle there. He rested his army for a week, during which he also accepted the surrender of Canterbury on 29 October. Feeling confident, he sent messengers to Winchester, where Harold's widow, Queen Edith, was in residence. That city too surrendered. William advanced to Canterbury.

From there, it was only a short march to Southwark and the banks of the Thames. But here he met stubborn resistance. He was prevented from crossing London Bridge and retreated, after destroying much of the town.

He withdrew further up river to Wallingford, ravaging the land as he went. He crossed the river at Wallingford and approached London from the north-west, reaching Berkhamsted in late November. The authorities in the city knew what was coming, and scrambled to do a deal.

Harold's young son Edgar was now the uncrowned king and it was agreed that he would abdicate, allowing William to be recognised as King of Britain. In return, the city would be spared. William's troops advanced on the city in mid-December, moving from Berkhamsted down Watling Street (Edgware Road) and moving west along what is now Oxford Street.

At St Giles High Street, William turned south down St Martin's Lane and past the royal palace at Westminster, then east through the city, along what is now The Strand. They reached the bridge of the River Fleet, near where it joins the Thames, and dug in, establishing siege works. They were close to Ludgate, hard by the Thames. Ludgate was the main western gate of London at the time. They had met fierce opposition two months earlier when they had tried to take London via Southwark and London Bridge, but this time they had done a secret deal.

On 20 December, Saxon nobles inside opened Ludgate and admitted William of Normandy. Here the young King Edgar, the Sheriff of Middlesex and the Archbishops of York and Canterbury, offered their surrender. William treated them graciously. But not all the citizens were happy with the surrender. As William's troops made their way towards St

Paul's and Cheapside, an angry mob surrounded them and attacked. The site of the attack is unclear, but it was probably open ground at the west of Cheapside.

The Londoners regarded themselves as free men of an independent city, and they fought valiantly. But they were no match for the disciplined, battle-hardened Norman troops. The battle was a rout. The defenders of the city had included women and many men still in their teens. They were slaughtered unmercifully.

The dead were removed to a promontory where the Fleet joined the Thames, a bleak and uninhabited spot outside the city walls. Some of the bodies were beheaded, and many were buried under mounds of stone on the foreshore of the river. Recent excavations just south-west of Ludgate found eleven bodies, eight of which had been dismembered. Only three skulls were found. The bodies included men, women and teens.

Thus ended the battle of London. With the triumph of William the Conqueror (he was crowned on Christmas Day), the modern history of Britain had begun.

Rebellion — the Harvest of Heads
A popular People's Revolt in the late medieval period was crushed at London Bridge after forces loyal to the king used the crossing as a desperate last stand. It happened during the reign of Henry VI, in 1450. The reward the rebels got for their pains was to become part of the gruesome harvest of heads displayed by the vengeful king on London Bridge after the rising was quashed.

Jack Cade was the leader of the popular uprising, which began in Kent. A bit of a rabble-rouser, Jack organised 5,000 people in support of his grievances. He organised the grievances into a manifesto, "The Complaint of the Poor Commons of Kent". This listed complaints against the government not only from the poor, but from several MPs, lords and magnates. In essence, the king was accused of injustice and ordered to punish the wealthy for their crimes against the common people.

Underlying the complaints was the anger many English felt about the Hundred Years' War with France, and how it was draining the country. In May 1450, the 5,000 rabble began to march on London, forcing the king to flee to Warwickshire. In early June, the rebels gathered at Blackheath, south-east of the capital. They were mostly peasants, but also included shopkeepers, craftsmen and landowners (including at least one knight, two MPs, and eighteen squires). Soldiers and sailors from the French wars swelled the ranks.

The rebels advanced to Southwark, which marked the southern end of London Bridge. They set up headquarters at the White Hart Inn, then crossed the bridge on 3 July. When they had advanced to the London Stone (still visible behind a metal grill opposite the entrance to Cannon Street Underground station), Cade declared himself mayor of the city. He then marched on the Guildhall and took the Tower of London to proclaim his demands in full.

The Lord High Treasurer, James Fiennes, was beheaded, along with his son-in-law, William Cromper. Their heads were placed on pikes overlooking the river, and made to kiss each other. The rebels then looted London before recrossing the bridge for the night. (It was closed every night, so they crossed that evening, billeting in Southwark again.)

But the following morning, London was ready for the rebels. The bridge was guarded. There was a stand-off all day, but as evening fell, the rebels got tired of sitting around and they stormed the guarded bridge. A prolonged battle ensued, with fighting on or around the bridge lasting from 10 p.m. until 8 a.m. the following morning. At that time, there were houses lining both sides of the bridge, which gave vantage points for the defenders. The road through the centre of the bridge, overlooked by all those houses, was narrow, making it a perfect ambush site. Many of the rebels were slaughtered in the narrow street, while some of the defenders also found a watery grave.

As a contemporary account puts it: "And that same evening London did arise and come out upon them at ten of the bell. And from that time unto the morrow eight of the bell they were ever fighting upon London Bridge, and many a man was slain and cast into the Thames. And the Captain of Kent (John Cade) did fire the drawbridge of London; and before that he broke both King's Bench and the Marshalsea Prisons, and let out all the prisoners that were in them."

After a night of vicious fighting that raged on the bridge and the surrounding streets and river banks, the rebels retreated with heavy casualties. The forces of authority had won the battle of London Bridge.

The aftermath of the rebellion — which was crushed by the defeat on the Thames — was sordid. The Lord Chancellor (Archbishop John Kemp) persuaded John Cade to call off the rising by issuing official pardons, and promising to fulfil the demands of Cade's manifesto. He lied: the pardons were voided by the king and a price was placed on Cade's head. He was killed a few days later. Many of his followers were captured and hung. None of the objectives of the rebels were met. The second battle of London Bridge was a decisive victory for the Crown — as the first had been.

It had a grisly aftermath: the king displayed the heads of sixteen executed leaders on spikes across London Bridge as a warning to future malcontents. It became known as the Harvest of Heads.

The Last Resistance to the Normans

The Norman invasion of Britain took months to achieve, but centuries to consolidate. Most of the conquered people knuckled down under the new rulers fairly quickly, but the more independent Celtic tribes held out for hundreds of years. Wales only capitulated in 1412, while Ireland fought bitterly on until the twentieth century. Scotland resisted until the battle of Culloden in 1715. The last bit of resistance in England came from Celtic Cornwall, with the rebellion of 1497. It featured one of the last battles to be fought in London, at Deptford Bridge.

Deptford Bridge crossed Deptford Creek, the tidal portion of the River Ravensbourne, less than a mile from where it joins the Thames on the south bank, near what is now Deptford Broadway. The rebels took the bridge but in the ensuing battle, 200 Cornish men were killed, to eight of the London army.

Lord Audley and Thomas Flanmark were taken on the battlefield, and Michael Joseph was captured as he fled towards Greenwich. All three Cornish leaders were taken to the Tower of London, tried and condemned to death; they were to be hung, drawn and quartered. Joseph and Flanmark were shown mercy. They were hung until dead, before being disembowelled and quartered. Such mercy was uncommon in those harsh times. Lord Audley's sentence was commuted. Instead of being hung, drawn and quartered, he was taken to Tower Hill in a procession, on a cart bearing his coat of arms. At Tower Hill, he was simply beheaded.

All three heads were displayed on London Bridge as a warning to others: mess with the Crown at your peril.

World War One

The Norman invasion was the last land attack on Britain — apart from the disastrous Spanish Armada in 1588, defeated by a smaller but superior British navy and bad weather. By the time the First World War came along, Britain had enjoyed eight centuries of glorious isolation. But distance could not keep the city out of harm's way.

Munitions Factory Blows Up

As you drift down the Thames, looking left and right as you travel from the edge of Greater London down towards the final bridge and the estuary, an industrial landscape meets your eyes. The river was the place for factories, store houses, wharfs and the great driving forces of the industrial revolution.

Rivers bring supplies, and they carry away the finished product. They are also a source of water for the industrial processes — and a convenient sewer to take away the waste products of manufacturing. The banks of the Thames are littered with century old stone factories, relics of the great growth in commerce in the Victorian era.

One of the largest factories on the river was a munitions factory in Silvertown, West Ham. During the First World War, it was one of the most important buildings in the city, supplying the daily barrages from the trenches. It was working at full capacity, round the clock shifts, to keep the big guns fed.

But on 19 January 1917, there was a massive explosion. Fifty tonnes of TNT went up, killing seventy-three people and injuring four hundred more, as well as causing extensive damage to the surrounding area. It was a crippling blow to the war effort, following a similar explosion in Faversham which killed 105. A year later, another munitions factory in Chadwell exploded, killing 137.

The West Ham factory was built in 1893 on the south side of the Thames on North Woolwich Road, to produce soda crystals and caustic soda. The business ceased in 1912, leaving the factory idle. The War Office decided it would be the perfect place to purify TNT, despite the fact it was in a highly populated area. Nine tonnes of the explosive were purified each day.

On 19 January 1917, a fire broke out in the melt-pot room, and the fire was being fought when 51 tonnes of TNT ignited at 6.52 p.m. The plant was destroyed in an instant. So were many of the surrounding buildings, including the local fire station. The sky above West Ham was lit a lurid red, and the shock wave broke windows in a wide circle around the plant. Even buildings across the river were rattled and severely damaged by the rain of rubble.

Debris was flung high into the air, with red-hot chunks of rubble landing miles away from the explosion site, causing many small local fires. A gasometer, or gas storage unit, at Greenwich Peninsula, four kilometres away, exploded when struck by the debris, creating a giant fireball. Seventeen acres (7 hectares) of warehouses were damaged or destroyed.

The explosion blew out windows in the Savoy Hotel, and almost overturned a taxi in Pall Mall. The fires from the factory and the gas storage unit could be seen as far away as Maidstone and Guilford, and the blast was heard for a hundred miles.

The human cost was horrific, with sixty-nine people killed instantly. Another four died of their injuries. More than four hundred people were injured.

The landscape around North Woolwich Road was transformed into a wasteland. 900 nearby buildings were either entirely destroyed or damaged beyond salvage, with a further

70,000 properties suffering some damage. The cost of the explosion was put in the region of £2 million.

It could have been far worse. If the explosion had happened two hours earlier, when everyone was still at work in the surrounding buildings, the death toll would have been far higher. Many workers had already left for the evening. Only forty were in the munitions factory itself, and they all perished. Had the explosion taken place an hour later, everyone would have been home, and many more would have been killed in the surrounding residential streets.

However, the community lost several firemen and volunteers who were fighting the earlier fire when the TNT ignited.

The emergency services responded rapidly, with the street outside the factory turned into an impromptu first aid camp to treat the walking wounded. Thousands were left homeless, requiring temporary accommodation in schools, churches and community buildings.

One thousand seven hundred men were employed in the clean-up and rebuild of the area. Four hundred new houses were built to replace those destroyed. Hundreds more had to be repaired.

To this day, the factory has not been replaced. The grounds are empty, not having been built upon since the explosion. A second building, part of the plant, was rebuilt and used until 1961, but is now also disused. A memorial commissioned in the 1920s was placed inside this second building, a tribute to those who lost their lives that day, and a memorial to the war dead.

There is a second memorial to the disaster which people can visit to this day. One of the dead was Police Constable Edward George Brown Greenoff. He was posthumously awarded the King's Police Medal, and is commemorated with a plaque on the Memorial to Heroic Self Sacrifice in Postman's Park, near St Paul's Cathedral.

Air Raids in World War One

Aircraft were just over a decade old when the First World War broke out, and they were small and primitive. But the military quickly saw the advantages of fighting from the air. The Germans were particularly enthusiastic and didn't confine themselves to the flimsy propeller planes at their disposal. They also used massive airships, the majestic silver torpedo-like Zeppelins. These floated across the channel and dropped their loads over London and the south-east.

In 1917, heavy bomber planes began crossing the channel, and unlike the Zeppelins these specifically targeted the capital.

Between 1916 and 1918, 250 tonnes of explosives were dropped on London. This represented 9,000 bombs. Nationally, the bombing raids killed 1,413 people and injured 3,500, as well as causing massive damage and spreading fear among the population. Over a third of the casualties were in London.

Air defences were put in place and the slow-moving Zeppelins were easy targets. By the end, the Germans had given up on the air offensive. London had survived the First World War.

World War Two

When Hitler declared war on Poland in 1939, years of tense diplomacy came to an abrupt end; Europe was at war again, and Britain was part of the forces ranged against Germany. Britain is on the periphery of Europe, protected by the English Channel and the North Sea. There was no immediate danger of a land invasion, but air warfare had improved immeasurably since the First World War and London, being so close to the channel, was in constant danger.

The authorities began drawing up plans for what seemed an inevitability. Stockpiles of cheap coffins were prepared, food rationing was introduced, women were pressed into essential war work and evacuation of children from the capital began. The government began to build large public air raid shelters, and private householders were given small bomb shelters for their own homes.

The two most common were steel sheds built in pits in the garden, or reinforced steel tables which people would sleep under at night, and which would withstand the collapse of a building on them. An evening blackout was enforced to give bombers no easy targets. But London itself was an easy target. The river winds through the centre of the city in a series of serpentine swirls, and that was often enough to guide an enemy plane. After a year of waiting, the first attacks came. The Blitz was on.

How One Ship Survived the Blitz

The Blitz was one of the most frightening periods in London's history. The German air force led bombing mission after bombing mission on the capital, in an attempt to break the British before an invasion. Hitler knew he needed to secure Britain, or all his gains in Western Europe were in jeopardy.

Throughout the winter of 1940-41 his air men dropped bombs and incendiary devices on London. Londoners got used to living in fear, crawling into shelters at night, or sleeping in the secure tunnels of the underground rail network.

The centre of London was particularly vulnerable. The blackout was in place, so German bombers could not make for the bright lights of the city. However there was no disguising the swirls of the river, a silver ribbon in moonlight or starlight. It led the bombers unerringly to the docklands, and the commercial heart of the city.

The Blitz deserves a book of its own, and several have been written. There was so much death and destruction along the Thames, it is difficult to know where to start. To simplify, it might be useful to follow the story of one boat, the Dutch freighter *Abbekerk*.

This 7,900 tonne vessel was built in 1939, and had a crew of fifty, with accommodation for twelve passengers. She was a fast ship and Dutch seamen crewed her during the war years. Adriaan Willem Kik (1919-2000) was the assistant engineer, and wrote his memories of the war before he died. His son Peter has kindly allowed us to quote from those memoirs, which are online at www.msabbekerk.nl.

Kik was in London, moored at Albert Dock, when the air raids began on 7 September 1940. It all nearly ended for him that same night.

Nine hundred aircraft crossed the channel towards London, not travelling singly or in small groups as people were used to, but in a dark cloud of bombers, clustered tightly. Their target was the London Docks.

"We saw them coming, and when the first bombs started to drop I ran like crazy down the gangplank and I flew into a small entrance under the silos under construction. Was I safe? We had to wait and see," Kik remembered.

"The time seemed to stand still. It was raining bombs. I saw items flying through the air which normally would be securely fastened to the ground, and all this under a curtain of dust and smoke from exploding bombs. The noise was fit to raise the dead and then some. It seemed that my clothes and my hair were blown from my body. It lasted an eternity but everything has an end, and so did this bombardment. When I went outside I did not recognise where I was. How was it possible that surroundings familiar for me could be changed so much in such a short while? Everywhere there were fires and explosions of time bombs. The stench of gunpowder and burning timber was very strong and stuck in your throat.

"The east end docks were surrounded by small homes of dockworkers. They also had suffered the full force and most of these houses had simply been blown over by the blasts, and all the people's belongings were lying in the streets. Ships were burning or had been sunk. It was a scene never to be forgotten."

The *Abbekerk* had been hit a number of times. A bomb had destroyed the engine room, and another exploded in the hold, making a sieve of the watertight compartment. Two bombs had detonated in the river beside the ship, damaging the hull and allowing water to pour in.

"With two holds and the engine room flooded our one and a half year old ship slowly sank to the bottom of the harbour, leaving the main deck about one and a half metres above the water-line," said Kik.

The *Abbekerk* had also been struck by debris from burning warehouses on shore. The crew abandoned the ship, with no injuries. The crew of two tugboats, the *Walbrook* and *Beverley*, spotted the burning, abandoned ship, and boarded her. Bravely they extinguished the flames, but they realised the vessel was still in danger from a neighbouring fire. With the help of volunteers from a nearby ship, the SS *Otaio*, and a tug hand acting as deck pilot on the stricken ship's bridge, they managed to tow her to a safer birth. She was moored to another Dutch ship at the docks. Two of the tugmen involved in the rescue were awarded George Medals for their bravery on the night.

But two nights later, a near miss shook the *Abbekerk*, allowing more water in, and she began to sink completely.

The ship was raised and over the winter remained in the docks, undergoing extensive repairs until the following April. The crew stayed in London, and endured the nightly Blitz. Kik and another engineer had to stay on board each night to quench fires caused by incendiary devices. It was not an easy job; from 7 September, when the Blitz began, London Docks were bombed fifty-seven nights in a row.

Initially, the bombing raids took place more during the day than at night, but as the British Spitfires began to win the Battle of Britain, the Germans were losing aircraft at a faster rate than they could replace them. So they began nighttime raids. That was when life on board the *Abbekerk* became really frightening.

In April, the ship was repaired and ready for sea again. She set out as part of a convoy, bound for Durban in South Africa. She never returned to London. In the Atlantic on 24 August 1942, she was sunk by a German U-boat, with the loss of two lives. Thus ended the Dutch freighter's war.

On Deck during the Blitz

"At night the Germans came back and had no trouble finding the docks again. The whole dock area was in flames and they just dropped their bombs into the middle of this," said Adriaan Kik, assistant engineer on Dutch freighter the *Abbekerk*.

"If during a bombardment any incendiary bombs fell on the ship, we could extinguish these with a couple of shovels of sand. Very fast action was required, particularly if a bomb had fallen on one of the timber hatches. In a very short time the bomb would burn through the wood and fall down into the hold burning. If that happened you really were in trouble," he said.

"Was all this justified? We were both 21 years old and were responsible for the safety of a large and helpless ship with a value of millions. Everything was pitch-dark because of the blackout. Today we would say 'no', but then everybody was in the same boat and let's be honest, we did not know any different and we did what we were ordered to do."

"The incendiary or fire bombs were raining down. Luckily only once two bombs fell on the ship which I, with much bravado, or maybe it was stark fear, or a bit of both, could render safe. We must take into consideration that I would swig half a flask of whisky beforehand. You'd be surprised how brave you can be even if you are no hero. These bombardments lasted till the beginning of January 1941; after that things got a little quieter."

The Opening Salvo

The Battle of Britain raged through the summer of 1940 as the German Luftwaffe began a concerted effort to soften up Britain by attacking air fields and air defences along the south-east. But the RAF proved more than capable of repelling the German attacks. Losses were heavy, but the RAF was still functioning. Germany could not establish air superiority, and Hitler was becoming frustrated. He decided on a change of strategy. If he could not win the air war, he could attack the cities. The Blitz was born.

The Blitz began on 7 September 1940. Anyone in their late thirties, or older, would have recalled the air attacks on London during the First World War. Those attacks filled people with terror, but could not have prepared them for the ferocity of the new German onslaught.

A whining noise filled the air long before the planes arrived, and people looked up in alarm. The planes were not coming in singles or simple formations. A swarm was crossing the channel. The first attack was aimed at the Port of London.

Late in the afternoon, an armada of 348 bombers and 617 fighter planes crossed the channel and headed straight for the unmistakable landmark of the Thames.

The change in strategy caught the RAF off guard, and most of the armada got through. Massive damage was caused, and civilian casualties were huge. Over 100,000 tonnes of shipping was damaged on the river — including the Dutch freighter *Abbekerk* — and 400 people were killed. Over a thousand more suffered injuries.

It was a huge blow to the city, and the start of fifty-seven days of continuous bombing.

The RAF did try to respond, and there was an intense battle in the air over London and the Thames Estuary. The Luftwaffe lost forty-one aircraft; fourteen bombers, twenty-three fighters, and four reconnaissance aircraft. The RAF lost twenty-three fighter planes, with six pilots killed and seven wounded. The others parachuted to safety.

That night, a second wave of bombers hit the docks, with 247 German aircraft dropping ordinance.

The following day, 8 September, the Luftwaffe returned, doing more damage to shipping and buildings along the docks, as well as killing 412 people and severely wounding 747.

Weather was poor on 9 September, but the Germans still came, determined to bomb Britain into capitulation. This time they concentrated on the suburbs, and the airfield at Farnborough. They lost twenty-four aircraft, to the RAF's seventeen. The RAF was winning the battle in the air, but the docks were still being targeted. A week of bad weather followed, but there was no let-up; each day bombs landed on the Thames. The Blitz was well and truly on.

Life in Hell
Life was hell for the civilian population of London. The war was no longer something going on in mainland Europe; it had come to their doorstep and destroyed the door. The government had favoured small domestic bomb shelters, but the population was having none of it; they wanted to stay in the Underground, safe from the carnage on the surface.

Authorities yielded to popular pressure, and by the second week of the Blitz, orderly queues of people were gathering outside the tube stations at 4 a.m., waiting for them to open. Many families sheltered regularly on the platforms, while others only took to the tunnels during periods of heavy bombing. By mid-September, about 150,000 a night slept in the Underground, with a peak of 177,000 on 27 September. The deepest stations muffled the sound of the bombing and people felt safe. But some of the stations suffered direct hits, including Marble Arch, Balham Bank and Liverpool Street. By mid-winter and the following spring, the numbers sleeping on the platforms had dwindled to less than 100,000 a night.

A rough census was taken in November 1940 and found that 4% of the population of London were sleeping in the Underground. Another 9% were using public surface shelters, big bomb-resistant bunkers. A quarter of the population were using what the government recommended: their own private back garden bomb shelters. But that meant more than half the population was unaccounted for. Presumably, they risked staying the night in their own homes. You can become habituated to anything, even Hell.

A staggering statistic is that a quarter of the population of the great city evacuated to the country — whole families upped sticks and relocated. Some moved because the factories driving the war effort were in the industrial midlands. Others left to avoid the bombs.

Those who remained, knuckled down to the business of war. Many joined the Home Guard, the Air Raid Precautions Service, or the Auxiliary Fire Service. The Boy Scouts, though well under age for military service, guided fire engines to where they were most needed. They became known as the Blitz Scouts, and many a boy, just out of short trousers, did his bit for the defence of London. Some gave their lives.

In 1938, there had been 6,600 full-time and 13,800 part-time firefighters in the country; now there are 138,000.

Battle of Britain Day

On 15 September, the weather had improved a bit, and the Germans launched their biggest yet attack on London. The Luftwaffe made two large daytime attacks on the city, concentrating on the estuary and targeting the docks and rail communications. The plan was to destroy the docks, crippling Britain's naval superiority, and to take out the transport infrastructure in the city.

A second objective was to draw the RAF into an air battle over London, and take out as many fighters as they could.

In both objectives, the Luftwaffe failed. Large air battles broke out and lasted most of the day. Dock workers could look up and see the dog fights overhead. The first wave of the German attack was on the Battersea rail network, but it merely managed to knock out rail transport for three days. The second attack failed all together. Its target was the estuary, including the warehouses of the East End, Surrey Commercial Docks south of the river, the Royal Docks (Royal Victoria Dock, Royal Albert Dock, and King George V Dock), and West India Dock. 1,500 German aircraft took part; the largest raid undertaken by them.

It was a resounding victory for the RAF, commemorated to this day as Battle of Britain Day. One in five German aircraft were downed. Very little damage was done to the rail network, and virtually none to the docks. The overwhelming victory turned the Battle of Britain in the RAF's favour and forced the Germans to a new strategy. Within a month, they decided to concentrate on night raids, targeting the civilian population and industry.

The Blitz would continue.

Nights of Horror

By October, most of the bombing raids took place at night. The blackout was in force, plunging the city into darkness. But it was difficult to hide the shining highway of the River Thames, giving the German bombers their bearings despite the darkness beneath them.

October 14 saw the heaviest night attack, with 380 bombers hitting London. Around two hundred people were killed, and another 2,000 injured. The following night, the bombers returned, mixing 450 tonnes of high explosives with 11 tonnes of incendiary devices. Around 900 fires were started in the centre of London and along the banks of the river.

By mid-November, 13,000 tonnes of high explosive and a million incendiaries had fallen on London alone. The docks had taken a heavy pounding. Over 13,000 had been killed, and nearly twice that number seriously injured in the opening two months of the Blitz. But life went on: London was not on her knees. Morale was high. The Germans moved on to the next phase of their plan: night raids on the industrial cities of England, such as Coventry and Birmingham. But they kept bombing London.

The Second Great Fire of London

The heart was ripped out of the city — but not out of its people — by the Luftwaffe on a wintery night just after Christmas, 1940. They dropped 100,000 incendiary devices, setting off a firestorm that raged out of control all along the river and the surrounding streets for miles.

The worst night of the Blitz began after dark on 29 December 1940. The screaming of high flying aircraft filled the air, and the first wave of bombers reached their target around 6 p.m. The blackout was in place, but the ribbon of the Thames guided the bombers unerringly to the heart of London.

As people in the streets heard the whine of the engines and the shriller whistle of the falling bombs, they ran for cover, quickly finding the bomb shelters and the tube stations.

The first wave of German bombers managed to get through the RAF defences, then swooped low over London and began releasing their bombs, before turning to head back to Germany. They were followed by wave after wave of enemy aircraft. The Spitfires of the RAF managed to down a number of them, but most got through with their deadly cargos.

Over the course of twelve hours — until 6 a.m. on 30 December — the bombardment continued. 24,000 high explosive bombs and 100,000 incendiary bombs were dropped — more than 300 a minute at the peak. The high explosive bombs destroyed buildings, while the incendiary bombs started a firestorm that raged across the entire city.

The damage was immense. Many Livery Halls (the historic headquarters of national trade associations) were destroyed, while the Great Hall in the Guildhall, off Gresham Street and Basinghall Street, was gutted. The Guildhall is the headquarters of London Corporation.

When Londoners emerged from their shelters the following morning, they found the largest continuous area of Blitz destruction ever caused. The damage was greater than that caused by the Great Fire of 1666, stretching from Islington to the edge of St Paul's churchyard. Many targets along the Thames were in flames.

In a cruel twist, the raid was planned to coincide with a particularly low tide on the river, making water scarce for the firefighters. The incendiary devices had started 1,500 fires, and many of these spread and joined, forming three major conflagrations. These in turn merged into a firestorm that spread the flames further, threatening areas that had not been hit by the bombers.

The attacks on London and other British cities were designed to demoralise the civilian population and pave the way for a German invasion. Instead, they had the opposite effect. Plucky Londoners got on with the job of living and rebuilding with stoic good cheer. The survival of St Paul's became a minor victory, keeping their spirits alive.

A famous photograph at the time was taken from the roof of the *Daily Mail* newspaper and published the following morning. It showed the dome of St Paul's rising in majesty and triumph over the noxious clouds of black smoke. If that survived, London would survive.

However, the picture was carefully cropped to remove the destroyed houses in the foreground!

Saving St Paul's Cathedral

St Paul's Cathedral, destroyed in the last Great Fire (1666), was again under threat, with flames licking at the edge of the graveyard attached to the church. The massive dome was a symbol of London, and its loss would be an irreparable blow to the morale of the city and nation. Prime Minister Winston Churchill insisted that the building be saved, whatever the cost.

Through the night of the bombardment, while the city huddled underground, a brave team of firefighters were on the streets among the falling bombs, struggling to keep the flames at bay. Volunteer fire-watchers of the St Paul's Watch worked with London firemen to put out fires caused by incendiaries dropping on the cathedral's roof. The 200 members of the St Paul's Watch were not professional firefighters. They were mainly recruited from the Royal Institute of British Architects, but they performed valiantly that night. They knew the vulnerabilities of the structure, and where to direct the firefighting efforts.

The cathedral was saved, but at a cost. 160 civilians died during the raid, while fourteen firemen died battling the subsequent blazes. Another 250 were injured. The Great Fire of the seventeenth century had destroyed over fifty churches. The worst night of the Blitz destroyed nineteen, along with thirty-one guild halls and all of Paternoster Row. This old street was where the clergy from St Paul's would stroll, chanting their prayers. It was the centre of the London publishing trade, and an estimated five million books were lost on the night of the fire.

The End of the Blitz

By early 1941, the losses inflicted by the RAF on the Luftwaffe were severe, with just 551 of their 1,214 bombers combat worthy. There could be no more nights like 14 October, or the second Great Fire. The Luftwaffe simply did not have the resources to mount such missions.

Realising that the battle was lost, focus switched to what could still be won. The North Atlantic kept the lines of communication open between America and Europe, and Germany desperately needed to control the sea. If America became involved in the war, it complicated things for Hitler. The focus of the air raids switched to ports on the sea.

London was still a target, but the heat was off. After sustaining fifty-seven continuous days and nights of bombing, there were now some periods when life could return to normal.

The last major attack on London was on 10/11 May 1941. The Luftwaffe sent 571 bombers, and over 800 tonnes of bombs. The attack came after a period of quiet, when Londoners had become convinced that the Blitz was over. So it badly dented morale. It also started 2,000 fires in the capital. The attack was continued the following night. 1,436 people were killed and 1,792 were seriously injured. Westminster Abbey and the Law Courts were damaged, while a chamber of the House of Commons was destroyed. One-third of the streets in London were impassable, and all but one railway line was damaged, taking out the rail network for several weeks.

It was the last hurrah of the air war. The objective of the Blitz — the softening of the British in preparation for an amphibious attack — was not achieved. Perversely Londoners rose to the challenge and a sort of aggressive patriotism ensued. That, at least, is the legend, and there is a certain truth to it. But many were severely traumatised, particularly in the poorer areas of the city where the resources to rebuild lives were not in place.

The Cost
Between 20 June 1940, and the end of March 1941, the Luftwaffe lost 2,265 aircraft over Britain. They had also seen 3,363 airmen killed, and a further 2,641 missing. Most of those were also dead. There were 2,117 injured. The Luftwaffe made 127 major air raids on Britain during the Blitz, and seventy-one of them targeted London. One hundred and twenty thousand houses were destroyed in and around London, with heaviest damage along the Thames in central London.

Across the country, 60,000 civilians were killed, and 87,000 were seriously injured. Of those killed, the majority lived in London. Until halfway through the war, more women and children in Britain had been killed than soldiers.

Living Through the Blitz
Several Londoners have given their accounts of living through the Blitz. This is the experience of Harry Meacham, who worked as an air raid warden. He told a reporter in 1987: "The streets were lit up like day. Houses were burning, shops were burning, it was a proper inferno. Heat was something terrible. The soles of your shoes were being burnt because of the heat of the pavement. In one period I never took my clothes off for six weeks.

"There was one outside shelter with, I suppose, fifty or sixty in the shelter. When I got to the shelter we could do nothing for them. They were literally blown to pieces. The next morning you could see pieces of them in the trees. Another time I came across nine bodies dead at a factory bench with no visual signs of injury. Blast had caused it. It had blown all their clothes off, including their socks.

"On another occasion people were walking over heads that had been blown off bodies. We brought out forty people on pieces of corrugated sheets. We used anything we could find. I remember bringing out one fellow who had lost his face down one side. His arm was gone. His leg was gone. He looked up at me and said: "Have you got a cigarette, mate? I lit it up for him and put it in his lips. He took a couple of puffs and said: 'Will you tell me landlady I shall not be home to tea.' And with that he closed his eyes, and was gone."

After the House of Commons took a direct hit, journalist Vernon Bartlett was on hand to record how Prime Minister Churchill took the news: "The bomb had fallen almost directly above the Speaker's Chair, which was crushed under a steep hill of smoking rubble. A cloud of dust still hung over the place. The stone of the doorway into the Chamber — later to be preserved and named after the Prime Minister — had been flaked and eroded in one night so that it looked as old and as weather-worn as the ruins of Ancient Rome.

"As I clambered up the hill of rubble, I was suddenly confronted by a figure clambering up from the other side. There stood Winston Churchill, his face covered with dust, through which the tears that ran down his cheeks had made two miniature riverbeds. 'I am a House of Commons man,' he used to boast; had that boast not been true, he would doubtless have surrendered to the temptation and the clamour to put a stop to Question Time, which caused him and his ministers so much extra work and worry, but which provided that safety-valve for public bewilderment or discontent, and which gave the British an advantage of morale over all the other belligerents. 'I am a House of Commons man.' And Churchill wept as he saw his beloved House in ruins."

Greed Causes Tragedy

There was great camaraderie during the Blitz, but not all was roses. Muriel Simkin worked in a munitions factory close to the Thames in Dagenham, and remembers the bosses playing a dangerous game of brinkmanship: "We had to wait until the second alarm before we were allowed to go to the shelter. The first bell was a warning they were coming. The second was when they were overhead. They did not want any time wasted.

"Sometimes the Germans would drop their bombs before the second bell went. On one occasion a bomb hit the factory before we were given permission to go to the shelter. The paint department went up. I saw several people flying through the air, and I just ran home. I was suffering from shock. I was suspended for six weeks without pay.

"They would have been saved if they had been allowed to go after the first alarm. It was a terrible job; we were risking our lives in the same way as the soldiers were."

This is London — Good Night and Good Luck

Ed Murrow was one of the great American crusading journalists of the last century. He came to Europe in 1937 and provided an eyewitness account of the rise of Hitler and the London Blitz. The accounts, broadcast on CBS, made him a household name. He began each night with: "*This* is London," and ended each broadcast with: "Good night and good luck," his twin catchphrases. His nightly reports brought home the frantic horror of the times: "For three hours after the night attack got going, I shivered in a sandbag crow's-nest atop a tall building near the Thames. It was one of the many fire-observation posts.

"There was an old gun barrel mounted above a round table marked off like a compass. A stick of incendiaries bounced off rooftops about three miles away. The observer took a sight on a point where the first one fell, then he picked up his telephone and shouted above the half gale that was blowing up there, 'Stick of incendiaries, — between 190 and 220 — about three miles away.'

"Five minutes later a German bomber came boring down the river. We could see his exhaust trail like a pale ribbon stretching straight across the sky. Half a mile downstream there were two eruptions and then a third, close together. The observer reached for his night glasses, took one quick look, picked up his telephone, and said, 'Two high explosives and one oil bomb,' and named the street where they had fallen.

"There was a small fire going off to our left. Suddenly sparks showered up from it as though someone had punched the middle of a huge camp-fire with a tree trunk. Again the gun sight swung around, the bearing was read, and the report went down the telephone lines.

"There was peace and quiet inside for twenty minutes. Then a shower of incendiaries came down far in the distance. They didn't fall in a line. It looked like flashes from an electric train on a wet night, only the engineer was drunk and driving his train in circles through the streets. One sight at the middle of the flashes and our observer reported laconically, 'Breadbasket at 90 — covers a couple of miles.' Half an hour later a string of fire bombs fell right beside the Thames. Their white glare was reflected in the black, lazy water near the banks and faded out in midstream where the moon cut a golden swathe broken only by the arches of famous bridges.

"We could see little men shovelling those fire bombs into the river. I must have seen well over a hundred fire bombs come down and only three small fires were started. The incendiaries aren't so bad if there is someone there to deal with them. As I watched those white fires flame up and die down, watched the yellow blazes grow dull and disappear, I thought; what a puny effort is this to bum a great city."

Doodlebugs to the Attack

Once the Blitz was over, London returned to the business of running a war — and a country — and training soldiers and arming them. The evacuees returned to the city, and rebuilding slowly began. The authorities had expected the Blitz to be devastating, and it was. But it had cost less than a third of the lives they had anticipated. Tens of thousands of papier-mâché coffins had been prepared in advance; and now were not needed. The war began to turn. The Americans had joined the Allied cause, and Germany was also facing battle on the eastern front. The heat came off London.

But after D-Day, the Germans were playing a desperate game. They gambled on one final attack on London. This time they had not the planes for bombing missions — and they did not control the airfields of Western Europe any more. But their researchers were working on more deadly munitions. They had invented the first guided missiles — the infamous V1s, or Doodlebugs.

These were huge, jet-powered rockets that would deliver massive bombs to targets up to 160 miles away. They were launched from the French and Dutch coasts at London, beginning on 13 June 1944. That was just a week after the D-Day landings, and a direct response to them.

Nearly ten thousand missiles rained down on London over the coming months, until all the launch sites were overrun by the Allies. The final attack on London came in October.

Bombing missions could target specific places, but the guided missiles were primitive. They were aimed at the city, and caused huge damage and loss of life. But they could not take out the docks and the riverside industry, the way the Blitz bombings had attempted.

While the damage was not specifically targeted, the Doodlebugs were a spectacular success. In three months, they destroyed almost as many houses as a year of the Blitz, with no loss of aircraft or crews. 22,000 people lost their lives. But it was the final hurrah — when the last Doodlebug landed in October 1944, the war was over for the people of London. The following decade would be devoted to the rebuild.

Britain at War Museum

For a full appreciation of what it was like to live through the war, you could visit the Britain at War Museum, 64-66 Tooley Street, near London Bridge. Check out their website www.britainatwar.co.uk for opening times.

Terrorist Attacks on the Thames

25 January 1885. The Fenians (an Irish independence movement) detonated bombs at a number of locations in central London near the Thames, including London Bridge, the House of Commons and the Tower of London.

15 February 1894. Greenwich Observatory was attacked by a French anarchist with a bomb. He blew his hand off and died thirty minutes later.

29 March 1939. The IRA took advantage of the war to strike for Irish independence. On 29 March they placed two bombs on Hammersmith Bridge.

17 June 1974. A bomb was planted by the IRA at the Houses of Parliament, causing extensive damage and injuring eleven.

30 March 1979. A car bomb at the House of Commons killed Shadow Northern Ireland Secretary Airey Neave. The bomb was planted by the Irish National Liberation Army.

10 January 1992. A small bomb exploded at Whitehall Place, but no one was injured.

28 February 1992. An explosion at London Bridge Station injured twenty-nine people.

10 April 1992. A large fertiliser bomb in a truck exploded at the Baltic Exchange, killing three people: Paul Butt (29), Thomas Casey (49), and Danielle Carter (15). It caused £800 million damage — £200 million more than the total damage costs caused by all 10,000 previous explosions in the Northern Ireland conflict. The Baltic Exchange has been replaced by 30 St Mary Axe, the most distinctive building in London. It's the giant gherkin that dominates the skyline, a symbol that the city always rises from the ashes.

16 November 1992. An IRA bomb at Canary Wharf was spotted and diffused by security services.

9 February 1996. Two people were killed and massive damage caused by a half-tonne car bomb at Canary Wharf.

1 June 2000. A bomb exploded on Hammersmith Bridge at 4.30 a.m., injuring no one.

IRA End Ceasefire with Canary Wharf Bombing
In recent years, London has become a target for Islamic fundamentalist attacks, but traditionally when there was a terror attack on the capital, the perpetrators came from

Ireland. The last major London atrocity in the conflict between Britain and Ireland was the Canary Wharf bombing in 1996, which claimed two lives and caused an estimated £100 million worth of damage.

Canary Wharf is a major business and financial district located in the West India Docks on the Isle of Dogs, Tower Hamlets. It is one of London's two main financial centres (alongside the traditional City of London), and contains many of the UK's tallest buildings. About 90,000 people work in Canary Wharf, and it is home to the world or European headquarters of many major banks, professional services firms and media organisations.

By the mid-nineties, three decades of bloodshed and conflict in Northern Ireland were coming to an end. The Provisional Irish Republican Army (IRA) and other terrorist organisations on both sides of the conflict were enjoying a prolonged ceasefire while negotiations went on.

In 1996, the IRA decided that negotiations were not going fast enough, and they ended the ceasefire. They telephoned a warning to the police that a bomb had been planted at Canary Wharf, and was due to go off at 7 p.m. It was timed to cause maximum physical damage, but to minimise injuries. Police immediately commenced an evacuation of the nearby buildings, and the road was cleared.

At one minute past seven, the bomb went off. It was a huge one, made up of half a tonne of ammonium nitrate fertiliser and sugar. The bomb was contained in a small lorry parked about 80 metres from the South Quay Station on the Dockland's Light Railway, directly under the point where the tracks cross Marsh Wall.

The police had done a good job evacuating nearby areas, but two men working in a newsagents directly opposite the explosion had not been evacuated in time, and were killed. They were Inan Bashir and John Jeffries. Thirty-nine people required hospital treatment for blast injuries and cuts caused by falling glass. Had the explosion been two hours earlier, and without a warning, the death toll would have been far higher.

The explosion left a 10 metre wide crater, 3 metres deep. Three nearby buildings (the Midland Bank building, and South Quay Plaza I and II) were severely damaged. The Midland Bank building was beyond repair and had to be demolished; the other two required complete rebuilding. The rail station was extensively damaged, but both it and the bridge under which the bomb was detonated, were reopened within weeks.

The bomb ended the IRA ceasefire, and put the Northern Ireland peace process back several steps. Eventually, James McArdle was convicted of conspiracy to cause explosions, and was sentenced to twenty-five years. He was not charged with the murder of the two men in the newsagents shop. McArdle served only a tiny portion of his sentence, as he was one of the prisoners released under the Good Friday Agreement in June 2000.

The IRA described the deaths and other injuries as "regrettable", but added that they could have been avoided if the police had responded to their warning promptly. Police Commissioner Sir Paul Condon replied: "It would be unfair to describe this as a failure of security. It was a failure of humanity."

Three weeks after the bombing, British Prime Minister John Major and Irish Taoiseach (Prime Minister) John Bruton announced that peace talks would resume, and the Canary Wharf bombing became the last major UK terrorist attack in the Northern Ireland conflict.

CHAPTER EIGHT: WEIRD TALES ON THE WATER

When you make a model airplane, there are always bits left over. It is the same when you tell the story of a river. There are stories and incidents that defy categorisation. This chapter is a bit of a lucky dip — tales of big fish, battling ambassadors and unusual entertainments. Enjoy.

A Fit Burial for a King

Families can be murder. In-fighting is particularly vicious when an inheritance is at stake, as Harold Harefoot found out.

Harold, called Harefoot because of his speed on the hunting field, inherited the throne of England by a happy accident in 1035. He was not next in line when his father, King Cnut, died. His half-brother Harthacnut was the heir, both to England and Denmark. But he was unable to travel to his coronation in England because the Danish kingdom was under threat of invasion from Norway and Sweden.

So Harold, still in his teens, stepped into the breach. He was crowned Regent in 1035 to keep the seat warm for his half-brother. But he held on to the crown, supported by his mother Aelfgifu. By all accounts, he was under her thumb and she was the real ruler.

But in 1036, Harold's half-brother Aelfred Aetheling returned from exile in Normandy. He immediately conspired against the king. So Harold had him captured and blinded. Aelfred died of his wounds. Family can be murder.

Four years later, Harold himself died in Oxford, still in his early twenties, just before Harthacnut launched an invasion against him. He was buried at Westminster Abbey, as befitted a king. But when Harthacnut took the throne, one of his first acts was to have the body of Harold dug up and dumped unceremoniously in a bog near the Thames.

The body slid into the river and began its passage towards the sea. Legend has it that some Danish fishermen got a shock when their nets snagged on the rotting corpse. The body was brought ashore and the supporters of the late king secretly reburied him at the church of St Clement Danes.

This church was one of the oldest in London, built by Danish invaders in the ninth century on the banks of the Thames between the City of London and Westminster. It has been rebuilt three times, and was almost destroyed in 1941 after being hit during the Blitz. It has been fully restored and is now the Central Church of the Royal Air Force.

If the church sounds familiar to you, it may be from the childhood nursery rhymes: "Oranges and Lemons say the bells of St Clement's".

The bells of the church still ring out that old tune on the hour.

Bloody Diversions on the Bridge

A thousand years ago, Londoners were a savage race, given to their own bloody diversions. The city regarded itself as almost a separate entity from the Crown, and Londoners were quick to defend their rights and entitlements. For this reason, they developed a hardihood and a callousness that extended to their sports.

Roman gladiators and Inca and Aztec football games involving human sacrifice aside, very few societies have the stomach for watching people die as entertainment. Medieval Europe was a glorious exception.

Public executions were a favourite treat for the lower classes. But the upper classes had their bloody pastimes too — tournaments and jousting. Knights thundered at each other on horseback, and fought to the death under the watchful eye of king and court.

The bustling City of London provided a great background for such spectacles.

One of the most infamous jousts took part across the river, with the champion of England taking on the cream of Scotland on London Bridge in 1390. It was a fight to the death, with sharpened lances; the result of a drunken encounter between Sir John Welles and Sir David De Lindesay.

Tensions were high between the two countries, but they were enjoying a temporary truce when the two men met at a banquet in Edinburgh. Sir John was the Champion of England — the finest tournament jouster in the service of Richard the Lionheart. He issued a drunken challenge to the Scottish Sir David, later First Earl of Crawford, saying: "Let words have no place. If ye know not the chivalry and valiant deeds of Englishmen, appoint me a day and a place where ye list, and ye shall have experience."

The day chosen was St George's Day (23 April), 1390, and the place was London Bridge. The challenge was a fight to the death. Most jousts were done with blunted lances, and were won when a horseman was unseated. But the fight to the death used sharpened war lances and the combatants were free to continue the battle with swords and axes on the ground.

A dais was erected on the bridge for King Richard II and his court. All the suitable positions — including top floors of the buildings that swarmed the bridge — were occupied by the nobility, while the commoners fared as best they could. Several thousand people crowded every available space on the bridge and the surrounding river banks.

Both knights abandoned traditional chainmail in favour of new suits of plate armour and visored helmets. They carried their lances and shields, and waited on their mounts for the signal. The heralds sounded their horns and both men spurred their heavy chargers into a gallop. The first clash was inconclusive. The spears were broken, but both warriors remained firmly in their saddles. Sir John had swayed under the lash of the lance, but did not fall. Sir David was like a rock.

A cry went out from the crowd that he was tied to his horse, but he quickly jumped down then remounted to kill that suspicion. Both men were given fresh lances and charged a second time. Again the lances splintered, but neither man fell. So they went at each other a third time.

This time there was no doubt. Sir David struck Sir John firmly in the chest, knocking him from the saddle. The Champion of England fell heavily to the ground. He lay there immobile for a few moments, and the crowd thought he had been killed. But then he managed to rise himself. Sir David was off his horse in an instant, sword drawn for the kill. He closed in on Sir John, but the Champion of England rose and drew his own sword. On the ground, the battle proved uneven. Quickly, the Scottish knight overpowered his English rival and knocked him to the ground again, standing over him with his dagger drawn and his foe's neck exposed for the kill.

He glanced up at the king. Richard had the power to stop the fight and offer mercy to the fallen soldier, but he just smiled and shook his head. He wasn't going to deny the crowd their fun. However, the Scottish visitor was made of more chivalrous stuff than his English hosts. He sheathed his kirk and held Sir John tenderly, until a physician came out and helped the fallen champion from the field.

The joust between Sir David and Sir John was the main event, but several knights from Scotland and England fought that day on the bridge. Many of the fights were with blunted instruments, but a number of knights lost their life under the baying howls of the blood-thirsty crowd. The vultures got their carrion.

It was an away win, with the Scottish, inspired by their leader, carrying the day. Richard II was a gracious loser, showering the northern Knights with rich gifts. He knew his London subjects had seen enough blood spilt that day to keep them happy for a while. And Sir David became a new favourite of the warlike king. Six years later, he organised the entertainment when Richard visited Perth. He chose a re-enactment of the battle of the clans; with many more brave men lost to the English craze for sport to the death.

Jousting with Boats

Jousting on the bridge was a rarity, but jousting under the bridge was a common sight in early medieval times. It was one of the popular occupations of idle young men.

A monk born in the reign of King Stephen gave us a late twelfth century account of the sport. William Stepanides, or Fitzstephen, wrote: "In the Easter holidays they play at a game resembling a navel engagement. A target is firmly fastened to the trunk of a tree which is fixed in the middle of the river, and in the prow of a boat driven along by oars and the current stands a young man who is to strike the target with his lance."

The lances were heavy oak spears, with a pummel near the end for gripping. They were heavier than a throwing spear, but a lot smaller and lighter than the later lances used by knights on horseback in full armour.

He went on: "If, in hitting it, he break his lance and keep his position unmoved, he gains his point and attains his desire, but if his lance not be shivered by the blow, he is tumbled into the river and his boat passes by, driven along by its own motion."

Throngs gathered on the bridge and the banks to watch, cheering lustily as young warriors were dunked into the cold water. The soldiers were not in full chainmail (the armour of the time), but the sport was not without its dangers. Two boats were stationed on either side of the target. These were prime positions to watch the sport, and they were crowded with eager young men. They would help pull the unlucky competitors out of the water to safety.

As Fitzstephen said: "In them (the two boats) a number of young men do take up the striker when he first emerges from the stream, or as soon as he rises again upon the wave."

Sometimes instead of jousting at a shield fixed to a tree trunk, they had a mechanical warrior fight back. This was a popular variation, on land as well as on water. A pole was placed in the river, with a shield on a swivel. Once you struck the shield it would spin around, and on the other side there was a heavy bag filled with sand that would strike you and knock you from the boat, unless you ducked. Many didn't duck in time.

This was even more dangerous than the regular version of the game because the heavy bag could wind the attacker, or concuss him. So the falls into the water were correspondingly more spectacular.

Londoners have always enjoyed such pastimes as bear-baiting, public hangings and witch burnings. The jousts under the bridge fell into that category, and the crowd often went home with their blood lust satisfied as young men disappeared under the water, sinking despite the best efforts of the rescue crews.

The Ducking Stool

During the height of the witch hunts in the mid seventeenth century, sadistic Witchfinder General Mathew Hopkins came up with a neat theory: witches rejected their baptism, so water would reject witches. This allowed him to create a foolproof test for witchcraft: throw someone in the water, and if they floated, they were convicted.

He didn't have to search hard for a way of putting his bizarre idea into practice. Ducking stools had been in use for centuries as a way of punishing aggressive or adulterous women (and occasionally men). Now they had a new use.

The ducking stool was a chair on a beam. The witch was strapped into the chair and swung over the water. She was let drop. If she floated, she was a witch and could be tried and burnt. If she sank, she was innocent. Unfortunately, she was also drowned, but Hopkins did not worry about such niceties.

Sometimes, the ducking stool was dispensed with. The woman's right thumb was tied to her left big toe, and she was thrown into the river with a rope around her waist. If she floated, she was condemned. If she drowned, she was innocent.

Actually, ducking stools long predated Hopkins, and were used as a punishment for scolds, loud and unruly women, among others.

At one point, ducking stools were quite common around the country and there were at least three prominent ones in London. The one in Kingston was used longer than any other, and was still in operation in 1745. There was also one at

Ducking Stool Court in Havering, and another at Sydenham, though that one was not on the Thames.

The witch-hunting period in English history was short, but the ducking stools were also used for punishing shrews, women who were loud, drunk or a nuisance to their neighbours. These women were strapped into the ducking stools and dunked a number of times before being released. It was more of a humiliation than an attempt to harm them. Dunking remained on the statute books in the UK as a punishment for "scolds" until 1967. But by the time it was struck off, it was already obsolete for two hundred years.

The last ducking stool to be used was the one in Kingston. The *London Evening Post* of 27 April 1745, notes: "Last week a woman that keeps the Queen's Head ale-house at Kingston was ordered by the court to be ducked in the River Thames, under Kingston Bridge, in the presence of 2,000 or 3,000 people."

The punishment was considered an amusement by bystanders. One French traveller, M. Misson, wrote in 1700: "This method of scolding women is funny enough. The scold being well fastened in her chair, and being lifted up behind, the chair, of course, drops into the cold element. The ducking is repeated according to the degree of shrewishness possessed by the patient, and generally has the effect of cooling her immoderate heat, at least for a time."

But the results were not always so benign. One account of a ducking in Ratcliff, in the East End of London, described an elderly woman being ducked. The people handling the ducking chair decided on one extra duck, and it proved too much for the frail lady, who drowned. That was also in the early eighteenth century, and was also witnessed by thousands of jeering onlookers.

One account described a typical ducking day: "Labour would be deserted. All the world would be out of doors. Men would shout; women would look timidly from doors; dogs would yelp. The recalcitrations of the peccant dame, her crescendo screamings and invectives, the final smotherment of her cries in the cold but not cooling element, must have furnished a scene for a Hogarth."

Of all the ducking stools along the Thames, the one at Kingston was the most used. In old account books, there are numerous mentions of money being paid for its repair and upkeep. In 1572, it had to be replaced entirely.

The first to try the new apparatus was the wife of the local grave digger, punished for being "a common scold and fighter". It was quaintly recorded that she was "set on a new ducking stool made of a great height, and so brought about the market place to the Thames bridge, and there had three duckings overhead and arse."

Nothing remains now of the horrific practice of dunking scolds. However, the "Wonder Wall" at Kingston Museum preserves the story for the curious.

The Battle of the Ambassadors

London knew how to do pomp and ceremony. When a foreign ambassador arrived at the Court of St James, the proper pageantry was observed. It began when the ambassador arrived in Dover. He would then proceed to Canterbury and on to Gravesend, where a Royal Barge awaited him.

The Lord Mayor and his Sheriffs were also waiting, on barges of their own, and there were barges on hand for the Ambassador's retinue. With their escort in place, they came down the river with flags flying and music playing, disembarking at Tower Stairs near the Tower of London.

There they were met by a convoy of state coaches, and paraded through the streets to Whitehall.

The pageantry was magnificent, but it didn't always go to plan. On Monday, 30 September 1661, early in the reign of Charles the Second, the Swedish Ambassador was being given the full diplomatic treatment. He arrived at the Tower Stairs to disembark from his barge.

It was the custom for other ambassadors to be on the steps to greet the new arrival. But there was a long-running dispute between France and Spain as to who would take precedence in the procession to Whitehall.

The two ambassadors were Baron de Batteville of Spain, and Comte d'Estrades, Marshal of France, and they were determined to use the arrival of the Swedish diplomat to sort out their differences. They came armed. And they brought backup. The king had heard rumblings of what was coming, but he wisely decided to keep out of it. He ordered that no Englishman should intervene.

He did, however, send a strong escort of guards and posted soldiers throughout the city. The Lord Mayor called out troops in expectation of a brawl.

It was as bad as they anticipated. The king pulled out from the wharf in his coach, with the Swedish ambassador behind him. The Spanish immediately joined the procession, but the French tried to cut in on them, supported by 150 horses and foot soldiers, armed with muskets, carbines and pistols. They opened fire on the Spanish.

One of the Spanish managed to crawl under the horses of the French ambassador's coach and hamstrung two of them, wounding a third. The three fallen horses stopped the French coach dead. The French coachman was dragged from his box, and one of the postilions was mortally wounded. He staggered into the crowd of onlookers and was caught by an Englishman, who stepped from the crowd to help him.

This Good Samaritan was immediately attacked and wounded by a Spaniard, and the crowd began throwing bricks and stones at the brawling diplomats and their entourages. Chaos reigned.

Shots were fired, swords flashed in the summer air, and before the smoke cleared, there were forty injured and a number dead. Seven men had been fatally shot on the wharf and near the Bulwark Tower, including a valet de chambre of the Spanish Ambassador, and an English plasterer who was among the bystanders.

The Spanish held the field, and the French had to retreat. The Spanish took their place in the procession, but by the time the French had reassembled, they were well back in the order. The unseemly fracas had been orchestrated on the orders of the French King Louis IV, adding to their embarrassment.

Samuel Pepys recorded the whole event in his famous diary that night: "This morning up by moon-shine, at five o'clock, to Whitehall to meet the Privy Seal, but he not being come as appointed, I went to the Red Lyon to drink my morning draft, and there I heard of a fray between the two Ambassadors of Spain and France, and this day being the day of the entrance of the Ambassador from Sweden, they intended to fight for the precedence!

"Our King ordered that no Englishman should meddle in the business, but let them do what they would.

"So I went to the Spanish Ambassador's and the French, and there saw great preparations on both sides; but the French made the most noise and vaunted most, the other made no stir almost at all; so that I was afraid the other would have had too great a conquest over them.

"Then to the Wardrobe, and dined there, and then abroad and in Cheapside hear that the Spanish had got the best of it, and killed three of the French coach-horses and several men, and is gone through the city next to our King's coach; at which it is strange to see how all the city did rejoice. And indeed we do naturally all love the Spanish, and hate the French.

"There were several men slain of the French, and one or two of the Spaniards, and one Englishman by a bullet. Which is very observable, the French were at least four to one in number, and had near 100 cases of pistols among them, and the Spaniards had not one gun among them; which is for their honour forever, and the others' disgrace."

The Winchester Geese

Graveyards can be melancholy places, reminding us of our mortality. But some graveyards carry a deeper resonance than others.

Cross Bones Cemetery, on Redcross Way in Southwark, is one of the saddest cemeteries in London. It was an unconsecrated graveyard, the last resting place of those who society scorned. It was reserved for fallen women, prostitutes and their bastard offspring. More than a third of the corpses there were under the age of one; unbaptised infants. Many of them died at the hands of their mothers.

Southwark was outside the City of London in medieval times, so became a haven for all things lawless. The Liberty (district) of the Clink was a part of Southwark that clung close to the river (near modern Bankside), and was well known as an area where the normal rules of the city did not apply. The district was exempt from the jurisdiction of the County High Sheriff, being under the jurisdiction of the Bishop of Winchester instead.

Theatres sprang up — including Shakespeare's Globe — and less salubrious entertainment was always on hand in the Clink. Bear-baiting was popular, and there were several dedicated pits on the river for the sport. Dog fights were also a draw.

But the Liberty of the Clink (The Clink was the famous gaol there) was also famous for its brothels and prostitutes. In 1161, the Bishop of Winchester was granted the power to license prostitutes and brothels in the district. It was a strange function for a bishop, but was retained by the clergy for centuries.

Because of this, the fallen women were known as Winchester Geese, giving us the term "goose bumps" for the symptoms of venereal disease. For centuries, men struck down by VD were said to have been "bitten by a Winchester goose".

Some venereal diseases, such as syphilis, were fatal in the days before antibiotics. Sufferers tended to go mad before dying, making the disease even more terrifying.

Many of the Winchester Geese ended up in the unconsecrated Cross Bones cemetery. By the turn of the fifteenth century, it was already well established as the final resting place of "single women", a euphemism for prostitutes. The church controlled the prostitution, but didn't want the women sharing their eternal rest with the faithful.

Why did the church agree to regulate the brothels? It seems a strange occupation for men of the cloth. One possible explanation is that they recognised that single men, driven by their hormones, wanted women. To protect the virtuous women, they regulated the unvirtuous.

The unconsecrated graveyard operated for four centuries, until it was closed in 1853 because it was "completely overcharged with dead".

The tragic women have not been forgotten. Every year at Halloween, there is a commemorative procession to the graveyard, with candles and songs. A local committee is campaigning to have the cemetery turned into a permanent memorial garden. And the gates in Redcross Way are permanently decorated by an ever-changing array of messages, ribbons, flowers and other tokens.

The Winchester Geese may have flown, but they have not been forgotten.

Digging up the Geese

An archaeological dig in the 1990s, in connection with an expansion of the Jubilee Underground Line, unearthed the full horror of the Winchester Geese. The Cross Bones cemetery was found to contain bodies piled on top of each other in chaotic heaps. The women had died from smallpox, TB, Paget's Disease, osteoarthritis and vitamin D deficiency. A dig in 1992 concentrated on the Victorian portion of the cemetery. Of the 148 bodies unearthed, a third were perinatal (between twenty-two weeks of pregnancy and one week of birth). This indicated a huge infant mortality rate, or a high instance of infanticide.

A further 11% were under a year old. The adults were mainly women, and mainly from their thirties onwards. There were roughly 80,000 prostitutes in London in the 1830s. By one estimate, one in ten died each year from the diseases they picked up and the grinding poverty they endured.

Frost Fairs

In "The Pickwick Papers", Charles Dickens has a delightful description of revellers on the ice at mid-winter. Despite our temperate climate, we still have the romantic notion of the

White Christmas, and skating on frozen ponds and rivers. But rivers in Britain rarely freeze. It takes extreme weather conditions to ice over a fast-flowing body of water. Lakes freeze occasionally, but rarely hard enough to cross safely. So it is a bit of a surprise that Frost Fairs were common for several hundred years in London. The Thames froze solidly enough to allow markets on the ice.

There are two reasons why the Frost Fairs happened — and why they do not happen anymore. The first is that Europe went through a mini-ice age between the sixteenth and nineteenth centuries. It was not a proper ice age, but glaciation in northern Europe increased, and winters were longer and harder than usual. The second reason is London Bridge.

The medieval London Bridge had nineteen arches and wide pillars supporting them. It was as much a dam as a bridge, and slowed the flow of the Thames considerably, creating a reservoir of sluggish water upstream. This sluggish water froze during hard winters, creating the conditions for the Frost Fairs. The new London Bridge, with its three wide arches, does not obstruct the flow of the river. And the construction of the Embankment in the nineteenth century also changed the flow of the river, ensuring there would be no more Frost Fairs. In earlier times, the Thames was broad and shallow; now it is narrower, deeper and flows swifter.

The first recording of the river freezing over is from the Roman period. In AD 250 the river froze solid for nine weeks. Such occasional frosts continued for the next thousand years. For instance, in 923, the river was iced enough to take wheeled traffic. For thirteen weeks, traders were able to cross the ice from north to south bank with their carts of goods. The freeze lasted for fourteen weeks in 1410, helped by the presence of the bridge.

Occasionally, the ice caused problems; chunks would break off, slam into the bridge, and block it further. Boats were also stove in by sheets of ice, and people were occasionally trapped when the ice broke. But people did not see the danger so much as the excitement. Frost was fun. Even the Monarchy agreed. In the winter of 1536, by now on wife number three, Henry VIII travelled from central London to Greenwich by sleigh along the river. He was accompanied by Jane Seymour, the only one of his six wives he truly loved.

Queen Elizabeth I also took to the ice in 1564. She developed a fondness for shooting at targets and was an accomplished archer. The exercise kept her warm on the cold winter days, and she went onto the river several times that winter. So did most of London, and football games between rival tribes of boys became common.

But it could not end well; the thaw came during the night of 31 January. It took five days for the river to become completely ice-free, and the thaw caused great floods and high tides. Bridges were damaged and houses plunged into the river. Many people were drowned in the chaos.

It did not deter people. The first proper Frost Fair was held in the winter of 1608.

Years the Thames Froze
From the thirteenth to the nineteenth century, there were twenty-three winters in which the Thames froze solidly, allowing people to cross easily from one side to another. That averaged one year in twenty. There were two further years in which the river froze almost completely.

These are the fully frozen years: 1408, 1435, 1506, 1514, 1537, 1565, 1608, 1621, 1635, 1649, 1655, 1663, 1666, 1677,

1684, 1695, 1709, 1716, 1740, 1776, 1788, 1795 and 1814. The river was partially frozen in 1768 and 1785.

The river froze ten times in the seventeenth century, as opposed to only twice in the fifteenth century, which illustrates the effect of the Little Ice Age. There have been no more big freezes since 1814.

Fun on the Ice, 1683/84

A contemporary account of a seventeenth century Frost Fair can be found in the diary of John Evelyn. The writer and horticulturist kept a diary for a number of decades, which throws light on life in London through those turbulent times. His description of the celebrated freeze of 1683/84 makes it all sound so jolly: "Coaches piled from Westminster to the Temple, and from several other stairs to and fro, as in the streets; sleds, sliding with skates, a bull-baiting, horse and coach races, puppet plays and interludes, cooks, tippling (drinking), and other lewd places, so that it seemed to be a bacchanalian triumph, or carnival on the water."

Vendors sold food, drink and souvenirs. But Evelyn, a committed environmentalist centuries before it was fashionable, saw the dark side: "The fowls, fish and birds, and all our exotic plants and greens universally perishing. Many parks of deer were destroyed, and all sorts of fuel so dear that there were great contributions to keep the poor alive. London, by reason for the excessive coldness of the air hindering the ascent of the smoke, was so filled with the fuliginous steam of the sea coal that one could hardly breathe."

Smog arrived before the industrial revolution!

A French writer noted: "Besides hackney-coaches, a large sledge, or sledges, were then exhibited on the frozen Thames, and King Charles passed a whole night upon the ice."

An English eyewitness wrote, in "The Beauties of England and Wales, Volume X": "On December 20, 1688, a very violent frost began, which lasted to February 6, in so great an extremity that the pools were frozen 18 inches thick (45 cm) at least, and the Thames was so frozen that a great street from the Temple to Southwark was built with shops, and all manner of things sold. There was also bull-baiting, and a great many shows and tricks to be seen."

But the fun and games came to an abrupt end on 6 February, as the same writer recorded: "In the morning I saw a coach and six horses driven from Whitehall almost to London Bridge, yet by three o'clock that day next to Southwark the ice was gone, and the next day all the frost was gone."

Many traders had set out their stalls that day, but had to remove them in a hurry. As the ice broke, people scrambled for the shore. Less nimble, several of the animals were lost, and many merchants saw their stock disappear into the inky waters.

As the ice broke rapidly up, large chunks of it began flowing swiftly downstream towards London Bridge. Several large chunks, weighing several stone, smashed against the piers of the bridge, destroying wooden structures under the arches, and also crushing small boats moored nearby.

It is not known how many lost their lives when the ice broke, as the poor, in those days, went unrecorded.

Public House Sinks
The rapid thaws that characterised the end of the Frost Fairs were very dangerous, and often led to loss of life and property. This happened in 1789, when the thaw came in January. The frost had set in on 25 November, and after seven weeks, people had got used to the ice. The breakup caught them by

surprise. Several boats had been trapped by the ice, moored to jetties and quays. One of the boats was anchored to the main beams of a riverside tavern at Rotherhithe. It had been firmly wedged by the ice for weeks.

But when the thaw sets in, the ice does not melt, it breaks up. Large sheets of it flow down river, being battered and crumbled. The breakup can be swift and dramatic. That evening, the ice began to break and people began to scramble to safety. Large cracks appeared, which had to be leapt over. Several of the boats that were trapped were suddenly free, but still tethered to their moorings.

But a boat at Rotherhithe was trapped in a large sheet of ice that broke off and began to move downstream. The boat was moored to the back wall of the tavern, and when it began to move, the weight of the ice and the boat was too much; the wooden structure of the tavern collapsed. Five people who were asleep in their beds were crushed to death.

Coldest Winter Leads to Tragedy

Europe's coldest winter in 500 years came in 1709, the peak of the Little Ice Age. Harsh conditions caused starvation throughout the continent; in France, an estimated 500,000 people died of starvation later in the year. There was a big impact in Britain too; the ground was too hard for agriculture, and food shortages followed in the summer.

Not just the river froze. Huge chunks of the North Sea turned to ice, making shipping difficult.

But Londoners lived in the now, and they used the freeze as an excuse for the biggest ever Frost Fair. A newspaper account reads: "The Thames seems now a solid rock of ice; and booths for sale of brandy, wine, ale, and other exhilarating liquors, have been for some time fixed thereon; but not it is in a manner like a town; thousands of people cross it, and with wonder view the mountainous heaps of water that now lie congealed into ice."

This Frost Fair featured a most tragic event, recorded in the archives of the Old Bailey courthouse. The poor suffered horribly in the cold weather, with food scarce and the prospect of dying of hypothermia a very real one. Their plight was in sharp contrast to the idle rich who could frolic on the ice then return to their opulent homes, their hot dinners and their roaring fires. Some desperate people were pushed by the conditions to extremes of despair.

On 9 January, a young mother, Elizabeth Cole, went out onto the frozen Thames with her three-year-old daughter. When she returned, she told shocked neighbours that she had put the child "under the ice and sent it to heaven."

She was tried for murder, but the jury showed compassion, unusual in those days. They took consideration of the fact that Ms Cole was suffering from "a great trouble of the mind" — perhaps what we would recognise today as persistent postnatal depression. She was acquitted.

Hurricane

Ice was not the only thing that made the winters of the past a hazard on the river. On 26 November 1703, London was struck by a hurricane. The storm force winds were funnelled by the Thames Valley, and thundered along the river, wreaking terrible damage.

Between London Bridge and Limehouse, almost every ship was torn from its moorings and tossed onto the shore, or broken in the current. Only four ships survived the night still moored and relatively undamaged. Over four hundred wherries, the small water taxies that were so important a part of the transport infrastructure, went to the bottom that night. More than sixty barges were dashed against the arches of London Bridge, while as many more were sunk or staved upriver of the bridge.

The loss of life was considerable.

Wind was not the only danger. On 1 January 1730, there was such a dense fog on the river that navigation became next to impossible. There were a huge number of collisions that day, and several deaths as a result.

In February 1791, there was an extraordinary high tide and all the low-lying districts on the Surrey (or southern) side of the river were flooded. Bankside and Tooley Street were submerged, and on the city side, Queenhithe, Thames Street and Wapping High Street disappeared under the water. The Palace Yard was flooded to 2 feet, and several people were drowned.

The Great Frost

The winter of 1739-40 was one of the most severe on record, with frost lasting from Christmas Day to mid-February. The usual Frost Fair was held, but the conditions caused great distress in the city. Watermen could not ply their trade, and other trades ran out of materials. Carpenters, bricklayers and labourers could be seen walking the streets begging.

A few days into the big freeze, a gale struck the city. Storm winds raged all day and night, dragging vessels from their moorings and flinging them against one another. Large sheets of ice broke loose and were dashed against smaller boats, breaking them up. Many sunk, taking their cargoes of coal and corn to the bottom of the river. Many a sailor also lost his life in the tumult.

The following day, the Frost Fair went ahead, the carnival atmosphere in sharp contrast to the misery suffered by those who made their living on the water.

Ice Floes on the River

Two hard winters followed each other in quick succession in the mid-eighteenth century. There were severe frosts in 1767 and 1768. Navigation on the river came to a standstill as ice turned water into land. But the ice never became fully solid from shore to shore. There were no Frost Fairs those years. However, the broken ice proved, in some ways, far more dangerous than the full ice cover of previous years.

The ice formed into floes and big blocks, uneven slabs as solid and as heavy as concrete. Some of the slabs were enormous, weighing several tonnes. They crashed into the bridges and also crushed the hulls of river vessels. Many were sunk or driven on shore, and a number of lives were lost in the carnage, both winters.

Elephants on the Ice

The last Frost Fair was held in the winter of 1814. Europe was emerging from the Little Ice Age, and London Bridge would soon be rebuilt, removing the tiny arches and speeding up the river. An era was coming to an end.

The river partially froze in January, and then a thaw set in. Huge fragments of ice were carried down the river on the ebb tide, smashing into London Bridge with great force and a noise like an artillery discharge. As the tide changed, the chunks were forced back again, but they became blocked under the arches, stopping navigation.

The area around the bridge became a jumble of jagged ice floes. Then the frost came back, temperatures dropped and the sluggish river water froze over. By 1 February, the Thames between Blackfriars and London Bridge was full of people moving across the broken ice in great numbers. The canny traders of the city decided it was time for another Frost Fair.

But society was changing. The staid Georgians had a less cavalier attitude towards death and danger than their forebears, and many people had a reluctance to trust their weight on the ice. Traders were desperate for the Fair to be a commercial success, and they needed to convince the public that it was safe to walk out on the Thames. Someone came up with a wonderful idea.

A full-grown adult Indian elephant was procured, and a solemn procession was made. The elephant stepped onto the ice close to Blackfriars Bridge, and slowly and sedately promenaded across to the other side. Seeing he came to no harm, the public followed. Swing boats and amusements were set up on the river; and the usual mix of games, amusements, shows, food and souvenirs gave people plenty to occupy themselves.

Whole sheep were barbecued on the ice, and people queued to sample the "Lapland mutton".

The Fair lasted only a few days. The ice was never as thick or even as in previous winters, and was unsuitable for a proper fair. Near Blackfriars — where the elephant had walked — it was quite thin and dangerous. High tides on 7 February suddenly broke up the ice. Many people were on the river at 4 p.m. when the breakup began. The ice gave way suddenly and swept through the arches of Blackfriars Bridge, carrying many boats and forty barges. They all came a cropper against the new Strand Bridge.

Many foolhardy people had remained on the ice to the last minute, and suddenly found themselves on floating icebergs.

Some managed to scramble into two derelict barges. One passed through the bridge safely, but the other became trapped under the arches, and ropes were thrown down to rescue the occupants.

But several people did not make the barges and were lost when the breakup of the ice threw them into the river. Death was a swift release: at those temperatures, even with a lifejacket (which no one had), hypothermia would have caused unconsciousness within a few minutes.

It was a sad conclusion to the last of the Winter Wonderlands on the Thames.

Frost Fairs Today

There will never be another true Frost Fair; changes in the topography of the river and global warming have guaranteed that. The river still freezes occasionally upriver — in 1947, it froze at Windsor so hard that cyclists were able to cross from one side to another. And in London, the banks can freeze, allowing brave people to walk out until the creaking of the thin ice drives them back to shore.

But the days of yore are commemorated every year on Bankside, between London Bridge and Southwark Bridge. It began with a one-day Frost Fair on 23 December 2003. It proved so successful that it has become an annual event, and now stretches over a week and two weekends. The Bankside Winter Festival is modelled on the popular Christmas festivals of Germany and central Europe, and features a market as well as entertainment.

In addition to the Christmas Fair, the Frost Fairs are commemorated by a series of grey slate engravings hanging in the pedestrian tunnel under the south bank of Southwark Bridge. The engravings are by local sculptor Richard

Kindersley, and depict the fairs, as well as the following lines of verse:

Behold the Liquid Thames frozen o're,
That lately Ships of mighty Burthen bore.
The watermen for want of Rowing Boats
Make use of Booths to get their Pence & Groats.
Here you may see beef roasted on the spit
And for your money you may taste a bit.
There you may print your name, tho cannot write,
Cause num'd with cold: tis done with great delight.
And lay it by that ages yet to come
May see what things upon the ice were done.

Shark Attack

On New Year's Day, 1787, fishermen from the East End hamlet of Poplar had a strange catch. Used to small river fish, they knew they had a big one on the line. It was putting up a hell of a fight.

But when they finally hauled it into their boat, they were shocked to find their catch was a large shark. The animal was still alive, but sickly. A few clubs on the head soon sorted that out. When it was taken ashore, the shark was cut open. The fishermen got the second shock of the day. The stomach contents included a silver watch, a metal chain and a cornelian seal, with some fragments of gold lace. They obviously belonged to someone who had fallen overboard on a sea journey. The rest of the body had been digested. The fishermen wondered if the shark had been sickly as a result of the watch and chain in its stomach, but just as likely the pollution in the Thames would have accounted for it.

The watch had an inscription. It bore the name Henry Warson, London, and a number, 1369. It was not in good working order, no surprise considering where it had been found. But the fishermen reported the details of their find.

Henry Warson came forward and revealed that he had sold the watch to a Mr Ephraim Thompson of Whitechapel. Mr Thompson had given the watch to his son as a present as he was embarking on his first ocean voyage. He was on the *Polly*, a ship under the command of Captain Vane.

When the captain was contacted, the full story came out. The ship had been nine miles off Falmouth when a squall hit it. The ship had heeled under the weather and bucked, and young Thompson had been flung overboard. He was never seen again.

The grief-stricken father bought the shark from the fishermen. As the Annual Register of 1787 recorded, he bought the shark "not for the sake of having it buried in consecrated ground, but to preserve it as a memorial of so singular an event."

It was described as the largest shark anyone could remember ever taking in the Thames, measuring 9 foot 3 inches. Its jaws were 17 inches across, and it had five rows of razor-like teeth.

Gonzo the Goner Whale

Whale watching is not one of the big tourist draws of London, but on Friday, 20 January 2006, the capital was consumed with nothing else. Everyone was talking whales.

The reason was simple; a juvenile female Northern bottlenose whale was seen swimming through central London. She might have been a juvenile, but she was not small. The aquatic mammal was 5 metres (16 feet) long, and weighed about seven tonnes. Full grown, they are double that size.

She was also way off course; her normal habitat would have been off the northern coast of Scotland or Ireland, and in the seas around the Arctic Ocean. It was the first time the species had ever been recorded on the Thames.

The initial sighting was made from the Thames Barrier the previous evening. The control team reported to the British Divers Marine Life Rescue that one, or possibly two, pilot whales had slipped through the barrier. It turned out to be one bottlenose.

A shocked commuter on a train phoned the authorities at 8.30 a.m., saying he believed he was hallucinating; he had just spotted a whale swimming in the river. More reports followed, then the whale was filmed by a TV crew, and the whole city was on the alert.

The whale was confused by the shipping and the narrow channel. She swam as far as Albert Bridge, then tried to swim back the opposite way. She beached several times as the tide went out, and members of the public gathered on the foreshore to encourage the whale back into deeper water. The problem was that there was no deeper water. The river depth was only 5 metres, while the bottlenose typically dives to 700 metres. People could see the animal was bleeding and suffering.

That evening, there were reports that she was trying to go with the current back out of the Thames. She was spotted near Greenwich, but later that night she was back in Battersea after the tide had changed.

The following morning, it was decided to help the whale out, as she was not strong enough to escape the river on her own. Now she was trapped near Albert Bridge. The British Divers Marine Life Rescue decided to deliberately beach her, which they did with the help of the Port of London Authority and the River Police. By midday, the whale was captured and her eyes covered to prevent her from panicking.

Two hours later, she was slowly eased onto a barge by a crane near the bridge. Thousands of people lined the banks of the river for the rescue, which was watched by a television audience of millions across the world.

As the barge rushed down the river towards the sea, news channels provided non-stop coverage of the race against time. There were serious concerns about the health of the young whale. The barge reached the Thames Barrier at around 5 p.m. Despite the falling dusk, huge crowds lines the Queen Elizabeth II Bridge to catch a glimpse of the rescue operation.

It was not going well. The whale had been out of the water for some hours, and she was being slowly crushed by her body weight. Due to the lack of suitable transport, plans to release the whale into the Atlantic were shelved. Instead, she was to be released off the Kent coast near Margate, at Shivering Sands.

But at 7.08 p.m. the whale, already breathing heavily, suffered convulsions and died. The post-mortem revealed she had died from complications of dehydration, including kidney failure. She also had several cuts and scars from collisions with boats in the river.

No one knows exactly why the Thames whale ended up in the city, but the most likely explanation is that she simply took a wrong turn, swinging west up the estuary rather than crossing it in a northerly direction on her way back to her usual feeding grounds in the North Atlantic.

The skeleton of the whale was salvaged and donated to the Natural History Museum. It is still on display there at the museum on Exhibition Road, South Kensington, London.

Naming the Whale

The media love nothing more than a lovable animal story, and they were quick to jump on the attempts to rescue the bottlenose whale. Each paper came up with its own colourful nickname to try and humanise the story. Many chose male names, as it was not obvious until after the post-mortem that the whale was female.

The *Evening Standard*, the local London paper, went for "Pete the Pilot", as the whale was initially reported to be a pilot whale. Pete refers to the pop star Pete Burns.

The Times went for a couple of different names. Not sure of the sex, they began with "The Prince/Princess of Whales". Later a columnist went for "Wilma the Whale".

"Wally" was the choice of the *Sun*, while the *Daily Mail* went for "Willy". The *Daily Mirror* stayed close to its fellow tabloids, with "Whaley".

But the most imaginative name was probably "Gonzo". The bottlenose has a very distinctive nose — as does *The Muppet Show* character Gonzo. The Lewis Whale Watch Group, which published regular online updates of the rescue attempt, christened the whale "Gonzo", in the mistaken belief it was a male.

Other Whales in the Estuary

The initial alert about the Thames whale came from the controllers of the Thames Barrier, who thought two whales had passed through. During the rescue operation, there were unconfirmed sightings of a second whale near the barrier at Southend-on-Sea. Whale song was also reported around the estuary.

But the mystery was solved when the body of a porpoise was discovered upstream at Putney the same day. Another harbour porpoise (a small animal related to the whale, but about the size and weight of an average human) was also spotted in the Thames in the few days leading up to the stranding of the bottlenose whale. This porpoise was spotted at Chiswick and Kew, and it too died in the water.

Humpback Dies in River

Three years after the death of the Thames whale, another whale washed into the river. But this one was not spotted alive.

The carcass of a whale was seen in the estuary on Thursday, 10 September 2009, and initially thought to be a minke whale. But when it washed up near The Queen Elizabeth II Bridge at Dartford two days later, it was seen to be a juvenile of the much larger humpback species.

The carcass was 28-foot long, making it almost twice the size of the famous Thames whale. It was the first humpback ever sighted on the Thames.

A post-mortem showed the two-year-old whale died of starvation. There is an average of one stranding every two years in the UK, but none so far into an estuary.

Whales in Less Compassionate Times

Earlier eras were more cruel and pragmatic when it came to stranded animals, and a whale that wandered into the river a few hundred years ago would not have evoked the sympathy that Gonzo did.

This was demonstrated on 3 June 1658, when a Greenland (or bowhead) whale was spotted near Greenwich. It was alive and well and attracted a big crowd. Second in size only to the blue whale, they are monsters of the deep.

According to John Evelyn, in his famous diary: "A large whale was taken betwixt my land butting on the Thames and Greenwich, which drew an infinite concourse to see it, from London and all parts. It appeared first below Greenwich at low water, for at high water he would have destroyed all the boats."

No attempt was made to rescue the whale. It was a different era.

"After a long conflict it was killed with a harping iron struck in the head, out of which spouted blood and water by two tunnels, and after a horrid groan, it ran quite on shore and died," said the witness.

The whale was a monster; his mouth was so big, a number of men could stand upright in it — though his throat was so narrow, he could only swallow the smallest of fish.

Strange Creatures on the River

Over the centuries, several strange creatures — not limited to whales and sharks — have washed up, dead or alive, in the Thames in central London. In 1891, in his twice-yearly magazine *The Kentish Notebook*, George Howell listed some of the more interesting.

In 1457, several whales came up the river. Two were caught off Erith, in the borough of Bexley, along with an exotic swordfish. These tropical fish grow to 10 feet, and weigh up to half a tonne.

In July 1642 a "terrible monster" was caught by fishermen near Woolwich, and afterwards exhibited at Westminster. "The Monster is like a toad, and may be called a Toad-Fish, but that which makes it a monster is that it hath hands with fingers like a man, being near five-foot long, and three feet over, the thickness of an ordinary man," according to a contemporary account. What it was remains a mystery.

Following a massive storm on 26 March 1699, a 56-foot long whale came up the river. It is not recorded what became of the beast.

A small whale came right up the river on 25 July 1746. It sunk three boats and was eventually killed near Execution Dock, at Wapping. The whale measured 5.5 metres (18 feet).

Just sixteen years later, in February 1762, a whale was caught in the Hope, a tributary of the Thames, and was chased by a number of boats. It was eventually killed and landed at Greenland Dock, Rotherhithe. It was 16 metres (54 feet) long and 4.5 metres (14 feet) wide. An estimated 50,000 people came to the dock that Sunday to inspect the animal.

In November 1842, a 5 metre (15 foot) whale weighing 2 tonnes was caught off Deptford Pier. The skeleton was taken to the British Museum.

CHAPTER NINE: PROTECTING THE CITY

A city puts a veneer of civilisation on a river, but we can never forget that the Thames is a force of nature. Under the wrong circumstances, it can rise up and overwhelm the city. The river brings pollutants and diseases with it. It brings floodwaters, fogs and dangerous ice. The Thames has been responsible for cholera epidemics, drownings, terrible stinks and smothering smogs. Thousands have died.

We think of environmental protection as a new thing, but the first measures to reduce pollution in London were introduced by Edward I in 1306. There are three main environmental problems London has to protect itself from: smog, river pollution and floods. All are caused or worsened by the river. Various clean air acts have reduced smog; Bazalgette's sewerage system vastly reduced pollution and eliminated cholera; and the Thames Barrier has minimised the risk of floods. The river is also policed to help reduce the amount of suicides.

A History of Smog

London had smog long before the industrial revolution. The Thames was the problem: thick fogs were common along the river, and those fogs trapped any foulness in the air. The first attempt to control air pollution, and eliminate smog, occurred as early as 1306. Edward I banned the burning of coal within the city in an effort to combat the noxious clouds of coal smoke that settled over everything. His ban also had a secondary purpose: to help eliminate the fires that plagued the city.

In both, he was unsuccessful. The ban was not enforced effectively, and London was one of the first cities in the world to suffer a serious air pollution problem. People just got used to it and got on with life. But the pollution could be lethal. In 1880, a toxic cloud of coal smoke choked, smothered and killed 2,200 Londoners.

This was the worst outbreak until the Big Smoke of 1952 finally forced the city to act.

The Big Smoke Kills 12,000

London is famous for its fogs. We cannot think of Sherlock Holmes without thinking of the notorious pea-soupers that defined his city. Fog is technically a low-lying stratus cloud that reduces visibility to below a kilometre. Fog forms in valleys and moist places, and the foggiest part of London is along the river. The moisture of the Thames soaks the air, creating a miasma of water droplets.

But when the fog mixes with air pollution, you get a deadly mix. Smog is a phenomenon of the industrial world, and has claimed thousands of lives along the river. The worst outbreak occurred in December 1952. No one realised what was happening at first — there were no bodies on the streets to alert authorities. Then undertakers began running out of coffins, and florists ran out of flowers. Slowly the city took notice.

"Only later was it realised that the number of deaths per day during the smog was three or four times normal," remembered medical researcher Robert Waller, who worked in St Bartholomew's Hospital. "Nothing like this had ever happened before."

The smog descended like a pall on the city on 5 December, and did not lift for four days. During that time, it claimed

4,000 lives. Another 8,000 people died in the aftermath. It all began with a cold spell, and an anticyclone settling on the city. Windless conditions allowed the normal river fogs to trap airborne pollutants into a deadly grey haze. The pollution came from a number of sources, but the worst offenders were the coal power stations along the river, at Battersea, Bankside and Kingston-on-Thames. Domestic coal fires and emissions from the recently diesel powered buses (which had replaced electric trams) also contributed.

A temperature inversion trapped the cold, dirty air under a lid of warmer air. By Friday, 5 December, the air was yellow-black and had an acrid, sooty smell that was very unpleasant. Visibility was down to a few yards. Public transport ground to a halt, and the ambulance service closed down. No vehicles could move. The smog even seeped indoors, forcing cinemas and theatres to close — the screens could not be seen!

Even walking outdoors became a problem, a delicate matter of shuffling feet to feel for kerbs, walls and lampposts. At night, it was even worse. But Londoners did not panic. They were used to fog and smog. Then the realisation slowly dawned that the Great Smog, or Big Smoke, had seen 4,000 people more than normal pass away. It was raised in Parliament in February 1953, with Lieutenant-Colonel Lipton suggesting to the House of Commons that the smog had caused 6,000 deaths, and that 25,000 people had claimed sickness benefits during the period.

At its height, people were dying faster than in the cholera epidemic a century earlier.

Most of the deaths were caused by respiratory tract infections and as a result of obstruction of the air passages by pus arising from lung infections. Recent research suggests that the number of fatalities was considerably understated, and the true figure was probably nearer 12,000.

The Big Smoke had such a huge public health impact that the government were forced to take action. In 1956, the Clean Air Act made the burning of coal in domestic fires illegal throughout the city. Only smokeless fuels could be used. Another Act followed in 1968, with the intention of reducing airborne pollutants, and making the famous pea-soupers a thing of the past.

The measures have been largely successful. London is a cleaner place than it was half a century ago. But the problem of smog has not been completely eliminated. Between 12 and 15 December 1991, thick smog descended along the Thames and claimed 160 lives.

An Open Sewer

The Thames is not the world's longest open sewer. That honour goes to the Ganges. But the Thames for a long time could well have been the dirtiest. The river, before recent environmental work, was a fetid, foul morass of dark inky water, carrying filth and disease to the heart of the city. It has always been thus.

Towns were built on rivers because they provided transport and water, two essential commodities. But try drinking from the Thames, and the only place you will be transported to will be the hospital.

People have been complaining about the filth not for decades or generations, but for centuries. Excavations at Cannon Street have shown that the Romans, 1,500 years ago, were pouring raw sewage directly into the river. This practice continued until 1856. That's a hell of a lot of effluent. Couple that with all the waste poured into the river upstream — from

Cricklade through Oxford, Reading, Windsor and on to the city — and the extent of the problem becomes clear.

Some of the waste flowed out to the North Sea, but much of it sank to the bed of the river, mingling with the silt and the clay. It festered for a millennium or more. Workers on the Thames Tunnel complained of the stench when they were digging under the riverbed. It caused their eyes to water, and in many cases led to blindness, temporary and permanent. More than one worker succumbed to the foul vapours.

The problem has been commented on for centuries. King Edward III, in 1357, remarked: "Dung and other filth had accumulated in divers places upon the banks of the river with fumes and other abominable stenches arising therefrom."

At the time when London Bridge was covered in houses and shops, there was a public toilet hanging over the parapet, showering waste on the waters below. Dominican Friars near Ludgate complained that the emanations from the river were causing illness and death among their congregation.

One writer noted in 1481: "At every ebb of the water there remain the entrails of beasts and other filth and carrion of great substance and quantity."

Dunghill became a common place name, with examples at Wapping, Puddle Dock, Whitefriars and Queenhithe, among others. And where was the dung flung? Into the river. Authorities built a public convenience with accommodation for sixty-four at Friar Lane, near Blackfriars Bridge. Human waste was washed away by the tides.

In 1535, Parliament decided to act, passing a law prohibiting the dumping of dung into the river since: "Till now of late divers evil disposed persons have habitually cast in dung and filth."

It didn't make much difference, as sewage was still flowing in by the thousands of gallons a day. Then, as the industrial age dawned, the effluent from the new factories — dangerous chemicals and poisons — flowed into the mix.

Scottish poet and novelist Tobias Smollett wrote in the year of his death (1771): "If I would drink water, I must swallow that which comes from the River Thames, impregnated with all the filth of London and Westminster. Human excrement is the least offensive part, which is composed of all the drugs, minerals and poisons, used in mechanics and manufacture, enriched with the putrefying carcases of beasts and men; and mixed with all the souring of all the washtubs, kennels and common sewers, within the bills of mortality." (The Expedition of Humphry Clinker, 1771)

This was a work of fiction, but the sentiments rang true to Londoners. As the population grew to three million, and the city became the centre of the world's greatest empire, the problem grew to monstrous proportions. Clothes washed in the water bore the smell for days, and London became known for its odours as much as for its wide fashionable boulevards. People who fell into the river and were rescued often succumbed to the effects of the pollution within weeks of their rescue.

Then, in 1815, legislation allowed sewage from households to be piped directly into the Thames. It was like pouring petrol on a burning building. Drinking water became infected, and cholera broke out in the city. Thousands died.

The city also had over 200,000 cesspits, many overflowing because it cost to empty them. The air was as foul as the water.

Things came to a head with the Great Stink of 1858, which shut Parliament, killed scores, and brought the city to a standstill. London finally accepted the inevitable and built a sewerage system, with modern sewage treatment plants. The river has not been won back from the pollutants, but the water today is purer than it has been for centuries.

The Great Stink

The Palace of Westminster is an iconic symbol of England. The magnificent building, constructed on the site of an earlier palace after the fire of 1834, is home to the House of Lords and the House of Commons, the twin institutions at the heart of British democracy. Its gothic exterior mirrors the dignity at the heart of the empire, but in the 1850s it was far from dignified inside.

Parliament sat by the Thames, and during the damp days of winter, the smell of the river permeated every corner of the building. In the warm days of the summer, the smell grew even worse. The drapes hanging on the windows were soaked with chlorine, but did little to combat the problem. Working conditions were slipping from appalling to intolerable.

Benjamin Disraeli, Chancellor of the Exchequer (later Prime Minister), was seen rushing from a meeting "with a mass of papers in one hand and with his pocket handkerchief clutched in the other, and applied closely to his nose, with body half bent, hastened in dismay from the pestilential odour".

He wrote himself that the river had become a "Stygian pool reeking with ineffable and unbearable horror."

Then came the Great Stink.

Many factors contributed, not least a thousand years of sewage, growing every year, being dumped into the river. The invention of the flush toilet did not help. Now a bigger volume than ever of water and waste was flowing untreated into the cesspits. These overflowed into the street drains, which also carried the outfalls from factories and slaughterhouses direct to the Thames.

A heatwave struck in the summer of 1858. The Thames and its many tributaries were overflowing with sewage. Bacteria thrived, releasing noxious gases such as methane and hydrogen sulphide (with its characteristic rotten eggs smell). That mingled with the normal smell of excrement and the smoke from houses and factories, creating a lethal miasma.

The Houses of Parliament, right on the river, were badly hit. Business was severely disrupted. There were attempts made to douse the drapes with chlorine to mask the smell, and candles and incense burned. But it made no difference. It became impossible to conduct business. There was serious consideration given to moving the entire parliament to Hampton Court. Other proposals included closing down the law courts and using them for parliamentary business.

But towards the end of the summer, the weather broke and heavy rain moved in from the west. The increased flow of the river brought some of the filth out to the estuary and the air became breathable again.

The Great Stink was over, and Londoners were able to walks the streets again without scented hankies. But it was a wake-up call; the city began to invest in the infrastructure to clean up the river and provide a proper sewerage system. The Great Stink was never repeated.

Cholera

Cholera was one of the many gifts the cruel Thames gave to the people of London. There were four outbreaks of the disease between 1831 and 1854, killing tens of thousands.

Cholera is a bacteriological disease of the lower intestine carried by poor water. The Thames is a natural breeding ground for the infection. However, for centuries, this was not known. It was believed that the disease was an airborne miasma. It caused severe vomiting and diarrhoea, often leading to dehydration and painful death. One in fifteen typically succumbed.

London got hit a number of times during the nineteenth century with cholera epidemics, wiping out thousands. Unknown to the doctors, it was the dirty river water that was causing the problem.

There were four major epidemics that struck the capital in the 1800s. The first hit in late 1831, and lasted into the following year. As its cause was not understood (and as a laissez-faire attitude prevailed in Government to such natural disasters as pestilence and famine), nothing was done to contain the disease. Thousands died. Two more epidemics followed, and the disease thrived in the overcrowded conditions of the capital.

The cholera epidemic of 1854 was centred on Southwark and Lambeth. Throughout late summer, 10,675 died. Soho was barely affected, with a few isolated cases in August. Then, on 31 August, the Soho strain became virulent, suddenly sweeping up the area around Broad Street. Within three days, 127 people on or near the street were dead. The outbreak claimed several hundred lives in a few short weeks. It was killing one in eight — almost double the national average.

One of those treating people was Doctor John Snow, who was based in nearby Firth Street. He finally linked the disease to waterborne bacteria, and the presence of human waste in the Thames. Previous research had convinced him that cholera was spread by a poison passed from victim to victim through sewage-tainted water. He traced the Soho outbreak to a pump operated by the Vauxhall Water Company. The company, who supplied Thames water to pumps around the city, was naturally reluctant to agree with him.

But Dr Snow interviewed families of victims and did some sterling detective work.

"I found that nearly all the deaths had taken place within a short distance of the pump on the corner of Broad Street and Cambridge Street," he wrote afterwards. Under the microscope, the water from the pump contained "white, flocculent particles" — the bacteria, which had not been identified yet.

He later found the probable cause of the whole infection. Just before the Soho outbreak, a child on Broad Street had become ill with cholera, and her nappies had been steeped in water that was then tipped into a leaking cesspit only feet from the Broad Street well.

Dr Snow managed on 7 September to persuade the Board of Guardians of St James's Parish to remove the handle of the pump. Immediately the spread of cholera stopped. In all, it had claimed 616 lives in Soho.

The survivors acted as a confirmation of Dr Snow's theory. Over five hundred inmates of Poland Street Workhouse survived — but they had their own well. None of the seventy workers in a Broad Street brewery succumbed — perhaps because they were given free beer and did not drink the water.

Still, people were reluctant to agree with Dr Snow. The Reverend Henry Whitehead, vicar of St Luke's Church, Berwick Street, believed divine intervention was to blame. But Snow's theories gradually gained credence. It took many years before sanitary conditions improved, but the cholera epidemic of 1854 was the last to hit London.

Dr Snow's work was the first step to finding a cure and ending the debilitating outbreaks. The Thames still carries small amounts of the cholera bacteria, but it is no longer a public health concern for the city.

Open Sewer of Thames Replaced by Underground System

It is a shame that no one can enjoy it, because the architecture of London's sewers is quite spectacular in places. The sewerage system was built in the late nineteenth century to replace the existing system. Up to that point, the River Thames was fairly much an open sewer. There were few fish or wildlife on the river. This caused huge problems for the public health, including numerous cholera epidemics. A decision in 1848 that all cesspits should be closed, and that house drains should connect to sewers and empty into the Thames, caused an epidemic that killed 14,137 people.

There had been proposals to build a modern sewage system, but the money could not be found. However, following the Great Stink of 1858, Parliament realised the urgency of the problem and hired civil engineer Joseph Bazalgette to sort it out for them.

He designed an extensive system of underground intercepting sewers that diverted waste from the river to the estuary, downstream of the main centre of population. Six main sewers, almost 160 kilometres (100 miles) in length, were constructed. Bazalgette incorporated stretches of some of London's lost rivers in the system. Three of these sewers were south of the river, and three north. The northern sewer closest to the river was incorporated into the Thames Embankment.

The intercepting sewers were fed by 720 kilometres (450 miles) of main sewers, that in turn were fed by 21,000 kilometres (13,000 miles) of smaller, local sewers. Gravity powered much of the system, but pumping stations were put in places such as Chelsea, Deptford and Abbey Mills. Sewers north of the river feed into the Northern Outfall sewer, which feeds into the treatment plant at Beckton. South of the river, the sewerage is piped to a similar facility at Crossness.

Further improvements in the twentieth century have led to dramatic improvements in the quality of water in the Thames, and a substantial reduction in pollution on the river and in the North Sea.

However the population of the city has exploded in recent years, putting the sewage system under increasing pressure. In redeveloping the Docklands in the late eighties, a major new drainage infrastructure was put in place. And plans are in place for a 35 kilometre (22 mile) tunnel that will have a diameter of 9 metres (30 feet) underneath the riverbed of the Thames between Hammersmith in the west and Beckton/Crossness in the east. The cost is estimated at well over £2 billion, but in 2007 the mayor of London Ken Livingstone announced that the new tunnel would be completed by 2020, and should serve the city for decades to come.

Joseph Bazalgette

Joseph William Bazalgette was born in Enfield, London, in 1819; the son of a retired naval captain. He began his career as a railway engineer, then gained experience in land drainage and reclamation works, allowing him to set up his own London consulting practice in 1842. He was appointed to the short-lived Metropolitan Commission of Sewers in 1849 (the body that had unwittingly caused the 1848-49 cholera epidemic), taking over as engineer in 1852. Soon after, another cholera epidemic killed 10,738.

Championed by fellow engineer (and builder of the first Thames Tunnel) Isambard Kingdom Brunel, Bazalgette was appointed chief engineer of the Commission's successor, the Metropolitan Board of Works, a post he held until 1889.

Following the Great Stink, Parliament passed an enabling act and Bazalgette's plans to revolutionise London's sewerage system finally began to be implemented. The job took until 1875. In a moment of inspired genius, he worked out the absolute maximum size of the pipes that would be needed for the system — and then doubled it. Because of that, his sewerage system is still in use today.

Joseph Bazalgette was knighted in 1875, and died in 1891.

Preventing Suicide

At one point, suicide was regarded as a very serious crime. If a person was saved from the river they could be charged, and even hung for the offence of trying to take their own life! There was no understanding of the forces that drove a person to such extremes. In 1850, Ann Wood was pulled out of the river and landed before the magistrate. He snapped at her: "Why did you not get under the water and make an end of it, instead of giving us all this trouble and bother?"

But in the last century, attitudes have softened and a real effort has been made to prevent suicides, and to rescue those who do go into the water. Authorities began by docking the Jumpers' Boat near Waterloo Bridge. This was a boat with a special roller system at its stern which allowed crew to pluck people from the dark waters and pull them on board easily. This was a necessary precaution, because pulling someone from the water could be a dangerous undertaking. Drowning people tend to clutch at anything, and could pull a rescuer in with them. And suicides are at the apex of their desperation. They would struggle against rescuers, often knocking them in.

The Jumpers' Boat was eventually replaced with a special floating police station, the only one in the world. It was moored at Waterloo Pier on the Victoria Embankment, almost under the bridge. As one Special Constable wrote: "It was there for a reason. Waterloo Bridge was known as the 'jumper's bridge'. If someone was going to jump, it was more often than not from that bridge, goodness knows why!"

Constable David van Vlymen was with the Thames River Police during the 1950s. He went on: "We may hear that a person was reported as having jumped from Battersea Bridge. At full throttle we would head for the spot and start our search. It was not unusual for Scotland Yard to radio us later that the person had been picked up by a private boat, and give us the location so we could collect the jumpers who, without doubt, would be suffering from shock.

"The best treatment for shock is a hot bath and that is exactly what our procedure was. Having wrapped the wet body in a blanket and radioed an advance warning to the floating station, it was full throttle to Waterloo Pier, which was equipped with a special bathroom.

"By the time we arrived the bath was all ready filled with warm water. Willing hands would take the body from us and without ceremony dump it into the bath fully clothed. An ambulance would also be standing by in case of injury.

"This bathing procedure was the same for males or females, and I remember one newspaper giving us a bad time when they reported, no doubt on a slow news day, that the Police were bathing women. What they did not say was that they were fully dressed!"

The River Police have their headquarters at Wapping, near the appropriately named Dead Man's Stairs. In the station is the occurrence book, often called "The Book of the Dead".

This registry lists all the bodies taken from the river in the district. It serves as a ghoulish roll call of despair.

In an entry on 26 May 1948, a policeman recorded launching a boat after hearing of someone jumping into the river: "I rowed out to try and save him but, as I was holding him, he struggled so violently that he pulled himself free from my grasp, and before I could catch hold of him again he sank. A little while later a gent's brown soft felt hat was found floating by."

Such little details add to the poignancy. One man was pulled out of the water with a large sum of cash strapped to his chest to cover funeral expenses. Two young girls — sisters — tied themselves together before stepping into the water. The reason for their decision is not known.

Suicide had continued to be a major problem. In 2002, the Lifeboat, River Police and Coastguard dealt with 400 incidents.

The Big Wind

London is not in one of the world's tornado belts. But freak windstorms have hit the city on occasion. The last was on the night of 16 October 1987, and tore a strip through the financial district, causing millions of pounds of damage.

Balconies on high-rise flats collapsed, walls came tumbling down, and roofs were stripped of their tiles in seconds. The glass from shattered windows danced on the air like lethal snowflakes. Market stalls were lifted and tossed about like they were mere beach balls, and thousands of trees were destroyed.

The destruction was confined to a small belt about 90 metres across. A tornado is a highly concentrated and local event, never lasting long, but leaving huge damage in its wake. Londoners looking at the mess the following morning could be forgiven for imagining they had had a glimpse of nature at her harshest.

They were deluding themselves.

Tornados are categorised on the Fujita Scale or the Torres Scale. A Fujita Four (F4) or Torres Eight (T8) tornado will level well-constructed houses. Structures with weak foundations will be blown away some distance, and trains will be overturned. Cars will be tossed into the air to form lethal missiles. Skyscrapers will be badly twisted and may lean to one side, and high-rises can be toppled and destroyed. Wind speeds reach up to 260 mph, and the tornado is normally between 600 and 900 metres across. This big a foot will leave a huge swath of damage.

These are kick-ass storms, and one hit London on 17 October 1091. It formed near the water and swept along the Thames, wreaking havoc as it moved. The church of St Mary-le-Bow was destroyed and 600 houses were demolished. Most of them were wooden and stood no chance against the tornado, which was both the first and the worst recorded in London.

But the most damage was done on the river itself. The raging winds drove the water in front of them, causing a swell several feet high which swept the shore. It is not known whether it was this swell, or the wind driving it, that hit London Bridge the hardest.

What is known is that moments after the tornado struck, the wooden bridge was in the water, with debris scattered over a wide area. The flying detritus were like missiles. Four rafters from St Mary-le-Bow church struck the ground by the river with such force that they were impaled more than 6 metres (20 feet) into the ground. Only their ends protruded above the surface.

Apart from St Mary-le-Bow, a dozen other churches also suffered catastrophic damage. Miraculously, only two people were killed. But Londoners were without their link between Southwark and the city. London Bridge had tumbled down once more.

The spectacle of the destruction caused a superstitious fervour in the city, with people turning to religion in their hour of need. There were demands for public penance to ward off the further wrath of God. On a more practical level, the next London Bridge was made of stone!

The Great Flood

Everyone thinks of rivers flowing down to the sea. But at the other end, the flow can reverse. In the tidal portion of a great waterway, sea water can come sweeping upriver. This makes the tidal portion of a river prone to severe flooding.

London lies on the tidal portion of the Thames, and has flooded badly several times. Now the Thames Barrier in the estuary protects the city from the worst of the storm surges, but in the past, rising waters carried death and destruction.

The last great flood in London was in the winter of 1928, an unwelcome New Year gift for thousands of householders. Flood waters poured over the top of the Thames Embankment, and part of the Chelsea Embankment collapsed. Fourteen people died within minutes as the water swept through unprepared streets. Several thousand were rendered homeless during the darkest days of winter.

A combination of factors caused the last major flood to affect central London. It all began on Christmas Eve, when unusually heavy snow fell in over the Cotswolds in central England. The Thames rises in those mountains.

On New Year's Eve, 1928, there was a sudden thaw, followed by prolonged heavy rain, doubling the volume of water coming down the river. But there was bad luck coming upriver too — the swollen river met with a storm surge caused by a major cyclone in the North Sea. With water rushing down from the Cotswolds, and sweeping in from the estuary, the city became a bottle neck. Water levels began to rise alarmingly.

What tipped it over the edge was a spring tide. Suddenly the water level at Southend was 4 feet above normal for a high tide. The funnelling of the water upstream caused its level to rise even further, producing the highest water levels ever recorded in the Thames in London.

The flood peaked at about 1.30 a.m. on 7 January, with a level of 5.55 metres (18 feet, 3 inches) recorded. This beat the previous record by more than a foot.

It also beat the embankments. The river overflowed at the Thames Embankment, and at embankments in the City and Southwark, up to Putney and Hammersmith. Serious flooding was also reported at Greenwich, Woolwich and other locations downriver, and there was huge damage to property.

As quick as it had arisen, the flood was gone. The high tide receded, the North Sea hurricane abated, and within a day the water levels had dropped to normal. But it took a lot longer to drain the many roads, tunnels, basements and cellars that had been submerged. The repair job ran to several years.

Houses were demolished and replaced with modern new buildings. A new bridge, Lambeth Bridge, replaced its dilapidated predecessor, and Horseferry Road was widened. The height of the embankments was raised, and the river wall strengthened along parts of the river.

It was the last great flood to hit the city.

The North Sea flood of 1953, which killed 2,551 people across northern Europe, (over 300 in the UK), raised the river to the top of the embankment, but it didn't overflow. Another half an inch would have spelt disaster — though Bermondsey was flooded on that occasion.

Flash Flood

At Millbank, a 75-foot section of the Chelsea embankment collapsed entirely, and a flash flood swept through the poor and run-down streets. Fourteen people drowned, unable to escape from the basement flats they lived in. Another 4,000 were made homeless, as water levels in the streets — and inside the houses — rose to 4 feet.

The flood didn't spare the well-off either. The Tate Gallery flooded to 8 feet, while Westminster Hall and the House of Commons also found themselves at sea. The Underground had to shut, as it became the underwater.

The Tower of London had its long defunct moat refilled, and the Blackwall and Rotherhithe tunnels were submerged.

According to the *Manchester Guardian* the following morning: "At the Houses of Parliament the water 'cataracted' over the parapet into the open space at the foot of Big Ben. The floods penetrated into Old Palace Yard, which shortly after one o'clock was about a foot under water.

"Flooding was worst at Charing Cross and Waterloo bridges, where the river sweeps around. Water poured over the embankment. At intervals along the Embankment stood tramcars derelict and deserted. Taxi-cabs and motor-cars splashed along the far side of the road. The public subway, Westminster Bridge, was flooded to a depth of 4 feet. There were miniature waterfalls at Cleopatra's Needle and the RAF

Memorial, and the training ship President floated at street level."

Other Floods

Central London will never flood again, thanks to the Thames Barrier. But several times in the last century, it came close. In March 1947, there was flooding along the Thames Valley and elsewhere. It was the worst overall flooding of the twentieth century, though London escaped lightly.

The flood was caused by the wettest March in 300 years. Over a short period, 4.6 inches of rain and snow fell, and the peak flow on the river was 61.7 billion litres of water per day. It caused £12 million damage.

Both the Thames and the Lea flooded in London, but the centre of the city was not affected.

There were also significant floods in 1968, 1993, 1998, 2000, 2003 and 2006.

Preventing Flooding into the Future

There is an inevitability about disaster. Fires will hit London again — but because of modern construction and advanced firefighting techniques, they will never, outside of war, engulf whole streets and districts again. Terrorist attacks may increase, but they will only hit single buildings and damage their neighbours. Hurricanes and tornados may come screaming in, but they will only cause structural damage.

London, as with most modern cities, is safe from all major disasters except one. If melting snow caused a swollen Thames to meet a spring tide, and that coincided with a storm surge from the North Sea, a huge swath of the city could disappear under the inky waters. Thames Street could become Thames Canal; and Tooley Street a reservoir.

The North Sea flood of 1953 devastated 1,600 kilometres (1,000 miles) of the UK coastline and killed 307. In the Netherlands, it sank much of the country and killed nearly 2,000. London escaped relatively unscathed, but it served as a wake-up call for the city authorities. It took twenty years to prepare a response, but in 1974 work began on the Thames Barrier. The job took eight years to complete.

The barrier is the second largest movable flood barrier in the world, and is downstream of central London. It regulates the river, preventing the city from being exposed to exceptionally high tides and storm surges. The barrier is raised (closed) during high tides: at ebb tide, it is lowered to release the water that backs up behind it.

The barrier stretches from Silvertown in Newham (on the north) to the New Charlton area in the Borough of Greenwich.

Built across a 520 metre (570 yard) stretch of the river chosen for its straight banks and for the solidity of the underlying chalk soil, the barrier divides the river into four 61 metre (200 feet) and two 30 metre (100 feet) spans. There are also four smaller non-navigable channels between nine concrete piers and two abutments. The flood gates across the openings are circular segments that can be rotated into place, giving the barrier its distinctive appearance, like an elongated Sydney Opera House. In addition, the flood defences for eleven miles downriver were raised and strengthened.

The gates swing closed when a combination of high tides and high river flows is forecast. If water levels are expected to rise above 4.87 metres (16 feet) in central London, the process begins. About nine hours before the high tide reaches the barrier, messages go out stopping river traffic. Smaller gates along the Thames tideway — including Barking Barrier, King George V Lock gate, Dartford Barrier, and the gates at Tilbury

Docks and Canvey Island — are closed first, then the gates of the Thames Barrier are swung into place, one at a time. The gates remain closed until the water level downstream drops to match that of the water level upstream.

After periods of heavy rain — or in winter as snow melts — floodwater can sweep down the Thames into London. A high tide can prevent the floodwater from escaping out to sea. So the gates are closed shortly after low tide, and a huge empty volume is created behind the barrier, which can act as a reservoir for the floodwater coming over Teddington Weir, the point at which the Thames becomes tidal. This has been the reason for about a third of the closures in the past thirty years.

Closures are not common: as it is a severe disruption to shipping, they are kept to a minimum. There were only four closures in the 1980s, but this rose to 35 in the nineties. In the first decade of this century, that figure rose to 75 — one closure every seven weeks, on average.

The barrier should continue to protect London until around 2060-70. But plans have already been drawn up to supersede it with a more ambitious 16 kilometre (ten mile) barrier across the estuary from Sheerness in Kent to Southend in Essex.

The Thames Barrier Information Centre (and café) is located at Woolwich, and is open Thursdays to Sundays. There is a small exhibition to show how the barrier was designed, built and operated. There are spectacular views from the café over the barrier and the river, and there is also a picnic area and a children's playground.

At the moment, London is safe from any catastrophe on the river — unless the *Montgomery* explodes. Then there really will be Death and Destruction on the Thames!

Sand Kite disables barrier

The barrier was designed to be wide enough to allow shipping to pass unobstructed, but plans and reality have a nasty way of not meshing. On 27 October 1997, the dredger MV *Sand Kite*, operating in thick fog, approached the barrier. It was 6.48 a.m. — three minutes after sunrise, but still pitch dark. The fog was dense. The bridge of the dredger contacted the Thames Barrier Navigation Centre at Woolwich, and asked, "Can we have the fog lights on please?"

The Navigation Centre replied, "Er, they are on, I'm afraid." To which the boat replied, "Oh dear…"

The vessel collided with one of the barrier's piers and was holed. She tried to reverse out of the barrier and pass through an adjacent one, but went down, bow-first, coming to rest across the second barrier, and effectively putting it out of commission.

In the accident, she also dumped her 3,300 tonnes of sand and gravel. Had there been a flood, the entire barrier would have been rendered useless. One estimate put the potential cost of the damage at £13 billion. With the risk so huge, efforts were made to refloat the *Sand Kite*. She was pulled off the barrier by early November — and just in time. On 9 November, there was the largest storm surge the country had seen since the North Sea surge of 1953. The barrier had to be closed twice in one day, the only time this has ever happened.

London had a lucky escape: the barrier held the water, as the surge did not coincide with high tide. The *Sand Kite* was refloated a week later.

A NOTE TO THE READER

If you have enjoyed this book enough to leave a review on **Amazon** and **Goodreads**, then we would be truly grateful.

Sapere Books is an exciting new publisher of brilliant fiction and popular history.

To find out more about our latest releases and our monthly bargain books visit our website:
saperebooks.com

Made in the USA
Middletown, DE
04 November 2019

77987244R00177